SPORT AND PHYSICAL EDUCATION: THE KEY CONCEPTS

An accessible and fully cross-referenced A–Z guide, this book has been written specifically for students of Sport Studies and Physical Education, introducing basic terms and concepts.

Entries cover such diverse subjects as coaching, drug testing, hooliganism, cultural imperialism, economics, gay games, amateurism, extreme sports, exercise physiology and Olympism.

This revised second edition, including fully updated further reading and web references, places a greater emphasis on sports science, with new entries on subjects such as:

- aerobic and anaerobic respiration
- blood pressure
- body composition
- cardiac output
- metabolism
- physical capacity

A complete guide to the disciplines, themes, topics and concerns current in contemporary sport, this book is an invaluable resource for students at every level studying Sport and Physical Education.

Timothy Chandler is Dean of the College of the Arts and Professor of Sport Studies at Kent State University.

Mike Cronin is Academic Director of the Centre for Irish Programmes at Boston College in Dublin. His publications include *Sporting Nationalisms: Identity, Ethnicity, Immigration, Assimilation* (with David Mayall, 1998), and *Sport and Nationalism in Ireland* (1999).

Wray Vamplew is Chair of Sports History and Director of Research in Sports Studies at the University of Stirling. His recent publications include *Encyclopedia of British Horseracing* and *Encyclopedia of Traditional British Rural Sports* (Routledge, 2005)

ALSO AVAILABLE FROM ROUTLEDGE

Sport Psychology: The Key Concepts
Ellis Cashmore
ISBN10: 0-415-25322-5
ISBN13: 978-0-415-25322-2

Primary Education: The Key Concepts
Denis Hayes
ISBN10: 0-415-35483-8
ISBN13: 978-0-415-35483-7

SPORT AND PHYSICAL EDUCATION

The Key Concepts

Second Edition

Timothy Chandler, Mike Cronin and Wray Vamplew

Routledge
Taylor & Francis Group

LONDON AND NEW YORK

First published 2002
by Routledge
This edition first published 2007
by Routledge
2 Park Square, Milton Park, Abingdon, Oxon OX14 4RN

Simultaneously published in the USA and Canada
by Routledge
270 Madison Ave, New York, NY 10016

Routledge is an imprint of the Taylor & Francis Group, an informa business

Typeset in Bembo by
Taylor & Francis Books
Printed and bound in Great Britain by
Antony Rowe Ltd, Chippenham, Wiltshire

British Library Cataloguing in Publication Data
A catalogue record for this book is available from the British Library

Library of Congress Cataloging in Publication Data
Chandler, Timothy John Lindsay
Sport and physical education: the key concepts / Timothy Chandler, Mike Cronin, and
Wray Vamplew.—2nd ed.
p. cm.
Includes bibliographical references and index.
1. Sports—Encyclopedias. 2. Physical education and training—Encyclopedias. I. Cronin,
Mike. II Vamplew, Wray. III. Title.
GV567.C43 2007
796.03—dc22
2006034560

ISBN10: 0-415-41746-5 (hbk)
ISBN10: 0-415-41747-3 (pbk)
ISBN13: 978-0-415-41746-4 (hbk)
ISBN13: 978-0-415-41747-1 (pbk)

CONTENTS

INTRODUCTION

At the start of the 2001/2 football season in Britain, there was a mass of media comment about the amount of football that would be screened on television during the season. It was claimed that by switching between the different terrestrial, satellite and cable providers, the avid fan could watch four live games every day, amounting to over forty hours of viewing per week. A fresh deal, signed in August 2004 with Sky television, and running for three seasons, netted the Premier League £1,024 billion for their television rights. This marked a massive increase on the figure for the previous deal, signed in 1998 and worth £670 million. Football is a booming industry, the home of multi-million pound players, the subject of huge media interest and a favourite of corporate advertisers. The 2006 World Cup finals in Germany were the product of €4.6 billion worth of infrastructure investment by the state and private business. During the tournament, while the eyes of the global television audience were on Germany, some 2 million spectators and tourists visited the country, spending an estimated €600 million. The presence of the World Cup in Germany created 50,000 new jobs, half of which would be permanent and outlast the duration of the tournament. Adidas sold 15 million replica shirts around the world in the six months leading up to the finals, while flag sales across Europe increased 1000 per cent as fans displayed their colours.

As evidenced by the World Cup, the scale of sports activity across the world at the start of the twenty-first century is immense. The multi-million pound figures that are paid for television rights, and to top performers in wages and sponsorship agreements, rely on the idea that there is an insatiable appetite amongst the viewing population for sport. Modern sport emerged as part of a range of social changes that were the product of the Industrial Revolution. In the ensuing century and a half since many of the major sporting associations came into existence, the sport and leisure industry has grown to be one of the biggest in the world. In recent years the continuing speed and scale of growth within the sports market on a global scale has appeared unstoppable. The costs of television rights for sporting events of all kinds have soared, sports clubs have been successfully floated on the stock market, and major events such as the football World Cup finals and the Olympics grow ever bigger and costlier. Whether sport can continue with its incredible level of success remains to be seen. The Athens Olympics of 2004 were not as successful as those held in Sydney in 2000. Mega events such as the Olympic Games and the football World Cup are fraught with planning and financial risks. It remains to be seen whether South Africa will be able to deliver the World Cup finals to the high standards of those set by Germany in 2006, and whether London will get everything ready in time for the Olympics of 2012. Other questions also continue to be asked of the sports industry. Will the viewers begin to desert televised football in large numbers? Will Nike continue to sign multi-million pound deals with sports stars to promote its products? All the answers to these questions lie in the future. They are, however, indicative of the importance of sport within the global society, and illustrative of its social, economic and political importance.

Sport, it can be argued, is everywhere. From children kicking or throwing a ball on any patch of ground, to the stars of the football pitch or basketball court, sport captivates us all. Its global presence is undeniable. We cannot turn on our television sets without seeing sport. General and dedicated radio stations keep us constantly abreast of the latest sports news, while the ever-growing number of daily sporting newspaper supplements and specialist magazines inform us of every minutia of sporting activity. The internet has been embraced by sports clubs and organisations, as well as fans across the world, as another medium through which sport can be promoted, discussed and enjoyed. In all forms of sponsorship and advertising, the sports star is dominant. There is not a product that is not connected to either individual sports players or an event. From Michael Jordan and Tiger Woods' embrace of Nike, through to the N-Power Ashes series in test cricket, companies believe that the sponsorship of sport will bring them much needed publicity, raise their profile and increase their sales. But big sponsors only remain with a sports star while they are successful. After his performance in the 2005 Ashes series against Australia, English cricketer Andrew Flintoff signed deals with Barclays, Red Bull, Volkswagen, and the Thwaites brewery, amongst others. If he continues to be the hero in the English side and results go their way, then the interest of sponsors in him will remain high.

However, if stars like Flintoff suffer long term injury or lose form, the sponsors will desert them for the next big thing.

Sport has a great cultural resonance. It is important in people's daily lives, and serves to bring people together. For many, sport is central to their sense of identity. It provides them with a focus for their lives, a group of friends with a common interest, and a series of games and events around which they can organise and centre their life. Sport is centrally important as an activity that promotes physical health and well-being, and is embraced as such by education, welfare and medical systems across the world. Physical and sporting activity, at whatever age, is to be applauded for improving health and sociability, as well as providing many people with an outlet for their competitive streak. Sport then, has a myriad of different functions. From the school child throwing their first ball as part of an educational process, through to the multi-million dollar pitcher on a major league baseball team, sport is an important focus for, and a central part of, the society in which we live.

Why sports studies and physical education?

The argument of what actually constitutes a sport is one that will keep any discussion group, whether in a classroom or over dinner, talking for hours. The argument is not one which is central here. We have taken a broad approach to the subject of what constitutes sports studies and physical education, and are more concerned with an area of activity that has a multitude of different forms, styles and influences across the globe. The approach taken here is one which, along with the majority of academic studies, is centred on an understanding of sport and physical education within a predominantly Western context. This is not to deny that sport has a great importance within non-Western societies, but a recognition that the majority of previous work has focused on Western sports, organisations and styles of play. The sports of the Western world, along with their sports stars, the products that they market, and the media that project them to the wider world, dominate the global sporting agenda. The work included in the text has sought to avoid an over-emphasis on elite forms of sporting practice, and to approach physical education and sports studies through an appreciation of activity at a variety of levels. However, one has to recognise that many of the dominant themes in contemporary sport, such as globalisation, can best be illustrated by reference to an elite performer, such as Ronaldo in football. As a result, professional or elite sport provides the majority of illustrations used in the text.

Sports studies and physical education have become increasingly important within the curriculum at both school, college and university level. Education has recognised that sport is not simply a human activity that has no importance within society. It is an activity that is worthy of study, from a variety of disciplinary approaches, so that the impact and importance of sport can be properly assessed and understood. This book has been constructed so that all the major disciplinary areas that constitute sports studies and physical education are included. That said, there are undoubtedly topics and concepts that have been excluded. Such exclusions are not the product of oversight, but the result of boundaries that had to be set at the outset of the project. For this new edition of the book some of the broader organisational themes that appeared in the first edition have been dropped in favour of a greater focus on sports science and physical education concepts. Also included are some general concepts, such as alcohol which, while not directly linked to sport, does impinge on the lives of athletes and has been a key issue in the area of sponsorship.

Why this guide?

The economic and cultural importance of sport, and the growth in popular and academic discussion of the topic, is the central justification for the book. As the Key Concepts series is well established and admired, we felt that it offered the best vehicle for an exploration of the terminology and major concepts that are attached to the study of sports studies and physical education. There is, as the bibliography in this book illustrates, a mass of literature on different aspects of sport. Much of this literature is the product of academic endeavour, and was aimed primarily at the peer group of the authors. Such work has often been written using complex specialist terminology, or else is placed in the context of a variety of often unfamiliar theoretical approaches. Even those general texts, which seek to introduce the student or reader to a particular disciplinary approach, often hide their definitions of the key concepts within the narrative, so that they remain unclear. As a result, many readers find it difficult to grasp the central purpose or definition of the different terms, concepts or ideas. This volume seeks, as with the others in this series, to provide, in a readable and accessible form, a comprehensive guide to the key terms and concepts present in the broad body of writing within sports studies and physical education.

As the study of sports and physical education embraces so many different disciplinary approaches, a definition of the key concepts is an ambitious undertaking. As such, all the concepts here have to be treated as introductions. They are not, and neither do they seek to be, definitive. The entries are designed to lead to a fuller engagement with, and usage of, the concepts and terms. It is hoped that all readers will make use of the extensive bibliography to further their understanding of any given concept or term, and see this book as a tool which facilitates understanding and further investigation. In the first edition we included a list of relevant website addresses, but as with many things on the internet, often these sites disappeared, were not maintained or else were renamed. Rather than provide a list of website addresses that might quickly become obsolete, we have taken the decision to omit them from this volume, and encourage readers to search for organisations and themes via a search engine.

Concepts

A concept, as used in this book, is a general idea, or class of objects. We have not been over-specific in our use of the term 'concept', so that we could include as many terms as possible that are important for an understanding of sports studies and physical education. The format of the book is alphabetical, but there are strings of related concepts that run throughout the book. These broad groupings include:

- **theoretical paradigms** and the methodological approaches associated with them. These include the major social and cultural theories, as well as the various 'isms', along with approaches such as anthropology or geography. At all times these concepts, as with all others in the book, are defined and discussed within the context of sporting examples.
- **research methodologies and typologies** are explored to enable the reader to understand how academic and scholarly research into the area of sports studies and physical education is conducted, and how it can best be approached.
- **key disciplinary areas** are identified throughout the text. As the study of sports studies and physical education is such a multi-disciplinary undertaking, we have tried, where possible, to outline the importance of any given discipline, e.g. history, sociology, sports medicine, and so on, to the wider study of the whole subject.
- **the sports business and sports organisations** are increasingly powerful and important, and have a huge effect on the general area of sports studies and physical education. While not seeking to

exhaustively define all such operations, we have identified the main ones, and the influence that they exert within the area.

- **associated businesses and themes** such as the media, have been key to the history and development of sport; and do much to enforce other concepts like globalisation. The book has therefore identified the main external influences on the historic and on-going development of physical education and sports studies, and defined them in the context of their sporting role.

We have not listed individual sports such as cricket or baseball as concepts here, and neither have we listed any individual athletes. Where either sports or individuals are mentioned, they appear only as exemplars of concepts. For example, Michael Jordan is not an entry as such, but is used as illustrative of the force of globalisation.

LIST OF CONCEPTS

Origins of sport
Outcomes
Over-training
Ownership
Patriotism
Patronage
Pedagogy
Periodisation
Philosophy
Physical capacity
Physical culture
Physical education
Physical literacy
Physical training
Play
Politics
Post-modernism
Price
Private goods
Private sector
Process orientation
Product development
  see commercialisation
Product improvement
  see commercialisation
Professionalism
Profit
Progressive resistance
Protective equipment
Psychology
Public goods
Public schools
Public sector
Racism
Rationalised
Rational recreation
Recreation
Reflection thesis
Regionalism
Regulation
Religion
Repetition training

Reproduction thesis
Residual volume
Resistance thesis
Respiratory system
  see anatomy and physiology
Restraint of trade
Retain and transfer
Risk management
Risk sports
Ritual
Rotation
Rules
Safety
Salary cap
Schema theory
Secular
Seniors' sport see ageism,
  veterans
Sexism
Shamateurism
Skeletal system
  see anatomy and physiology
Skill
Skill acquisition
Social behaviour
Social capital
Sociology
Specialisation
Special Olympics
Speed
Sponsorship
Sport
Sport education
Sport for All
Sporting associations
Sporting conduct
Sporting deviance
Sporting heroes
Sport science
Sportsmanship
Sports medicine
Spread betting

SPORT AND PHYSICAL EDUCATION

The Key Concepts

ADMINISTRATION

The field of sports administration is one that has grown rapidly throughout recent decades. With the emergence of modern competitive and organised sport, committees were formed to ensure the smooth running of any given sport, to draw up rules, organise fixtures and competitions and to discipline unruly elements. These early sports administrators were usually drawn from the upper or middle classes. At the national level they were to be found in organisations such as the Royal and Ancient Golf Club at St Andrews to oversee golf, the MCC to run cricket, or at the Football Association to control football. In this early form, administration relied heavily on former members of the **public schools**, or else, as Mason and Collins have demonstrated with respect to football and rugby, local businessmen. Whatever the social origins of such committees, the overwhelming majority of nineteenth- and early twentieth-century sports administrators were **amateur**. As sports clubs and organisations developed and were increasingly run as businesses, so paid secretaries and other administrators were appointed. At the highest level, sports associations began paying salaries and employing officers to take care of areas such as press relations, marketing and sponsorship. Since the 1960s, sports administration has been a definite career choice, and one that is often made after studying aspects of the subject at college and university level. With the growth of allied areas within the sports business, such as **law**, **economics**, **marketing** and the **media**, sports administrators have continued to become more numerous and ever more important. They are vital in sports organisations, such as Sport England, in lobbying government for funding, and in administering whatever money they do receive.

See also: **bureaucracy, leadership, management**

Further reading: Collins (1998), Mason (1980)

ADVENTURE SPORTS

There is an ever-broadening array of activities that are outside the traditional mainstream of organised, codified, rationalised sport, termed 'adventure', 'risk' and 'extreme' sports. They differ from traditional sporting and physical activities in terms of their location, equipment, emphasis on endurance, and/or the degree of danger involved. The fact that a number of these 'extreme' activities have been termed 'outlaw' sports is because they have been banned in certain places due to their level of danger. The terms 'adventure', 'risk', 'extreme', and 'outlaw' all bear witness to the search for thrills and the underlying ethos of freedom from authority and authority figures (such as coaches, managers, trainers and administrators who control traditional sport), which best exemplify both the motivations and the attitudes of many extreme athletes.

The list of adventure/risk/extreme sports continues to grow as such activities become more widely practised. Among the best known adventure sports are eco-challenge and sport climbing, both of which pit individuals against nature and the environment. In eco-challenge, contestants traverse difficult and unfamiliar terrain, using canoes, rafts, kayaks and even mountain bikes as they challenge themselves over a number of days to complete a course. This test of man against nature is often conducted in exotic and 'out of the way' places, where control of the environment is limited and where predictability of outcome is very limited. By contrast, sport climbing, while closely related to rock climbing, requires participants to climb artificial rocks, thereby standardising the events and offering some degree of uniformity of contest among participants who compete in tests of speed, strategy and difficulty.

Amongst the major risk sports are those which have developed from recreational activities such as bungee jumping, sky surfing and even barefoot water ski jumping, where points are awarded on the basis of 'stunts' or tricks performed during the activity. In bungee jumping, this involves 'diving-type' moves such as twists, turns and somersaults, on which a performer is judged. Inspired by the vine jumpers of Pentecost Island, and first attempted in Britain with jumps off the Clifton Suspension Bridge in 1979, this sport is thought to have developed in Australia. Sky surfing, which involves athletes being videotaped by a team-mate as they perform stunts on a surfboard whilst free falling from about 4,000 metres, was developed in France. However, while many Western nations, including Britain, have influenced the growth and development of extreme sports, none has been more influential than the United States. In the 1970s and 1980s, a teen culture of risk and rebellion against the established and traditional institution of sport was largely responsible for the growth of extreme sports, from recreational activities of a few 'outlaws' to the proliferation of such sports and the organising of them into festivals and games such as the X-Games and the Gravity Games.

Activities such as BMX dirt biking and jumping, in-line skating, mountain-biking, street-luge, skate-luge and skateboarding, were largely developed as sports in California, where the landscape and the climate afforded opportunities for such activities and where the surfing culture of the 1960s was transformed with the development of technology of a different sort to produce a broad array of on-land activities. BMX dirt biking, which got its start on the trails and fire roads of Mount Tamalpais, involves racing, jumping over and off dirt mounds and riding on vertical ramps. Competitors are judged for difficulty, style and amplitude. In-line skaters compete in three types of events over three different courses. The vertical event uses a horseshoe-shaped half-pike ramp in which skaters perform jumps, twists, turns, spins and flips, earning points for the quality and style of their performance. On the 'street' course, performers have to manoeuvre down obstacles such as stairs, along railings, up and down ramps and over walls, again earning points for style and difficulty of stunts. The down-hill course uses streets or roads, as do street and skate-luge competitions.

While the **World Wide Web** has enabled extreme sports enthusiasts to communicate more readily and thus develop a base of support for their activities, it has been the influence of the media through the development of the X-Games and Gravity Games, alongside the exploitation of these emergent sports and their appropriation by corporations such as McDonalds and Disney, which have changed these 'outlaw' activities into increasingly mainstream sports. As Pope and Rinehart note, enthusiasts in search of a unique recreational experience pioneered most of these sports. They developed local contests and championships as a means of testing their skills against others. It was only in the late 1980s that such activities began to attract media attention, and with this came sponsorship and career possibilities. The inclusion of snowboarding in the 1996 Winter Olympics typified the incorporation of extreme sports into the mainstream. Thus activities that began as recreational outlets for some of society's 'outsiders' have increasingly become formalised, institutionalised sports with their own corporate sponsors, national and international competitions, records and heroes, and as such part of mainstream sport in many Western nations.

Further reading: Allen (1993), Bane (1996), Donnelly (2006) Karinch (2000), McMillen (1998), Pope and Rinehart (2001), Wheaton (2004)

ADVERTISING

Advertising is the publicising of goods with the aim of increasing sales. It is the most visible sign of sport's commercialisation, with sports stars being used to endorse sports equipment and also non-sporting goods. This is nothing new. In the late nineteenth century the famous cricketer W. G. Grace was used to advertise not only cricket bats but also Colman's mustard, and in 1934 the FA Cup finalists promoted trousers, shoe polish and Shredded Wheat. Whether the public really believes that sporting success can be associated with and derived from buying the advertised product is a moot point. The development of televised sport has led to an expansion of the relationship between sport and advertising, with product logos on team shirts and playing surfaces, eye-catching revolving hoardings around grounds, and Formula One race cars becoming virtually mobile advertisements.

See also: **endorsement, sponsorship**

Further reading: Andrews and Jackson (2004), Groves (1987), Johnes (2000)

AEROBIC EXERCISE

The American College of Sports Medicine (ACSM) defines aerobic exercise as 'any activity that uses large muscle groups, can be maintained continuously, and is rhythmic in nature.' (1998) Aerobic means with oxygen and refers to the need for oxygen in the process of generating energy in muscles. The benefits of aerobic exercise include improvement in heart and lung functioning, (such as lower heart rate and blood pressure,) increased VO_2 Max, reduced body fat, improved weight control, and improved psychological well-being.

See also: **anaerobic exercise, exercise, fitness, periodisation**

Further reading: *Medicine and Science in Sports and Exercise*, 30, 6 June 1998.

AESTHETICS

Aesthetics is that part of **philosophy** which studies those values associated with beauty and ugliness. Beauty in sport is generally not rewarded save for appreciation by the cognoscenti. Most established sports have a 'classical' way of performing such as the timing of a drive in cricket, the smooth golf swing or the delicate drop shot in tennis. Yet these do not guarantee a win, for victory often goes to those who develop their own style, which may be less graceful but more effective. In some sports, however, such as ice-skating and synchronised swimming, marks are awarded for artistic interpretation. This raises the major issue of subjective judgement as there is no clear definition of artistry in sport.

Further reading: Best (1995)

AFFIRMATIVE ACTION

Affirmative action policies embrace the idea of positive discrimination to increase the participation of groups previously marginalised or discriminated against. This has been central to United States sport since 1972, and European Union law now has provision for the introduction of such measures. So far it has not occurred in Britain, where attempts to challenge sex **discrimination** in sport have generally used normal employment law to oppose such practices as unequal salaries for male and female administrators.

See also: **discrimination**

Further reading: McCardle (1999)

AGEISM

Sport has often been seen as the preserve of the young and the fit. Developmental theory once emphasised the importance of the period of childhood and adolescence as central to the successful development of the adult. It was as a result of such thinking that much of the effort in promoting sport was centred on the young. Whether in nineteenth-century English **public schools**, or through the modern educational curriculum, sport was used to teach young people good values and bring about fitness and physical strength. For many older people, especially prior to the 1960s, active sporting participation was rare. There were no leagues for senior players, and no encouragement of the elderly to keep fit through sport. It was argued by many supporters of developmental theory that as adults were already fully formed, they would not benefit from the positive effects of sport as they need no further development. An additional problem for many willing older sports participants were the arguments of many in the medical profession. Prior to the Second World War many health specialists argued that sport was too rough and involved over-exertion that would damage the ageing body.

Thankfully these negative views of the ageing body and sport have changed. People live longer, and most Western industrialised societies now have a dominantly elderly population that lives well beyond retirement age. The medical profession now argues that an active life, including sport and exercise, will give good or improved health to the elderly. The embrace of sport by the ageing population has been assisted by the rapid growth in the number of gym clubs across the Western world, and the provision of public facilities such as swimming pools. Role models have been provided by senior leagues in sports such as tennis and golf, which receive money from **sponsorship** and are regularly aired on **television**. **Olympics**-style athletics gatherings that are based around the elderly allow for competition and record setting, as competitors are classified on the basis of their age. The most important effect of the embrace of sport by the ageing has been to challenge the assumption that old age necessarily means a life of inactivity and illness. This has been the most central challenge to the ageist argument that old age leads to the end of physical activity and sporting competitiveness.

See also: **discrimination**

Further reading: Wearing (1995)

AGENTS

Players are often at a disadvantage in negotiations with experienced management over the terms and conditions of their contracts. Additionally, some players feel that direct negotiations might harm their working relationship with club management. In recent years both these factors have led to the employment of agents, specialised in the area, who represent their clients in discussions with clubs and other employers, usually obtaining a commission from any deals that they negotiate. They are in a fiduciary relationship with their clients and must always act in their best interest. Hence, for example, they can only act for one party within a negotiation. Although in the United States some agents have been guilty of manipulative practices to induce players to sign with them, this has not emerged as a major problem in British sport. In some sports, licensing systems have been introduced in order to ensure propriety. In Premier League football, for example, special permission to act as an agent must be obtained except for close relatives, FIFA-licensed agents and barristers and solicitors. Several restrictions are imposed, for instance, that agreements between agent and client must be in writing, can last only two years, and cannot be transferred to another parry.

See also: **sporting heroes**

Further reading: Greenfield, Osborn and Taylor (2001), Steinberg (1991)

AGGRESSION

Despite the fact that many coaches will tell their players that they need to be more aggressive if they are to be successful, sport psychologists suggest that aggression is one of the most persuasive negative aspects of sporting performance. Aggression can be thought of as 'any form of behaviour directed toward a goal of harming or injuring another living being who is motivated to avoid such treatment' (Baron and Richardson 1994: 7). In sport, an aggressive act is generally defined as an act performed to harm or injure, physically, verbally or psychologically.

There have been three classic approaches to explaining aggression: instinctual, drive reduction and social learning. Instinct theorists contend that aggression is innate and that sports, and particularly contact sports, may well attract those who are naturally aggressive, since it is an aggression-releasing environment, and the opportunity for catharsis or aggressive relief. Drive reduction theories reflect the belief that aggression is a response to some external drive, such as a build-up of frustration caused by the inability to attain a desired goal. Thus we find that aggression is more likely to occur late in a contest when players realise that they are not going to attain their goal of winning. Social learning theory suggests that aggression is a learnt behaviour, and therefore that coaches who encourage players to be aggressive and reward it are increasing the likelihood of aggression. This theory also suggests that when an athlete plays aggressively and perceives that such a style leads to a successful outcome (rather than frustration) then they are more likely to continue to play aggressively. The same three theories apply to spectators as well as players, and various forms of typical spectator aggression have been identified, such as rowdyism, exuberant celebration and riots. A large body of work on football rowdyism and hooliganism suggests that the key factor in triggering spectator aggression is the presence of a leader.

See also: **motivation, violence**

Further reading: Bandura (1973), Baron and Richardson (1994), Gill (1986), Marsh (1983), Wann (1997)

AGILITY

A key component of motor-performance-related fitness, agility is defined as the ability to change direction of the entire body in space with speed and accuracy and is related to athletic performance potential.

Further reading: Pate (1983)

ALCOHOL

The relationship between sport and alcohol is a long-standing one. Historically, the publican played an important role by organising sporting events, providing a meeting place for sports teams (often sponsoring them), and offering a results service. In the nineteenth century, attempts to reform sport and render it less disreputable forced the drink trade to realign itself with new forms of 'respectable' sport. Darts, snooker and lawn bowls, among other public-house sporting activities, replaced brutal animal and human blood sports as an attraction to a drinking clientele. As team sports emerged among the working classes, sponsorship came from landlords and hoteliers, and at the elite level, as sports clubs adopted limited liability company status, those in the drink trade came to the fore as shareholders and directors. In the twentieth century the alcohol sector has promoted its wares through sport via media advertising; promotion at the event itself on perimeter boards, shirt fronts and the actual playing area; and in the naming of leagues, races and other competitions.

Today it is recognised that alcohol depresses the nervous system, impairs both motor ability and judgement, reduces endurance, and, as a diuretic, can cause dehydration, none of which are conducive to sports performance. In the past, however, the drinking of alcohol, particularly ales and porters, was positively encouraged as a perceived aid to strength and stamina. The UK Sports Council has legislated against the use of alcohol as a performance-enhancing drug in those areas where there is an advantage to be gained from its use as an anti-anxiety drug, an isometric muscular strengthener, and for improving steadiness in 'aiming' sports.

Undoubtedly the alcohol industry has brought benefits to British sport: at the elite level via major sponsorships of events, teams and leagues; and lower down the sporting pyramid by assistance in the construction of club premises and the support of junior coaching. Yet at the same time there have been less positive aspects to the relationship through crowd disturbance from 'lager louts', the promotion of drinking to excess, and the risk of alcoholism to sportspersons and others.

Further reading: Collins and Vamplew (2002), Dixon and Garnham (2005), Vamplew (2005a)

ALEXANDER TECHNIQUE

The Alexander Technique was devised in the late nineteenth century by Frederick Matthias Alexander, a Tasmanian actor who suffered from vocal cord problems that threatened his career. He found that if his head and body were properly aligned he no longer had difficulties with his throat, and his breathing, voice and posture all improved. It is not a form of exercise, but a method of moving that realigns the limbs and improves balance and coordination. By reducing physical tension, it also helps ease stress and create feelings of calmness and confidence. Central to the technique is learning how to loosen the neck and allow the head to balance freely on top of the spine.

ALT-PE

A useful means of accessing current views/data on physical education worldwide is to look at ALT-PE. It is part of the newsgroup service carried by most e-mail browsers and requires the user to 'subscribe to newsgroups'. This is a free service but, as it does not appear to be moderated, caution should be exercised in utilising the contents. In North America and elsewhere ALT-PE (Academic Learning Time Physical Education) also refers to a unit of time in which a pupil is engaged in activity set by the teacher at an appropriate level of difficulty. Early studies conducted in the 1980s using this measure showed that students in physical education classes were not spending a great deal of time (about one third of class time) engaged in appropriate practice of physical skills. While more recent research has shown that practice time is one important factor in predicting learning outcomes in physical education, ALT-PE researchers have also discovered that other factors such as the quality of practice are also important in promoting the learning of physical skills.

See also: **World Wide Web**

Further reading: Rink (2002)

AMATEURISM

Amateurism is a British invention, its growth being largely reflective of a lengthy process of appropriation and gentrification of sport from the late eighteenth century onwards. It began as an ideal and ended as an ideology. In its strictest sense – amateur as 'lover' or absolute enthusiast – it represented the peak of intention rather than the manner of performance. The ideal became consolidated in the gentlemanly activities of public schoolboys in the first half of the nineteenth century, so that, as Wigglesworth (1996: 85) notes, 'by 1868 Trollope could suggest that playing billiards was an amusement of a gentleman but to play billiards eminently well is the life's work of a man who in learning to do so can hardly have continued to be a gentleman "in the best sense"'.

It was in trying to further the distinction between the sporting gentleman 'in the best sense' – the sense of the amateur as the ideal, and the sportsman concerned with performance – the professional player of the game, that other distinguishing features of being a professional emerged. These included: financial reward, occupation and social class. And it was in attaching social class characteristics and overtones to the concept of the amateur, and fostering a simple binary of amateur and professional to match the upper and lower class, gentleman and non-gentleman, respectable and not-respectable designations, that provided the basis for these terms as important 'social markers'. The terms amateur and professional also became instruments of social control, epithets of support and disdain, and measures of social standing and moral worth.

The key people behind the development of amateurism appear to have been the new Victorian administrative elite. As Holt (1989:110–11) notes,

> Just as the civil service was now open to all who had the classical education required to pass the entrance examination, so the running of sport was in practice confined to those with the necessary time, income and organisational experience. Very few outside the liberal professions had such qualifications and even then a measure of social influence via the old-boys network was important.

Thus we find institutions such as the Amateur Athletics Association, the Football Association and the Amateur Rowing Association being set up and run by such individuals during the mid-to-late Victorian era.

It is important to note that amateurism was never an uncontested notion, nor were negative responses to it always provided by professionals or the working classes. In the split between the Northern Union and the Rugby Football Union over broken-time payments, we find a geographic fault line in the amateur versus professional debate. In the split between the Amateur Rowing Association and the National Amateur Rowing Association, we find a split based on occupation and not on social or economic circumstances. Huggins suggests that in the years from 1850 to 1910 few sports were purely amateur. Occasionally, upper-middle class amateurs founded organisations specifically to preserve the nature of their activities and limit access to them. Wandering cricket clubs such as the Band of Brothers and the Free Foresters are examples. In other cases, such as in the founding of the Corinthians Club, the Barbarians Rugby Football Club and the I Zingari Cricket Club, they wished to distance themselves from developments in association football, rugby union or cricket that they found to be diminishing or tarnishing the amateur ideal.

Throughout the twentieth century, the amateur ideal has been eroded as high-level performance has become increasingly important in sport, as sport has become increasingly available to the masses, and as working at sport has become laudable and to be a professional athlete (as opposed to a 'rank' amateur) has been a sign of prestige. Being an amateur was an ascribed status, being a professional is an achieved status.

See also: **professionalism**

Further reading: Allison (1980; 2000), Cannadine (1998), Collins (1998), Holt (1989), Huggins (2000), Taylor (2006), Wigglesworth (1992; 1996)

ANABOLIC STEROIDS

Anabolic, or tissue-building, steroids are synthetic forms of the male sex hormone, testosterone, and are one form of steroids. They were first developed in the 1930s for medicinal purposes such as building body weight for the malnourished, treating gastrointestinal disorders, anaemia, and even osteoporosis. Anabolic steroids work by accelerating the natural cellular processes that build and replenish muscle. It is for this reason that athletes have been attracted to them in their search for improved performance, particularly in activities requiring both strength and speed.

While it is clear that athletes have been using anabolic steroids since the 1960s, and their use was banned by amateur athletic associations and the International Olympic Committee in the 1970s, it was not until the 1988 **Olympic Games** in Seoul, Korea, that the issue of **drugs** and **drug testing**, and more particularly the widespread use of steroids, became widely discussed. It was in the blue ribbon speed event, the 100 metres, at the 1988 Seoul Olympics that Canadian sprinter Ben Johnson achieved a world record time of 9.79 seconds and the title of fastest man on earth, only to be stripped of his gold medal after testing positive for drugs. Concern over the issues surrounding the use of anabolic steroids have continued ever since.

Among the reasons for widespread concern beyond the issue of cheating have been the purported health problems and severe side effects which use of these substances can entail. In addition to their being addictive, the use of anabolic steroids has been associated with sterility, increased aggressiveness, heart disease, and kidney and liver dysfunction in males. In females such use has been associated with increased facial and body hair, a deepening of the voice and disruption of the menstrual cycle.

See also: **drugs**

Further reading: Williams (1998), Yesalis (2000)

ANAEROBIC EXERCISE

Anaerobic exercise refers to the initial phase of physical activity, or short burst of effort, where energy is generated without the use of oxygen. Such exercise employs muscles at high intensity and a high work rate for a short period of time and is used as a means of increasing muscle strength or developing speed. As such, weight-lifting, jumping and sprinting are the most common forms of anaerobic activity. The benefits of anaerobic exercise include increased caloric consumption, increased metabolism and building lean tissue or muscle mass.

See also: **aerobic exercise**

ANATOMY AND PHYSIOLOGY

In order to understand the workings of the human body, biologists have focused on the body's structure (how it is put together) and its function (how it works). Anatomy is the study of the body's structure, and ranges from the study of cells (microanatomy) to the study of parts and systems (gross anatomy). Physiology is the study of the function of cells, organs and systems.

Anatomists typically divide the body into nine systems when analysing structure. These systems are: the skeleton, the muscles, the circulatory and respiratory systems, the nervous system, the glandular system, the digestive system, the urinary system, the reproductive system, and the skin. Physiologists study the functions of these systems and how they interact. A basic tenet of physiology is that the body tends to make internal adjustments so that its internal environment remains as stable and unchanging as possible. This is known as homeostasis. Physiologists study the ways in which the body achieves and maintains homeostasis. For those interested in sport and physical activity the skeleton, muscles, and the nervous system and the circulatory and respiratory systems are perhaps the most critical.

The skeletal system

The skeleton is a combination of bones, joints and cartilage. Its function is to support and protect the organs of the body and the soft tissue that surrounds them, while providing points of attachment or insertions for the muscles that enable us to move our bodies. Some of the body's 206 bones also produce blood cells in the bone marrow. Joints provide various forms of movement, and cartilage serves as a protective material between bones to cushion and facilitate that movement.

The muscular system

Muscles enable such movement to take place through their contractions since they are attached to bones by tendons. The control of such movement requires the development of motor skills in which the nervous system provides the necessary control of muscle activity. Unlike striated muscle which facilitates human movement, the two other forms of muscle found in the human body, smooth muscle and heart muscle, are not under conscious control.

The nervous system

The nervous system, which includes the brain, the spinal cord and the nerves, controls the body's activities. While the lower part of the brain controls autonomous functions such as breathing and heart rate, the higher part of the brain directs voluntary muscular activities and performs the important integrating and processing functions required for skilled movement. The brain receives and sends information to the nerves via the spinal cord, processing such information in order to provide appropriate and integrated movement that we associate with displays of sporting skills and excellence when conducted at the highest levels. The control of movement or motor control is an important area of sport science research.

The circulatory and respiratory systems

These provide the body with the nourishment and oxygen necessary to function and grow The circulatory system includes the heart, blood vessels and blood. The respiratory system includes the trachea, lungs and alveoli. The constant delivery of oxygen is necessary to sustain life. The respiratory system functions to bring oxygen into the blood for use at the tissues, as well as being responsible for the disposal of carbon dioxide. Regular exercise produces important changes in the circulatory system. Thus exercise undertaken to enhance endurance serves to increase blood flow to the working muscles, thereby providing the muscle cells with increased fuel and oxygen. Endurance training also increases the number of red blood cells and the volume of blood, both of which also enhance the capacity of the working muscles to perform.

See also: **biomechanics**

Further reading: Mottola (1992), Peronnet and Gardiner (1992), Wells and Luttgens (1976)

ANIMAL RIGHTS

Activists for animal rights argue for the dissolution of the ethical boundaries separating people from animals, thus mandating the moral consideration of animals and their protection from human exploitation. They question the morality of sportspeople who interact with animals, not merely in hunting, shooting and fishing, but in show-jumping, sheepdog trials and pigeon racing. In the nineteenth century some brutal **animal sports** such as cockfighting and bull baiting were made illegal, but this owed more to attempts to civilise the urban working class than to the precursors of the modern animal rights movement, the antivivisectionists. There are three strands within the animal rights activists: the welfarists who believe that animals deserve compassion and protection but allow that there are some boundaries between species; the pragmatists who argue that animals deserve moral and legal consideration, with a balance between human and animal interests, and who accept that there is some hierarchy of animals; and the fundamentalists who believe that animals have absolute moral and legal rights to autonomy with equal rights for all species. Obviously their goals and strategies vary. The welfarists aim to avoid cruelty and thus support reformist legislation and humane education; the pragmatists wish to avoid all unnecessary animal suffering but are prepared to negotiate and accept short-term compromise; the fundamentalists seek total and immediate abolition of animal exploitation and are prepared to use direct action and civil disobedience to support their protests.

See also: **animal sports, field sports debate**

Further reading: Collins et al. (2005), Franklin (1999), Kean (1998), Thomas (1983)

ANIMAL SPORTS

Animals have featured in sport as combatants, as prey, and as performers. Most of the first category have now been outlawed but, from the seventeenth- to the early nineteenth centuries, bull, bear and badger baiting, where dogs were set on a staked animal, were part of the sporting scenery. Cockfighting and matches between vicious dogs, often to the death, also offered opportunities for wagering and public entertainment. The animals were bred and trained especially for this combat. Throwing objects at cocks where a tethered bird was stoned to death also provided cheap entertainment in an era where concerns over animal welfare were minimal. Ratting too was a popular urban sport, in which a dog was timed in the killing of a number of the vermin in an enclosed pit. Now such activities are minor, clandestine affairs rather than the popular, public sports that they once were. Hunting, shooting and fishing were more associated with participation than with betting or watching, although sometimes involvement was restricted by social position. Coursing is one of the oldest of animal sports and involves competition between a pair of hunting dogs, usually greyhounds, in pursuit of live prey, usually a hare but sometimes a rabbit. Generally this sport has given way to groups of dogs chasing a mechanical hare around a track, though the Waterloo Cup, established in the 1820s, is still competed for with live quarry. Other sports involving animals performing include pigeon racing, horse racing, and other equestrian activities such as polo, show-jumping, and three-day eventing – which is still referred to in many parts of Europe as 'militaire' as it evolved from cavalry exercises in which horses had to prove their obedience, boldness and fitness.

Generally it is accepted that humans have become more civilised in their treatment of animals, though this has necessitated the intervention of the law to ban bull baiting in 1800 and cockfighting and other cruel animal sports in 1835. The use of RSPCA inspectors has aided the modern enforcement of this legislation, but certainly cockfights are still held surreptitiously in some areas. Hunting generally escaped legislation because of its friends in high places, but also because a case could be made for its importance in the rural economy. In recent years the debate over the alleged cruelty of hunting in its several forms has resurfaced, and Parliament has now outlawed most of its varieties. Live pigeon shooting, a sport in the 1904 Olympics, has given way to the clay variety.

As in most British leisure activities there is class differentiation. It occurs in the distinction between owning greyhounds or thoroughbred racehorses; in practising coarse angling or fly fishing; and in shooting grouse rather than rabbits.

See also: **animal rights**

Further reading: Collins et al. (2005), Franklin (1999), Kean (1998), Scherer (1995), Thomas (1983), Vamplew (2005b)

ANTHROPOLOGY

Anthropologists study the interaction of human culture, biology and environment; and while they are concerned with the study of the individual human, they are also concerned with broader comparative analyses of these elements, both across time and across different cultures. In studying human biology and human culture, anthropologists have developed two major sub-areas of focus: cultural anthropology and physical anthropology.

Cultural anthropologists have demonstrated that play, sport and physical activity are universal features of cultures past and present and yet, in their individual forms, these activities represent opportunities for assessing a particular culture and provide a way of assessing that culture's qualities and social problems. Early anthropologists of sport, such as Tylor and Culin, looked at the sports and games of non-Western tribal and pre-literate peoples. From these initial efforts, anthropologists have developed sophisticated studies of sport from a cross-cultural perspective. They have described and defined sport and physical activity in a range of cultures, analysing its language and symbols in an attempt to illustrate the depth, complexity and meaning of sport and physical activity in human society. TAASP (The Association for the Anthropological Study of Play), founded in 1974, signalled the growing interest in this area of study.

Blanchard has noted a number of major theoretical concerns that guide anthropologists studying sport and physical activity. These include the following:

- Sport is an integral part of culture and, as an institution, complements other aspects of culture. Thus to watch a game of cricket in the West Indies provides insight into the broader culture of those islands.
- The importance of the play aspect of sport in studying sport and physical activity.
- The fact that continuity and change in sport are both reflective of and yet factors in continuity and change in a culture. Thus while cricket continues to provide a sense of sporting and cultural continuity, the introduction of American football to the UK suggests change.

Anthropologists can help provide solutions to social problems such as violence because of the unique insights that they bring to such behaviour. The issue of soccer hooliganism has provided them with a rich area of study.

Physical anthropologists are interested in understanding biological variation and attempts to interpret meaningfully the wide range of variability characteristics of humans. In physical education and sport this concern is manifested in studies of human growth and development in relation to physical activity, and increasingly in studies of how our environment impacts our biology. Thus the effects of modern technologies such as the motor car, the computer and other labour-saving devices, have had an impact on the levels of physical activity of the populace in general, but certainly on the activity patterns of children (and thus on their growth and development) in particular. It is in this area that scholars such as Malina have made significant contributions to our understanding of the significance of physical activity to normal growth and development, and the impact that both excessive and minimal amounts of appropriate physical activity can have on the human organism, its structure and function.

Further reading: Blanchard (1996), Culin (1907), Huizinga (1950), James (1963), Malina (1983), Marsh (1983), Tylor (1879)

ARBITRATION

The idea of avoiding legal process and expense by turning to arbitration for the resolution of disputes has been slow to emerge in sport, though the International Olympic Committee has established a Council of Arbitration for Sport based in Lausanne, Switzerland and Sydney, Australia. In the UK the Central Council for Physical Recreation is considering the introduction of a similar body for British sport.

See also: **law**

Further reading: Fewell (1995)

ARCHIVES

Alongside the preservation of sporting venues and memorabilia in personal and public collections, one of the most important ways of understanding the sporting past is through archives. Without archival material, it is difficult for researchers wishing to understand sport in a historical context to conduct their work. As the awareness of the importance of sports history has increased, since the 1970s, so more sports clubs, associations and organisations have preserved material relating to various aspects of their operations. Unfortunately, as with **museums**, very few sporting archives can afford the luxury of purpose-built facilities or the employment costs of a professional archivist or librarian. There is, however, a wealth of material available both in private and public collections throughout the world. Much archival material is held by sporting clubs, but increasingly national repositories and libraries have begun to collect sports-related material. Many international sporting bodies, such as FIFA and the IOC, have archives dedicated to collecting all material relating to their activities.

AROUSAL

In the sport **psychology** literature, arousal has been defined in a variety of ways but is generally thought of as a physiological state of readiness to perform. As such, arousal is viewed as neither positive nor negative and as having both beneficial and detrimental effects on an athlete's performance. For humans, physiological arousal is a homeostatic process in that each individual has an optimal level of arousal. Arousal should not be confused with stress, which is an individual's response to an environmental demand. The fact that stress can, and often does, induce physiological arousal does not mean that the terms are interchangeable. And while some types and levels of stress can produce positive outcomes, they can also induce arousal in association with the negative form of stress we term anxiety.

Interest in the relationship between arousal and athletic performance has led to two major theories: drive theory and the inverted-U theory. Drive theorists posit that there is a positive linear relationship between arousal and performance. The higher the level of arousal, the higher the level of performance. Inverted-U theorists state that athletic performance will be facilitated by moderate levels of arousal. An athlete's performance will be less than optimal if they are either under-aroused (or 'not up for it') or over-aroused ('over the top'). Additionally, such theorists have also noted that different activities require different levels of arousal. Thus, for a biathlete to be successful, they need to be able to alter their levels of arousal when skiing and when shooting for optimal performance. Recent research has focused on the anxiety/performance relationship and on an individual's subjective understanding and interpretation of anxiety because it seems that successful athletes tend to view their anxiety as a means of helping rather than hindering their performance. They like the 'big occasion' and seem to be able to rise to the challenge which an anxiety-inducing situation, such as an Olympic final, can provide.

See also: **aggression, psychology**

Further reading: Landers and Boutcher (1986), Wann (1997), Yerkes and Dodson (1908)

ASSESSMENT

Assessment is a means of quantifying ability, performance or progress in practical and/or theoretical areas of the subject. It can be on-going, which measures progress (formative assessment), or it may represent a final attainment (summative assessment). Some assessments may be objective, such as a distance or a height attained in an athletic event, and any awarded marks or grades would therefore be self-evident to both the assessor (e.g. teacher or examiner) and the subject (e.g. the performer or student). In other cases, assessment is almost entirely subjective (e.g. tactical ability in a game or a performance in dance), and this type of assessment must be supported by a clear and well structured framework of objectives or characteristics against which performance may be interpreted and measured with some con-sistency. In physical education, assessment occurs most commonly within the framework of the National Curriculum and in GCSE examinations for students up to the age of sixteen years, and in AS, A2, GNVQ, etc. examinations for sixth-formers. Under the rules of the recent qualifications framework, assessment is conducted through unit based systems of credit accumulation and transfer.

ATHLETICISM

During the nineteenth century, as sports and games grew in popu-larity in the **public schools**, the ideal of athleticism emerged. For the schoolmasters who were promoting sports, their decision to have boys playing football or doing gymnastic exercises was ideological. Sport was not played solely for its own good, but was a method of inculcating the boys with Christian values through physical exercise. The core value was the promotion of **muscular Christianity**. Key amongst the early proponents of athleticism was Thomas Arnold at

Rugby School, who argued that by playing games and sport, boys would channel their excess energies. Such physical preparation made the boys better citizens, and kept their minds and bodies away from damaging pursuits which challenged the social order. Effectively, athleticism was about the development of good character and an instrument of social control. Athleticism taught the boys loyalty, integrity, obedience, magnanimity in victory, dignity in defeat and fair play. Although initially promoted in certain leading English **public schools** such as Rugby or Charterhouse, the concept of athleticism was one that was rapidly diffused throughout the educational system, and eventually across the British Empire. It was held that boys who were trained in all the good virtues of athleticism would be good leaders in education, business, the military and throughout the empire, and would use their experiences to control and educate others. The muscular Christian ethos of athleticism, with its accompanying embrace of manliness, was central in transferring leadership, gentlemanly conduct and fair play from the playing field to the wider world.

See also: **muscular Christianity, public schools**

Further reading: Brailsford (1992), Holt (1989), Lowerson (1993), Mangan (1981)

ATP (ADENOSINE TRIPHOSPHATE)

ATP, the body's major source of energy, is a complex nucleotide. It is found in all cells in the body, but chiefly in muscle tissue. When ATP breaks down into adenosine diphosphate (ADP) and an inorganic phosphate (Pi), energy is released.

See also: **energy metabolism, energy systems**

AUTONOMIC NERVOUS SYSTEM

The autonomic nervous system (ANS), sometimes known as the visceral or automatic nervous system, regulates individual organ function such as control of heart rate, blood vessels and glands. The ANS is divided into two separate divisions, the parasympathetic and the sympathetic systems. Physiologically the parasympathetic system is concerned with the conservation and restoration of energy, whereas the sympathetic system enables the body to be prepared for flight or fight, and controls such responses as heart rate, blood pressure and cardiac output.

BAT AND BALL GAMES

Scholars have puzzled endlessly over the origin of ball games, and have come to no solid conclusion about the genesis of these activities, which are to be found in all cultures and which we know have existed in various forms across time. Henderson has suggested that all modern games played with bat and ball come from one common source – an ancient fertility rite observed by priest-kings in Egypt. He notes that in practically all early cultures we find traces of religious rites practised in spring involving two parties that dramatised the conflict between winter and summer and in which the ball represented the sun, source of life, warmth and energy and fertility for the growth of crops and thus food. Primitive and ancient sports, such as the ball games of the Mayans and the Aztecs, were played within the sacred precincts of a temple, and were probably forms of worship. They ended with an act of human sacrifice. The ritual quality of such activity has led Sansone to suggest that sport can be best thought of as the ritual sacrifice of human energy. These pagan games took on religious significance in a Christian world. We find ball games played in churchyards and against the walls of churches between buttresses, games which are precursors to handball, fives and other 'wall' games. By contrast, in Greek and Roman societies, the ball was generally used as a means of conditioning the body – the medicine ball – although harpastum is thought to be a forerunner of football and perhaps hurling.

As Money (1997: 2) notes, the first possible mention of football in England is in William Fitzstephen's 'Descriptio nobilissimoe civitatis Londoniae' (1174) written as a preface to his *Life of Thomas Becket*. Fitzstephen notes that 'Every year on the day which is called Carnival [now Shrove Tuesday] ... the entire youth of the city goes into the fields for the famous game of ball'.

Ball games that involved kicking a ball or hitting a ball with the hand required very little equipment and could thus be readily played by people of all classes. Thus, we find calcio in Italy, la soule in France, but we also find hurling in Cornwall and in Ireland, and shinty in Scotland. With the development of bats and later rackets, the traditional hitting, catching and throwing games could be enhanced. The development of different types of balls – wooden, those of leather or cloth filled with stuffing, and those made from animal bladders and filled with air – led to further variations on the themes of kicking and hitting, catching and throwing.

Games such as bandy, shinty, croquet, cricket, hockey, golf, baseball, rounders, stick ball, bat and trap, trapball, lacrosse, stoolball and bowling all required particular types of open space in which to be played. Some required specific 'goals'. Tennis, rackets, fives, handball, squash and pelota all require spaces with particular structures (walls, buttresses, etc.) to facilitate play. As we have moved from traditional to modern societies, these spaces and structures have undergone the kind of **modernisation** which Guttmann describes in his treatise on the nature of modern sport, so that the rationale behind the playing of bat and ball games in Western societies has changed from being for ritualistic purposes to the achievement of records. The degree of technical sophistication and rationality now attached to bat and ball games bears continuing witness to this development.

In trying to classify bat and ball games, no obvious system has emerged or been developed. **Categorisation** has been attempted in a number of ways varying from number of players (team vs. individual) to type of equipment and facilities (racket games, net games, court games, wall games) to the goal of the game (invasion games). None of these categories helps codify clearly the broad range of bat and ball games played in cultures and countries around the world, suggesting the diversity of contexts, motivations, meanings and benefits which bat and ball games offer.

Further reading: Brailsford (1992), Guttmann (1978), Henderson (1947), Money (1997), Sansone (1988)

BENEFITS

Benefits provide an additional source of income for sportspersons. Usually they have taken the form of the net proceeds from either a specially organised 'friendly' match – most common in the football codes – or from a competitive championship fixture. This was risky as expenses were fixed but revenue was not. Sometimes clubs might guarantee a minimum sum in case of bad weather or unanticipated events lowered expected attendance. In the past this was not always the case and some county cricketers actually lost money when rain prevented play. To counter this problem, supplementary fund-raising events are now often held alongside benefit matches to generate more revenue and to spread the financial risk.

Benefits originated in cricket in the nineteenth century as money-raising events for veteran professionals nearing retirement in an era when there were no state pensions. The intention was to provide a nest-egg to enable players to set themselves up after retirement from the sport, usually at an age when their contemporaries were still employed. Initially benefits were designed to encourage player loyalty, only being awarded after many years' service. Historically this was around fifteen years for cricketers and five or more for footballers. More recently, there has been a trend for star players rather than the journeyman professionals to be offered a benefit; indeed many such players have this written into their contracts. This has, of course, changed the nature of the benefit from a tax-free one to being part of expected income and thus liable to normal taxation procedures. Players now commonly employ professional fund-raisers to arrange and run their benefit appeals. It is likely that the benefit will become less important as personal, portable and contributory pensions come on stream for professional sportsmen.

See also: **economics, sporting heroes**

Further reading: Vamplew and Sandiford (1999)

BIOMECHANICS

Often described as involving the interrelationship of the biologic and material properties of the **skeletal**, articular and neuromuscular systems and the laws and principles of mechanics, biomechanics is concerned with factors that affect movement of the body both internal (e.g. muscular form) and external (e.g. **gravity**, friction). In sport and physical activity, it is also concerned with the movement of implements or equipment used in athletics, exercise, games and sports.

Efficient and effective human movement is dependent upon the coordinated integration of the **skeletal**, **muscular** and **nervous** systems. Thus appropriate neural stimulation activates muscular contraction that in turn generates muscular force which moves our anatomical **levers**. When combined with mechanics, which is the branch of physical science which deals with the physical laws and principles relating to objects at rest or in motion, biomechanics is the study of the body in motion (dynamics) and in equilibrium (statics), and provides both descriptive (kinematic) and **force** (kinetic) analysis of human movement. Applying biomechanical analysis in sport and physical education generally takes one or more of three forms: teaching fundamental movements; improving performance techniques; and/or remediating or re-establishing movement patterns after illness or injury.

See also: **anatomy and physiology**

Further reading: Adrian and Cooper (1995), Bartlett (1999), Hay (1993)

BLOOD PRESSURE

Blood is carried from the heart to all parts of the body through the arteries. Blood pressure is the force of the blood pushing against the walls of the arteries. It is at its highest when the heart beats and is called systolic pressure, and then drops when the heart is at rest (i.e. between beats) and is called the diastolic pressure. Blood pressure is measured in millimetres of mercury (mmHg) and is expressed as systolic pressure/diastolic pressure. Normal pressure is 120/80 mmHg. Physical activity increases systolic blood pressure and can typically reach 200 mmHg with heavy endurance exercise. By contrast diastolic pressure changes little with exercise. Normal pressures above 140/90 mmHg are considered to be indicators of hypertension.

See also: **heart rate**

BODY

Studies of the body, and its importance within sport and physical exercise, have become increasingly important since the late 1980s. Researchers across a range of different disciplines realised that the body could no longer be considered an unchanging and constant fact, but was something that had to be assessed within the context of its social and cultural setting. Historically and contemporarily, it has now been realised that the body is defined and constructed by its social setting. Therefore our understanding of the female body, and its capacity to participate in sport, is radically different at the beginning of the twenty-first century, to how it was conceived a hundred years

27

ago. If we are open to different conceptions and constructions of the body, then we have to rethink, as Coakley (1998: 11) argued, about 'sex, sex differences, sexuality, ideals of beauty, self-image, body image, fashion, hygiene, health, nutrition, eating, fitness, racial classification systems, disease, drugs and other things that affect our lives'. In essence, studying the body, in the context of sport and physical fitness, offers a whole new way of thinking about human beings and their interaction with society. Sport has encouraged us to think of the body in a variety of different ways. Sports medicine and training have made bodies stronger and fitter, and many elite bodies are artificially tailored for their sports. Sports such as aerobics, which are essentially concerned with body image, and concepts of beauty, offer challenges as they seek to change the shape and style of the body. Sports sociologists, by examining the body, have been able to question the idea of what we mean by 'natural', have allowed us to place the excesses of training and preparation in context, and have forced us to explore the possible costs of current sporting technologies that are used to manipulate the body. Many new areas of research are still being uncovered, especially with relation to the cultural and historical understanding of the body.

Further reading: Booth (2001), Coakley (1998), Hoberman (1992), Loy et al. (1993), Shilling (1994)

BODY COMPOSITION

The human body is composed of a variety of different types of tissues, which are generally categorized as 'lean' tissues, including bone, muscle and organs, and adipose or 'fat' tissue. Total Body Composition is a lean-to-fat ratio and is generally referred to as the percentage of body fat. The average percent body fat is 15–18 per cent for men and 22–25 per cent for women while amongst highly trained endurance athletes these figures may be as low as 5 per cent for men and 12 per cent for women. Figures below this are considered unhealthy as are figures over 25 per cent for men and 32 per cent for women since they correlate highly with illness and disease. Body composition can be estimated and assessed in a number of ways. Among these, hydrostatic or 'underwater' weighing is considered the 'gold standard'. Bio-impedance is a more easily conducted but controversial assessment technique. Use of skin-fold measurements is still among the most widely employed and reliable techniques when performed by a trained and skilled tester. While body composition is based in part on heredity, per cent body fat is related to lifestyle and can be altered through nutrition and exercise.

β-OXIDATION

The process by which fats are broken down in the mitrochondria to generate Acetyl-CoA.

See also: **Krebs cycle**

BOXING DEBATE

Boxing is a controversial sport that has always drawn criticism from physicians and moralists alike. The moral controversy that surrounds boxing is embedded in two differing ethical stances, the one stressing individual autonomy, the other paternalism. Based on the harm principle, those arguing for individual autonomy conclude that boxing should be allowed. Those arguing that we have a paternalist duty to protect each other argue that boxing should be banned. For those who believe that boxing should be allowed, the arguments are straightforward. Those who freely choose to box, knowing full well the potential injury and damage they can cause themselves and their opponents, should be granted the autonomy to do so. Others have no right to prevent such freedom of choice, and freedom of action and activity, among fully informed and consenting adults. Furthermore, risk of death or brain damage is in fact less than in other high **risk sports** such as hang gliding, sky diving and motorcycle racing.

For the paternalists who argue against boxing, the argument is very different. While some paternalists would argue that they have an obligation to prevent an individual from boxing because they are likely to harm themselves, all paternalists would agree that boxing involves the intentional harming of another. Since such harms are morally objectionable in a civilised society and we claim to be a civilised society, then boxing should be banned. The British Medical Association, which has long argued against boxing, can provide evidence to support their claim that there are serious neurological, and non-neurological, injuries which occur as a result of boxing and that these injuries constitute significant 'costs' to society, the boxer's family, etc. In response to the intractability of this debate, both sides have attempted to make boxing safer by encouraging the use of **protective equipment**, limiting bouts and increasing medical surveillance.

Further reading: Jordan (1993), Rose (1988), Sugden (1996)

BOYCOTTS

With the advent of international sporting competition, such as the **Olympics**, it was perhaps inevitable that **politics** would enter sport. Rather than making political capital on the battlefield or in diplomatic negotiations, it was easier for nations to score political points in the sporting arena. As interest in sport grew from the **media**, and **television** coverage was extended to become international, so any political actions were instantly relayed to the whole of the world. The act of **boycott**, simply refusing to attend a sporting event, is an immensely powerful weapon. Any major sporting event bestows honour, prestige and attention on the host nation or city. By refusing to attend the event, a nation effectively withdraws support and legitimacy and makes the whole spectacle less impressive. A policy of boycott was discussed by many nations in the context of the 1936 **Olympic Games** in Berlin, but rejected. As a result Hitler was able to claim that he had hosted one of the greatest games to date, that was fully attended. Such attendance, it was argued, legitimised his regime internationally. On the international stage, two events in the second half of the twentieth century provoked boycotts of international sporting events and fixtures. The first was the politics of the Cold War, which led to the refusal of many Western nations to attend the 1980 Olympics in Moscow in the wake of the Soviet invasion of Afghanistan. In response, the Soviets led a reciprocal boycott by Eastern Bloc nations of the 1984 games in Los Angeles. The second issue, that of South Africa and its policy of apartheid, caused many more problems. The 1976 Olympics in Montreal was the victim of boycotts, as were the **Commonwealth Games** of 1986, in Edinburgh. Whether the decision to boycott a major sporting fixture or event actually changes any government's policy is hard to say. What is clear is that such decisions demonstrate the importance of major international sporting events, and their clear link with **politics**.

See also: **government policy, politics**

Further reading: Hain (1982), Ramsamy (1984)

BRANDING

The creation of a brand image is important for any business that hopes to secure repeat sales via customer recognition and appreciation of its product. This objective did not have much impact on sport until the advent of **merchandising** of official club products revealed a potential important source of revenue, in addition to the more traditional gate receipts and season tickets. Logos now feature on a host of endorsed products, many of them not at all connected with sport. As clubs increasingly move into non-sports areas of marketing, it is likely that sport branding will shift to a more generic club or company name. As is often the case in the business of sport, Manchester United have paved the way and have now dropped the FC from their logo, leaving chocolates, beer and numerous other goods branded simply as an official Manchester United product.

See also: **marketing, merchandising**

BRIGHTON DECLARATION

The Brighton Declaration took its name from the English seaside resort that hosted the first World Conference on Women and Sport in May 1994. The conference was attended by 280 delegates who represented sports, governmental and educational institutions in 82 countries. The Declaration was a statement of principles with the objective of developing a sporting culture that enabled and valued the full involvement of women in every aspect of sport – as athletes, administrators, coaches and officials. To some extent it was a wish list with no practical operational mechanisms but with the aim of being a useful tool to persuade those who could make decisions to allocate resources and take other action.

Further reading: White (2001)

BUREAUCRACY

In the nineteenth century, alongside the birth of modern sport, there emerged a growing dependence on the need for bureaucracy in sport. During the period when sport first emerged in its modern form, sports were steadily codified, leagues and cup competitions organised and gate receipts, wages and other income had to be accounted for. In Britain, the middle and upper classes were central in the formation of committees that would oversee the drawing up of rules, and who presented themselves as the custodians of sport. While such committees, the first embodiment of sporting bureaucracy, were amateur, this work rapidly became professionalised: club secretaries, accountants and other officers were appointed on a paid basis to ensure that any given sport, association or club ran smoothly. In the post-Second World War era, as the sports business rapidly expanded and became increasingly global, so paid officials became ever more important. No major sporting organisation can now function without an extensive bureaucracy, which is able to lease with television companies, players, agents, national governments and international federations.

See also: **administration, management**

Further reading: Hall (1987)

BURN-OUT

Unlike **over-training**, burn-out can affect both athletes and coaches alike, because it is as much, if not more, related to individual factors as it is to job or activity demands. Burn-out tends to accompany those with a high need for success. These individuals have a tendency to shoulder responsibilities themselves, and often believe that the only way to get things done properly is to do it themselves. They tend to take total responsibility for success (and failure) and thus carry enormous pressures and burdens. For professional coaches at the highest levels, in particular, where a job is dependent on on-going success, the tendency to burn out is particularly strong. The impact of burn-out on interpersonal relationships amongst players or between players and coaches tends to be one of alienation, so that coaches and athletes tend to become less concerned about others and more concerned about themselves. Feelings of lack of appreciation and a tendency towards 'blaming' – either others, themselves or the situation – are typical responses to such problems and are indicative of burn-out. Appropriate emotional, psychological and social support, along with 'well defined' periods of involvement in sport (a limited-term contract) are some of the methods being used to limit burn-out amongst players and coaches at the highest levels. However, it should be appreciated that burn-out can take place at all levels of sporting performance and amongst athletes of all ages. Examples of young athletes suffering burn-out after being pushed by parents and coaches to succeed, abound and offer sobering examples of the impact of the pressure for success.

See also: **over-training**

Further reading: Dale and Weinberg (1990), Henschen (1996), Kallus and Kellman (2000), Weinberg and Gould (1999)

CALLISTHENICS

Callisthenics is a form of free body exercise. Callisthenics emerged in the nineteenth century and was promoted by pioneers in the modern gymnastic world such as Adolf Speiss and Friedrich Ludwig Jahn. Although having its original base in the European nations of Sweden and Germany, callisthenics spread around the world. In the United States, Catherine Beecher was an important figure in its promotion and development. Beecher promoted callisthenics as an ideal form of exercise for women, but ultimately it would appeal to both sexes.

Although some light apparatus is sometimes used (such as rings), callisthenics is largely apparatus free. The exercises, which are supposed to stretch all muscle groups, include movements such as bending, swinging, jumping and so on. Callisthenics promotes general well-being, and specifically advances strength and flexibility. The exercises are especially useful in that they promote cardiovascular activity. Although often used as stand alone exercises, callisthenics are also used by many other athletes as a way of warming up.

CARDIAC OUTPUT

The product of heart rate (HR) and stroke volume (SV), cardiac output (CO) is the total volume of blood pumped by the left ventricle per minute, and is measured in litres per minute (L/min). During exercise, cardiac output increases in order to supply adequate amounts of oxygen and nutrients to working muscles and clear away waste products. The resting value for cardiac output is approximately 5ñ0 L/min and increases between 20 and 40 L/min depending on the individual and their level of training, with the relationship between cardiac output and exercise intensity being essentially a positive linear relationship.

CARTELS

Some economists view the various sports leagues as business cartels, created in order to reduce economic competition. They see an arrangement of firms (football clubs, basketball clubs, etc.) that agree to pursue joint policies with respect to key aspects of the environment in which they operate (super league, county cricket championship, etc.). Such policies might cover pricing (minimum admission charges), distribution of revenue (pooling of gate receipts), output (fixture schedules), supply of inputs (restrictions on player mobility), or cost of inputs (maximum wages). Sports cartels emerge from the mutual interdependence of clubs: the gate revenue of any club depends on the performance of all clubs. Clubs may be sports competitors but they can be economic partners. Only one team can win the championship but, in an effective cartel, all clubs can make profits. In many respects sports cartels resemble industrial ones, but with two major differences. First, most clubs have some degree of geographical monopoly with regard to their fan base, hence there is less danger than for a business cartel of a price-cutting war erupting to secure customers. Second, there is little chance of a club unilaterally opting to increase its output: indeed it is hard to conceive of any club voluntarily quitting a league and remaining an effective competitor in the industry. Sporting leagues are cartels where entry and exit is rigidly controlled. They are not competitive industries in which firms can freely come and go.

The effective operation of a sports cartel requires a central, decision-making body with the power to discipline members for rule infractions, to impose cost-minimising regulations such as **salary caps**, maximum **wages**, territorial restrictions on recruitment, maximum team rosters and impediments on player **mobility**, and to operate group revenue-raising policies, especially with regard to the sale of media rights.

See also: **economics**

Further reading: Gratton and Taylor (1985)

CATEGORISATION

It is a useful analytical device to divide sports into types. A simple format is to talk of invasion games such as football and rugby, where moving into an opponent's territory is a key feature; court games such as tennis, badminton and fives where a net or wall is used; target games such as golf and archery; and conquest sports such as mountaineering. One of the first to present such an analysis was Huizinga, whose categorisation encompassed pursuit (chase), enigma (mental), chance (gamble), vertigo (heady), strategy (planning), imitation (pretence), dexterity (skill) and exultation (excitement). Then Caillois in 1961 promoted a four-part categorisation of agon (competition), mimicry (pretence), alean (chance) and ilinx (vertigo). He was followed three years later by McIntosh, who proposed competition, aesthetic, combat, chance and conquest. Crum, for the purpose of examining the motivation of participants, has produced a more recent set of categories that identifies seven groupings. In elite sport the dominant motives are absolute achievement, status and money. At competitive club sport level, the participants are attracted by a mix of the excitement of competition, the pursuit of subjective achievement, and social contact. In recreational sport relaxation, health and togetherness come to the fore. The dominant motive in fitness sports is obviously physical fitness, whereas that in risk and **adventure sports** is thrill. Hedonism and exclusive pleasure feature in what Crum terms the 'lust sports' that focus on sun, sea, sand, snow, sex, speed and satisfaction. Finally, he identifies physical appearance as being the main thrust of **cosmetic** sports.

Further reading: Caillois (2001), Crum (1999), Huizinga (1950), McIntosh (1979)

CENTRAL NERVOUS SYSTEM

The central nervous system (CNS) is divided into two parts: the brain and the spinal cord. These serve as the main processing centre for the whole of the nervous system, gather information from both inside and outside the body, and control all of the workings of the body. The brain sends messages to the spinal cord and body through neurons. These messages are sent in electrical signals that are converted into chemical signals at the synapse. The spinal cord conducts sensory information from the peripheral nervous system to the brain and conducts motor information from the brain to the muscles and glands. Both the brain and the spinal cord consist of 'white matter' – bundles of axons each coated with a protective sheath of myelin, and 'grey matter' – masses of cell bodies and dendrites each covered with synapses.

See also: **anatomy and physiology**

CHARACTER BUILDING

Sport, particularly in mid-Victorian England, was often viewed as character building in that the individual would subsume self-interest under that of the team, obey the orders of the captain without question, and develop the virtues of courage, manliness and *esprit de corps*. Such arguments are still advanced by purists. Others, however, suggest that the assumption that sport will develop 'good character' is a false one. Vamplew, for one, has postulated that such virtues may be fine at the micro level of the game or the sport, but not within wider society, where manliness might lead to brutality and arrestable offences, and team solidarity to xenophobia.

See also: **muscular Christianity**

Further reading: Vamplew (2005b)

CHILDREN

Sport is seen as having positive advantages for **children**. It can provide enjoyment and promote physical **fitness**; it can result in improved posture and a healthier lifestyle; and it can help develop hand-eye coordination and motor **skills**. Then there are the perceived social goals of **sportsmanship**, teamwork, responsibility, commitment and self-discipline. Schools have a major role in assisting this sporting development of the child. Outside the school, sport for children is a twentieth-century phenomenon. Prior to that, and indeed well into the century, the maxim was that if they were big enough they were old enough to participate in adult sport. Fortunately, a major development of the past two decades has been the introduction of games with modified rules, which has assisted participation as sport has spread down the age scale to the physically immature. Progressively these special rules are eliminated as the children gain the necessary skills, so that when old enough they can play fully competitive sport.

A major problem with children's sport is the adults associated with it, the pushy parents and the coach who seeks victory rather than fun and participation. Moreover, following the withdrawal of many teachers from extracurricular activities after the union disputes of the 1980s, one major source of protection for children disappeared, leaving many youngsters to be coached by unqualified personnel.

Nevertheless, perhaps too much critical emphasis can be placed on the negative aspects of children's sport. There are coaches who are trying to improve their qualifications to teach young persons, and who set realistic targets for their charges, and there are parents who want their offspring to enjoy their sport irrespective of the result.

Further reading: Grisognono (1991)

CHOKING

Research suggests that stress management is a very significant factor in successful athletic performance. After a poor performance, athletes often report having experienced feelings of self-doubt, and when these self-doubts become so great that they radically affect performance in an adverse manner, athletes refer to this phenomenon as 'choking'. Numerous theories have been proposed to explain this phenomenon, the most common of which is the inverted-U hypothesis, which holds that an optimal or medium level of arousal and stress results in optimal performance, whereas low or, in the case of choking, very high levels of stress result in inferior performance. While this theory has intuitive appeal, critics have suggested that it is inadequate and overly simplistic, in that arousal and stress are multifaceted concepts and athletes may well 'choke' for a variety of reasons. Thus alternative theories have been posited, including the optimal functioning model, the catastrophe model, and more recently, a reversal theory model. All of these models make contributions to our understanding of choking, but it remains a subject of considerable continuing research interest.

See also: **psychology**

Further reading: Gould and Damarjian (1998), Hanin (2000), Hardy (1990), Kerr (1997)

CIRCULATORY SYSTEM *see* **anatomy and physiology**

CIVIL LAW

In simple terms, civil law covers those legal areas where individuals or groups can sue others for damages; for example, if a professional sportsperson is injured by the foul or negligent play of an opponent, he or she may seek redress through the courts for the resulting loss of income and career prospects. Generally, required standards of proof are less in civil than in **criminal law**.

See also: **criminal law**

CLASS

The notion that society is made up of a range of different and hierarchical classes has long been central to studies in areas such as **history** and **sociology**. Although some form of societal distinction has always existed, the class system has its origins in the process of industrialisation which began in the eighteenth century. In Britain, the creation of an urbanised workforce, dependent on factory owners for employment, led to the emergence of the working class. Traders, some professionals and factory owners were grouped together as the middle class, while members of the old professions such as the law, the landed gentry and the social elite formed the upper class. The class system in Britain was, as Lowerson (1993) has demonstrated, central to the emergence of modern sport. The codification of sport was viewed as essential to the wider control of the leisure time and activities of the working classes. The better that sport and other forms of recreation could be controlled by the hierarchy, the easier it was to maintain the social order. The on-going class distinctiveness of sport featured well into the twentieth century. In cricket, the **amateur/professional** divide that was maintained until the 1960s, was effectively a distinction that revolved around the concepts of gentlemen and players. Broad assumptions were made about the class following of any given game, so that football was seen as the 'people's game', that is, working-class, while rugby union was predominantly understood as a middle-class and southern-based pursuit.

In theoretical terms class relations have been understood, according to Coakley (1998: 35), as the 'social processes revolving around who has economic power, how economic power is used, and who is advantaged or disadvantaged by economic factors in a society'. Many historians and sociologists have examined the issue of class as one that serves as an agent of change within society, yet one that perpetuates and heightens social inequalities. The concept of class control that emerged during the industrial revolution is little changed. Sport is still used by those classes who possess power in society to organise sports and games that protect the status quo. Sport can be used to separate one social class from another through the use of exclusive clubs. Private members' clubs in sports such as golf, polo, or even gyms, exclude those who do not have the economic or social power to join. It has been argued that in the wake of the Taylor Report, and the construction of new football stadia in England, ticket prices have been raised to such an extent that working-class supporters can no longer afford to enter the ground. Despite its exclusivity, sport has been successfully used by many athletes to break out of their own social class. Boxing has been one sport where athletes have been able to escape from the ghetto, and in the process achieve wealth. One would question however, whether a boxer such as Mike Tyson, who has undoubtedly become rich through his sport, has been able to break out of his class location into the elite ranks of class society, given his brushes with the law and his time spent in prison.

The most important element of class control in sport has always been the issue of ownership. Throughout history the majority of sports associations, federations and organisations have been run by the elite within society. Any assessment of the men and women who have made up the committee of the International Olympic Committee, the Jockey Club or the Football Association would demonstrate how few working-class people have been represented. The same is true of the media and sporting goods industries attached to contemporary sport. Power in these industries predominantly rests with a small group of white, well educated and well connected men. Class, then, is an essential instrument through which the power relationships in sport can be understood.

Further reading: Eitzen (1995), Hargreaves (1986), Lowerson (1993), Sugden and Tomlinson (2000)

CLOSED LOOP

A closed-loop model has a processing loop to bring information into the motor system while movement is occurring, rather than waiting until the completion of the movement, as in the open-loop model. This means that the closed-loop model can provide on-going feedback and correction, thereby reducing errors during the movement. Supporters of the closed-loop model point to the deterioration of performance when feedback is withdrawn as evidence of support for this model. Movements that take larger than 200 milliseconds to perform appear to enable on-going corrections to be made.

Further reading: Adams (1971), Magill (1998), Schmidt and Lee (1999)

COACHING

Reasons why individuals participate in sport and physical activity are as wide ranging and varied as the opportunities available. These may range from the pure joy of participation in physical activity, to espoused social and moral benefits, to economic and material reward. The 'coach' is generally the person charged with imparting the knowledge and skill necessary to achieve those desired ends through coaching.

While there is little disagreement amongst those involved in sport and physical activity that good coaching can enhance a performer's level of performance and degree of enjoyment, the question of who should be coaching, what qualities and characteristics they should possess, what experience they should have had and what qualifications they should hold, have long been topics of debate. Since the late 1970s in Great Britain, there have been efforts to develop a strategy to enhance coaching education, and each individual sporting association recognised by Sport UK has developed coaching education programmes, coaching structures, coaching levels and examinations. In recent years, the **National Coaching Foundation** has been set up to help in these efforts and, in so doing, has attempted to bring some degree of **standardisation** to qualifications.

The vast majority of coaches are volunteers who themselves were enthusiastic and often skilled performers. Many elite performers who wish to continue their association with and participation in a sport, once their own playing days are over, turn to coaching. An on-going and apparently irresolvable issue in coaching is whether experience as an elite performer is a necessary and/or a sufficient condition for coaching success. Generally, it has been assumed that the elite performer's experience is not a sufficient condition for coaching success at any level, but it may be a necessary condition for coaching success at the elite levels, since the coach who has experience at the elite level can more readily identify with the issues faced by elite athletes, and also has more in common with elite athletes. By contrast, the coach who was an elite athlete may be less able to help athletes who are not as gifted in terms of talent and ability.

The most widespread source of coaching expertise lies with those who have trained as physical education teachers, since they combine pedagogical skills with an understanding of movement skill development, and an appreciation for individual differences in ability, motivation and commitment amongst athletes. It is largely for these reasons that this group of individuals offer the most in both the development of coaching and in the practice of coaching.

See also: **National Coaching Foundation**

Further reading: Armour et al. (2003), Cassidy et al. (2004), Lyle (2002)

COGNITION

Cognition is the technical term for thinking. In sports, an athlete's thoughts and emotions can influence performance quality and outcome both positively and negatively. Researchers have attempted to ascertain the thoughts and feelings of elite, consistently successful athletes both before and during the contest in contrast to less successful competitors and non-athletes in order to ascertain the impact of cognition on performance. Many elite athletes now employ a range of cognitive strategies, such as imagery and visualisation, positive self-talk, attribution training, and mental practice in order to improve performance.

COLLECTIVE MEMORY

Sport has the ability to have a powerful impact on society. Since the advent of modern sport, there has been a host of events that have become seminal, legendary and mythologised. In the same way that people remember where they were when Kennedy was shot, or a man landed on the moon, so sports events become part of the collective memory. Such memories are not solely the product of having been in the stadium and seeing the game 'live', but can also be produced through the **media**, and live broadcasts on **television** or radio. Modern communications now allow entire nations, indeed the entire globe, to be present at a sporting event. Sporting events that are indicative of collective memory are often those that are connected with major international sporting festivals and projected to the wider population by the **media**. However, as many forms of collective memory are nation-specific, the force or poignancy of the memory will vary depending of an individual's nationality. Examples of sporting collective memory for English people might include their victory in the 1966 football World Cup finals, Cathy Freeman's success at the Sydney **Olympics** would serve Australians, while Americans might all recall the career of Michael Jordan on the basketball court. On the global level, events of significance that enter the collective memory include the killings of Israeli athletes at the 1972 Olympics, the gymnastic perfection of Olga Korbut, or the French victory in the 1998 football World Cup finals.

See also: **media, sporting heroes, television**

COLONIALISM

A product of the formal process of **colonisation**, colonialism was historically understood as the ideological spread of the ideas of the occupying nation to the population of the colonised country. The British Empire was a major force in the process of colonialism. The spread of British ideas, practices and values across the world was aided by its control of a large proportion of the world's countries. While many of the features of colonialism were connected to formal concepts such as military control, the law and finance, informal aspects such as sport were equally important, and the effects just as long-standing. The process of colonialism in the British Empire was central to the global spread of specific sports such as cricket, football, golf and rugby. It was equally powerful in transferring the ideologies of **fair play**, **muscular Christianity** and gentlemanly conduct across the globe.

The process of sporting colonialism has not ended with the retreat of nations such as Britain from formal empire. Rather than being spread through military conquest and colonial governments, ideas and practices are now diffused by multinational corporations, the media and advertising. Colonialism, it can be argued is still an on-going process, although more often understood and labelled as **globalisation**. Companies such as Nike use sporting icons such as Michael Jordan in advertising to ensure that their products are sold throughout the world. Sports organisations, whether the International Olympic Committee or FIFA, can also be understood as agents of colonialism, as they see one of their primary functions to spread their sport, organisation and ethos throughout the globe.

See also: **colonisation, cultural imperialism, decolonisation**

Further reading: Bale and Cronin (2002), Guttmann (1994), Mangan (1992), Sugden and Tomlinson (2000)

COLONISATION

Many European nations, in search of new territory, wealth and raw materials, undertook a policy of colonisation from the seventeenth century. Foremost in this process were the nations of Britain, France, Holland, Portugal and Spain. In the nineteenth century they would be joined by Germany and Italy. Formal colonisation, that is placing another country under the jurisdiction of the colonising nation, produced a situation where European values, ideas, religion and pastimes, amongst other things, were transferred to Africa, Asia, South America and the Caribbean. The transfer of sporting forms and values was a key part of the colonial mission. That is not to say that all indigenous sporting forms were destroyed by the process of colonisation, or that the colonisers were left unaffected by the local sporting practices that they witnessed. It is clear however, that sports such as cricket, football, rugby, horse racing and many others were spread around the world by those European nations that were colonising their imperial possessions. The process of colonisation was formalised through the process of organising international sporting organisations. Bodies such as the ruling body of cricket, the MCC, invited colonial nations into the club of cricketing nations. By accepting the legitimacy of the MCC, colonial nations accepted the domination of Britain and the power of its empire. Sports such as cricket and rugby, which have spread as a result of colonial enterprise, became symbols of loyalty to the empire. The acceptance of the 'white' empire nations such as Australia or South Africa, and later the 'black' nations of India and the West Indies into cricketing competition, demonstrated that the process of colonisation had been successful, as British values had been championed across the globe.

See also: **colonialism, cultural imperialism, decolonisation**

Further reading: Birley (1995), Cronin and Holt (2001), MacKenzie (1989), Mangan (1992)

COMMERCIAL DEEPENING *see* **commercialisation**

COMMERCIALISATION

The commercialisation of sport refers to sport becoming subject to the market forces of commerce. Commercialism has never been absent from sport. What has changed has been its extent and intensity. In the eighteenth century, and even earlier, some profit-seeking entrepreneurs created special premises for sporting activities, such as cockpits and bear pits, to which they charged entry fees. Publicans also laid out bowling greens beside their alehouses to attract a drinking clientele. Later, boxing saloons served the same purpose, though more for spectators than participants. The late nineteenth century saw the burgeoning of gate-money sport organised regularly at specific sites created for the purpose, to take advantage of the market created by a wealthier, urbanised population with time to spare. These attempts to attract paying spectators led inevitably to the emergence on a large scale of **professionalism** in sport, as the skilled players – whom the crowds paid to see – demanded a share of the revenue which their talents generated.

Commercial widening occurs when more revenue is obtained from traditional gate revenue sources, such as the playing of more games or the expansion of stadium capacity, when there is excess demand for the event being sold. Commercial deepening involves the development of new revenue sources such as sponsorship, merchandising, signage and media rights. Today, at the elite level, sport and commerce are irreversibly intertwined, though gate money is becoming a less significant source of revenue as income from television rights and **merchandising** increases in importance. **Product improvement** involves modifying the original sporting competition so as to attract larger audiences, either for one event or over a season. Such changes include the establishment of new competitions within the sport or the introduction of play-offs for promotion from one division to another, matches that add excitement to the sporting calendar but do not change the essence of the traditional game. **Product development**, on the other hand, can drastically change the nature of a sport and the way in which it is played. A prime example here is one-day cricket which, although still a contest between bat and ball, requires different tactics and some different rules from the normal first-class match.

See also: **economics, marketing, media**

Further reading: Lewis and Appenzeller (1985), Vamplew (2005b)

COMMERCIAL WIDENING *see* **commercialisation**

COMMONWEALTH GAMES

The roots of the Commonwealth Games lie with their forerunner, the Empire Games. The first Empire Games were held in Hamilton, Canada in 1930. The Empire Games were designed specifically to bring together the nations of the British Empire in friendly competition. In effect the games were building on the sporting links that had been established through the process of British **colonisation**. In the wake of the Second World War, the rise of **nationalism** and the rapid development of **decolonisation**, the games were renamed the British Empire and Commonwealth Games in 1952. By 1974 they were known solely as the Commonwealth Games. The games, which have been staged in venues across the Commonwealth, are built on the Olympic model. They are held in the summer every four years, and play host to athletes from all the nations of the Commonwealth. The games have suffered from **boycotts**, especially that of 1986, but these have never been on the scale of those that have afflicted the **Olympics**. Despite the positive messages that underpin the games, they have been largely dominated by white Commonwealth nations. Despite the encouragement that was given to the nations from Africa, Asia and the Caribbean in the era of **decolonisation**, only Jamaica in 1966 and Malaysia in 1998 of all the 'new' Commonwealth nations have hosted the games. With the increased pace of sporting **globalisation**, the demands made by **television** and the need for sporting events to make a profit, there are concerns that the Commonwealth Games are no longer relevant as they champion nineteenth-century imperial ties that have ceased to be important.

Further reading: Bateman and Douglas (1986), Dheensaw (1994), Moore (1988)

COMPETITION

The basis of most sports is competitive. Whether contests involving humans, humans and animals or animals, sport will be a competition. The competition can take the form of a race (sprinting, horse racing and so on), a match based on goals or points scored (football, baseball etc.) or routines that are awarded a mark (figure skating, gymnastics and so on). The competition will allow athletes to measure their performance against each other, and for one player or team to emerge as the winner. In addition to direct competition against another contestant, many sports people will also get a sense of achievement in competing against the elements. For example, mountaineers or sailors may not be involved in a direct contest against anyone, but will be competing against the forces of nature.

When modern codified sport emerged in the nineteenth century, the spirit of competition was enshrined in the rules. All sports used rules and scoring systems so that a clear winner emerged. Historians have argued that the embrace of the competitive ethos in modern codified sport replicated the prevailing sense of competition that was inherent in nineteenth-century life. All aspects of life were seen as competitive. This included competition in business, educational systems that were based on academic competition and even the battles between nations for imperial possessions.

While competition is accepted as the basis of modern sport, especially at the elite level, there have been questions raised about whether such an emphasis on winning the competition is damaging. While comments such as 'winning isn't everything; it's the only thing' (attributed to Green Bay Packer's coach Vince Lombardi), are seen as exemplifying the purpose and spirit of competition, others have challenged this perspective. In the Olympic Games, for example (and in many school sports for younger children), the emphasis is on taking part in the competition, rather than winning it. The spirit of the Olympics is summed up by the famous statement, 'the most important thing in the Olympic Games is not to win but to take part' which favours competing over competition based on victory.

Further reading: Bailey (2000)

CONDITIONING

When coaches and athletes talk of **fitness** and **conditioning**, a central component is aerobic fitness. It is generally agreed by exercise scientists that to maintain and develop aerobic fitness, the training principles of specificity, overload and progression along with individual differences need to be addressed when developing conditioning programmes. However, it is also recognised that overall conditioning can aid both health-related and motor performance fitness. Accordingly, exercise scientists, coaches and trainers recommend a total exercise programme which includes strengthening exercises to maintain overall body strength and muscle mass, as well as stretching and flexibility exercises to maintain mobility, and proper joint function, appropriate for a particular individual.

In recommending aerobic fitness programmes for conditioning of athletes, exercise physiologists have developed a number of formulae based on norms, to ensure desired conditioning effects. These formulae are based on the need for control of three important factors pertinent to how hard, how often and how long we exercise. These factors are intensity of exercise, frequency of exercise and duration of exercise. The intensity of exercise is perhaps the most critical of these factors since if a sufficient level of intensity is not reached there will be no conditioning or training effect. On the other hand, if intensity is too high then injury is likely. The standard measures of intensity are target heart rate (expressed in terms of percentage of maximum) and target **VO_2 Max** (expressed in terms of percentage of VO_2 Max). Such measures enable athletes to monitor the level of intensity and the degree of stress they are undergoing during conditioning. The level of intensity employed will depend on the individual athlete and the goals of the conditioning programme.

How often an athlete trains again depends on their goals. However, general conditioning rates vary from between three times a week to six or more times per week. Those who train more frequently than this are more subject to the effects of **over-training** and injury, because their bodies are not able to adapt to this level of frequency. With regard to duration, again, the length of a conditioning session must depend on the goals being attempted. For cardio-respiratory or aerobic fitness, at least twenty minutes of reasonably intense exercise is necessary to engender adaptations in the system. Obviously, for those training to run marathons the specificity principle will ensure that greater duration of conditioning will be necessary!

Further reading: Brooks et al. (1996), Corbin and Lindsey (1984, 1997), Fox et al. (1987), Howley and Franks (1997), Wilmore (1982)

CONFLICT THEORY

Whereas the supporters of **functionalism** believe that a balanced society works for the good of all, proponents of conflict theory argue that society is not based on equilibrium. It is argued that certain sectors of society, especially in market economies, pursue their own self-interests, yet project their vision in such a way that the majority support them. Those studying conflict theory focus their research on how powerful groups in society use sport to promote values and aspirations that enable them to maintain their position of power and privilege. It also illuminates how sport is a force of discontent and inequality in a society that perpetuates the uneven distribution of power and wealth. Areas that have been studied in the context of conflict theory include the effects of commercialism in sport, the negative impact of **nationalism** and militarism, the role of sport in maintaining racial and gender imbalances, and the role that sport plays in controlling society.

See also: **control, functionalism, sociology**

Further reading: Brohm (1978), Coakley (1998)

CONSUMPTION

In economic terms, consumption refers to the expenditure on goods and services that are then used not stored. Hence both sports spectators (who pay to watch events) and sports participants (who purchase equipment) are consumers in the sports market. In 1995 the sports sector was responsible for £10.4 billion of consumer spending (about 2.3 per cent of total consumer expenditure). Most of this is spending in the mass participation market, with 19 per cent going on subscriptions and entry fees and a further 23 per cent being expended on sports clothing and footwear. Another 28 per cent is spent in gambling activities associated with sport.

See also: **economics**

Further reading: Gratton (1998)

CONTROL

The question of who controls sport is a vitally important one. Control should not simply be thought of in administrative terms. While it is true that FIFA controls world football, there are other forces and questions

that have to be taken into account when understanding power relationships that underpin control. What market forces affect football? What
power does **television** have over sports organisations? How far do
political issues dictate the awarding of the World Cup finals to a
country? All these wider issues will affect the workings of an organisation
such as FIFA, and shape how it responds to any given situation.
Control is thus not simply a question of administrative organisation,
but the product of competing power bases. Control is most properly
understood as a concept that lies at the heart of many sociological
definitions of sport, and one that is especially important in considering
conflict theory. Control is a product of power, and power emanates
from a variety of sources. Control in sport may be a product of a
dominant **gender** or **ethnicity**, be economic or market driven, or
else will relate to the intervention of **government** and **politics**. On
the actual sports field, the level of control will be a product of the
power of the referee or umpire, or might refer to the dominant skills
of one team over another, and their ability to 'control' the game.

See also: **class, conflict theory, sociology**

Further reading:: Coakley (1998)

CORINTHIANS

A 'wandering' football club founded in 1882 by N. L. Jackson with a
membership of fifty on the model of cricket's I Zingari club, the
Corinthians was intended to be an antidote to **professionalism** in
football. Membership was restricted almost entirely to those public
school and Oxbridge amateurs whose own status was most threatened
by the rising tide of professional teams such as Blackburn Rovers and
Preston North End. The term 'Corinthians' had previously been
applied to fashionable young men who were involved in elite horse
and coach clubs, and who were concerned with style and manners
rather than racing and winning. The idea of playing in a gentlemanly
manner and in an open and attractive style was continued by Jackson's
Corinthian footballers, who despised the tactics and style which a
need and desire to win was thought to promote among professionals.

Many members of the Corinthians football club were also talented
cricketers, and thus the term 'Corinthian' came to be attached to
those talented amateur all-round athletes, such as C. B. Fry, who could
turn their hand to a variety of sports and play them well. As professional

sport has grown and seasons have lengthened, it has become increasingly difficult for such Corinthian figures to survive. It was for this reason that Geoffrey Moorhouse, in the Daily Telegraph of 4 June 1979, suggested that M. M. Walford, who was educated at Rugby School and Oxford in the 1930s, and gained blues in cricket, rugby and hockey, may have been the last of the Corinthians. Whilst a schoolmaster at Sherborne School, Walford topped the county batting averages and went on an England cricket tour, was an England trialist at rugby, and would have been capped against Ireland if he had not been playing hockey for the Great Britain team which he captained at the 1948 **Olympic Games**.

See also: **amateurism**

Further reading: Birley (1993), Cashmore (1996), Doggart (1999), Grayson (1996), Taylor (2006)

CORRUPTION

Generally the result of a sports event is determined on merit, with perhaps some intervention by luck. Sometimes, however, corruption plays a role in that the winner or loser may be predetermined or a competitor cheats to gain an advantage. It has been argued that the growth of **extrinsic** rewards in modern sport, fuelled by commercialisation, has encouraged a widespread increase in corrupt practices, but there is no strong evidence to support this view, though some would suggest that there has been a decline in **sportsmanship**. **Intrinsic motivation** may be sufficient to persuade participants to break the **rules** if they feel that it will help them win and they will not be found out. Both historically and today, most serious corruption in sport stems from its relationship with gambling and the money that can be made in the betting market if it is known that a competitor or team will not be trying their best. It could be argued that corruption in sport is to the extreme of a spectrum which also includes cheating and gamesmanship and is distinguished by breaking not just the written and unwritten rules of the game but also the law of the land.

COSMETIC SPORTS

In cosmetic sports the focus is on the appearance of the participants, as in the styling and shaping of the physique in bodybuilding. To a degree, it can be seen as part of a narcissist culture where participants become preoccupied with self-image. As a competitive sport, body-building is unusual in that little physical activity takes place save for a series of poses. The real physicality of the sport comes in pre-competition training, in working out with weights to reshape the physique by adding muscle mass, and by increasing both the separa-tion and definition of the muscle groups. Modern bodybuilding emerged from the popularity of the 'strong man' demonstrations by Eugene Sandow in the late nineteenth century. But for some decades, displays of strength and athletic feats, rather than of physi-que, remained central to competitive physical culture. Nevertheless, by the late 1940s bodybuilding had made the jump from exhibition to competition. Bodybuilding for women has struggled more than most female sports for public recognition. Early twentieth-century bodybuilding competitions for women were prosecuted as porno-graphic; those of the 1970s derided as beauty pageants. The past two decades have seen the acceptance within the sport of female body-builders, but there is still societal disapproval of women who pursue it. Western society has generally equated femininity with curva-ceousness and softness, not the muscularity and hardness of the bodybuilder.

See also: **aesthetics**

Further reading: Crum (1999)

COST-BENEFIT ANALYSIS

In order to assess the merit of investment in a project, economists often undertake a cost-benefit analysis that compares the perceived benefits of an activity with the costs of undertaking it. In sport such benefits might include the increased health and fitness of partici-pants, the employment that could be generated by an event or pro-ject, and the **externalities** that could be generated. These would have to be quantified in money terms so that they could be weighed against the costs and a rate of return on the money invested calcu-lated. In this way different projects, or variations of the same project, can be compared and rational investment decisions made. **Private** investors will be concerned solely with the direct financial benefits and the economic rate of return on their investment, whereas those calling on **public** funds will also take account of the social rate of return which includes the **externalities** and other community benefits.

See also: **economic impact statements**

CRIMINAL LAW

In contrast to **civil law**, where an aggrieved individual or group sues for redress, the initiative for prosecution under criminal law lies with the agencies of the state. Hence it is the police who can bring charges of assault against a violent player, with of course penal sanctions as a possible punishment.

See also: **civil law, law**

CRITICAL THEORY

Primarily concerned with power in social life, critical theory has emerged from the debates that centred on the respective merits of **conflict theory** and **functionalism**. Those studying critical theory are not normally seeking to assess the whole of society, but prefer to focus on particular problems. The definition of power is far broader than that allowed for in **conflict theory**, and is not so dependant upon an appreciation of power as a product of economic determinism. In the realm of sport, critical theory seeks to understand how sports are shaped and influenced by the interaction of social relations. Proactively, it seeks to identify alternative sport forms that would better serve the needs of people than those that currently exist. As such, critical theory is popular amongst those wishing to promote groups of people such as women or ethnic minorities, that are currently marginalised by sport.

See also: **conflict theory, functionalism, sociology**

Further reading: Birrell and Cole (1994), Coakley (1998), Hall (1996), Hargreaves (1994), Mesner (1992)

CULTURAL ANALYSIS

Sport, as learnt behaviour, is a product of the society within which it occurs. So sports culture encompasses sports events themselves, but also their history, development, myths, icons, and the social, economic and political issues surrounding them. One form of cultural analysis examines the way that different societies, both historically and contemporarily, function by looking at the customs, attitudes and values of the population within each society. Such an examination of lifestyle includes sport and physical recreation, which often reflect the pattern of traditions and values of the wider society within which they exist. Most analysts differentiate between ancient cultures, where sporting activities are revealed by the work of archaeologists; primitive cultures of tribal societies, for which the ethnographic studies of social anthropologists are invaluable in revealing the meanings of rituals attached to physical activities; emergent or developing countries, who use sport as part of nation-building; and advanced societies where sport has become an institution in an industrial, urban-based culture. Another cultural analysis approach distinguishes **mass culture** from **high culture**.

See also: **anthropology**

CULTURAL IMPERIALISM

There are two distinct periods and types of cultural imperialism. The first, which belongs to the period of formal **colonisation**, led to the spread of games such as cricket and football, as Britain and other European nations built up their empires. By introducing foreign games to colonial nations, and encouraging the indigenous population to play them, imperial powers were undertaking a process of cultural imperialism. In addition to playing 'native' games, the indigenous population were accepting the sports of the imperialist, as well as the codes of conduct and ethos that accompanied them. It was not simply a matter of playing cricket or rugby, it was also accepting the allied ideologies of Victorian masculinity **fair play**, gentlemanly conduct and the word of the umpire. Cultural imperialism was the exportation of colonial ideals through the use of cultural forms such as sport. A similar process has been evident in the years since the end of the Second World War. It has been argued that **globalisation** or, as it is sometimes referred to, Americanisation, is the contemporary form of cultural imperialism. Although no state is formally seeking to annex another and make it a part of an empire, companies such as Nike, Reebok, and the NFL and NBA, have sought to expand their market reach around the world. In doing so they have changed customs, habits and thinking. Assisted by the **media**, **sponsorship** and

advertising, the major corporations and sports organisations have been able to gain access to markets across the world, and people have responded by transforming their points of cultural reference. In the Caribbean, for example, sporting dreams are no longer dominated by images of test cricket, but instead hinge on playing major league baseball or basketball in the United States. Men such as Michael Jordan are accepted as global sporting icons in countries such as Australia or Britain, where basketball is far from being the top sport, but where companies such as Nike, who have used Jordan to spearhead advertising campaigns, have been successful in dominating the marketplace. Cultural imperialism takes many different forms, but it is a process that is active in the contemporary world, and one which, with the increasing power of the **media** and the wealth of sporting organisations such as the IOC or FIFA, continues to grow unabated.

See also: **colonisation, colonialism, decolonisation**

Further reading: Klein (1991), Maguire (2000)

CURRICULUM DESIGN

Curriculum design embraces the overall philosophy/purpose of a course and the means by which this is to be implemented. This should not simply address such issues as curriculum content and/or structure, but should include an identification of desired learning outcomes and the learning experiences that might best facilitate those outcomes. Curriculum design must also include the delivery process, performance assessment, quality assurance, and a review process that allows the identification and implementation of necessary changes to any of its component parts without undue delay or wholesale restructuring.

A curriculum design process might include:

- curriculum theory and structural model
- curriculum needs – both material and consultative
- identification of learning outcomes
- course structure (and sequencing if more than one component/level)
- quality assurance
- approval and accreditation (internal and external)
- planning: including course delivery, media and assessment.

DANCE

Dance is a form of human movement that has long been used to convey and express emotion, physicality, stories and other elements of the human condition. Dance takes many forms. In addition to traditional forms of dance (folk dancing) and regionally or ethnically specific forms (Irish dancing, classical Indian dancing), there are forms which are used commonly in public performance (ballet and modern dance) and those for competition (ballroom dancing or swing dance).

All forms of dance can be physically exerting, and all are connected with and promoted as pursuits that will increase levels of physical activity, sociability and well-being. Dance has long been embraced by educators as a valuable tool for teaching children forms of movement. In Britain dance is part of the National Curriculum and is used as a means of expressing and communicating ideas and feelings. It is also studied as a way of introducing students to various cultures and differences between societies.

Competitive dancing has become increasingly popular in recent years due to its prominence on television through shows such as 'Strictly Come Dancing'. In the United States, dance is a key activity within High Schools, and organisations such as the American Dance Awards organise national competitions with cash prizes in the form of scholarships.

DECOLONISATION

The process of decolonisation followed the withdrawal of imperial nations from those nations that they had colonised. The major formal period of decolonisation was after the Second World War, but other nations had freed themselves from their imperial powers before then. Once the imperial power had departed, those nations that had previously been colonised had to find their own way in the world, and establish their own identity. This process involved deciding on aspects of liturgy such as the national flag and anthem, establishing diplomatic relationships with other countries, and joining, where applicable, international bodies such as the United Nations. Sport became part of this process. Nations such as India and those that constituted the West Indies were faced with a dilemma. As part of the process of **colonisation**, they had begun to play imperial games such as cricket, and had been accepted as formal test-playing teams. As free nations, should they continue to play these colonial sports that were organised and ruled from England, or should they retreat to indigenous sporting forms? This is at the heart of the postcolonial dilemma. Most nations that have been through the process of decolonisation have continued to play imperial sports, have prospered at them, and taken great delight at beating the 'mother' country. Such victories were seen as the triumph of postcolonial nations. However, other nations that have been through the process of decolonisation, such as the Republic of Ireland, chose to leave the Commonwealth, and thus the **Commonwealth Games**, and have also continued to champion indigenous sports such as hurling and Gaelic football. In recent decades there is a growing feeling that some decolonised nations, especially those in the West Indies, have been subject to the forces of **cultural imperialism**, and have steadily turned their backs on imperial sports in favour of baseball and basketball.

See also: **colonialism, colonisation, Commonwealth Games, nationalism**

Further reading: Bale and Cronin (2002), Cronin (1999), Cronin and Holt (2001)

DEMAND

In looking at what influences the demand for sport in general and for specific sports, economists would examine how the variables of price, income, **taste**, time and **demography** operate in the market for sport. The demand for sport is a composite one, involving the demand for free time, the demand for equipment and clothing, the demand for travel and the demand for facilities. Additionally the demand for sport can relate to both spectating and participation, though these generally are in distinct markets.

See also: **consumption**

Further reading: Gratton (1998)

DEMOGRAPHY

Demographic influences can have a significant impact on both the **demand** for and **supply** of sport. In aggregate, a larger population will generally demand more goods and services, including those of the sport and leisure industries, though this can be further influenced by age and gender variations. Similarly, of course, so can the demand for particular sports: netball and rugby tend to have significant gender differences both in playing and watching, and the same applies to the generally different ages of athletes and bowls players. Sports suppliers also take the distribution of the population into account, as a populace concentrated into urban areas is likely to produce a greater effective demand than one spread sparsely over the countryside.

DIFFERENTIATION

The term differentiation refers to the ways in which groups separate themselves from each other by appearing or behaving differently. The aim of differentiation is to make either the group or the individual distinct. This may work with football supporters in the ways that they dress and behave. For example, Scottish football supporters are known for the kilt wearing, carnivalesque behaviour and good humour. This differentiates them from other groups, and allows them to stand out as uniquely Scottish.

More widely differentiation can be used to measure the ways in which different social groups access and consume sport. Recently issues concerning social differentiation and social inequality in sport have received a great deal of attention in the sociology of sport. Many writers have argued that the opportunity to participate actively in sport is stratified according to sociocultural characteristics. Thus there is a differentiation amongst those who participate in certain sports because of factors such as class, gender or race. For example, golf clubs would be seen largely as the preserve of the white, suburban middle classes, while boxing clubs would have a multiracial membership of urban working class males. Each sport will mirror societal divisions and be differentiated precisely because sport, and participation in it, reflects the sociological basis of the population. Differentiation is therefore a useful tool for understanding debates relating to identity and participation issues in sport.

Further reading: Giulianotti (2005), Scheerder et al. (2005)

DIFFUSION

One of the major issues in both sports **history** and **geography** has been the movement of different sports and games across the globe.

This process, known as diffusion, helps explain how sports spread throughout the world. It can be used to analyse the **origins** of modern sport, as well as illustrating the distribution of sport through either **imperialism** or **globalisation**. The process of diffusion explains how the transformation was made between localised **traditional sports**, and eventually the globalised modern sports organisations such as the International Olympic Committee or the **marketing** power of the National Basketball Association (NBA). It has been argued that the process of diffusion can be best illustrated by examining pre-industrial sport. Gillmeister argued that the origin of many bat and ball games, especially tennis, could be traced back to the Picardian game of cache. Throughout Europe there were a host of games similar to cache, albeit ones with adapted local rules and with specific regional names. Cache therefore, while being understood at one level as an antecedent of modern tennis, is also a prime example of the process of diffusion. The game, despite changing form as it travelled across Europe so that local variants dominated, has clear origins. Guttmann has also explored the process of diffusion in the context of imperial powers and the more recent advent of a sporting globalisation. The process of diffusion has, it can be argued, led to the blunting of many national distinctions in sport, and has hastened the development of a global system of international competition and organisation.

Further reading: Bale (1989), Gillmeister (1981), Guttmann (1994), Maguire (2000)

DISABILITY SPORT

While advances in medicine, the development of prostheses, and the need to find activities appropriate to the needs of disabled soldiers after the First World War created limited impetus for sport for the disabled, it was the prevalence of service-connected injuries such as paraplegia and amputation that led more directly to the development of **disability sports**. Following the Second World War, sports and recreation were increasingly recognised as being significant components of therapy and rehabilitation for disabled servicemen. The shift in terminology from 'sport for the disabled' to 'disability sport' is indicative of changing social views of those with disabilities from being lesser beings to being equal – if different – beings performing in separate events. This drive for equality has led some disability athletes to suggest that wheelchair athletes should compete against able-bodied athletes in Olympic events.

The oldest international organisation for sport for persons with disabilities is the International Committee on Silent Sports. Founded in 1924, it has a close affiliation with the World Games for the Deaf. However, it was the founding of the National Spinal Injuries Centre at the Stoke Mandeville Hospital in Buckinghamshire in 1944 that signalled a new direction and emphasis for disability sport. Through the work of neurologist Ludwig (later Sir Ludwig) Gunman, who believed passionately in the vital role that access to sport played in the rehabilitation of those suffering spinal injury or disease, the first wheelchair sports programme was born, and in 1948 the first orga-nised wheelchair games were held at Stoke Mandeville. Since that time, disability sports, and most notably the Olympics for the disabled – founded in 1960 – which were renamed the Paralympics in 1980, have grown to become a world-wide phenomenon. There are now nine Paralympic categories of disability, and athletes compete in nineteen different sports, fourteen of which are Olympic sports.

The disability sports movement is still trying to change media and public perceptions that such activity is for therapy and recreation for the participants. Through the efforts of many of these athletes, the understanding that disability athletes are elite athletes involved in elite athletic endeavour, is finally being realised. The 1988 Seoul Paral-ympics saw significant changes in this direction, with the first IOC **drug testing** of some of the 4,000 athletes from over sixty countries who were competing. The controversy surrounding drug testing in the Paralympics is even more fierce than in the Olympic Games themselves, because while the rules applied to the Olympics are being applied to the Paralympics, many of the Paralympic athletes' condi-tions require medications which are currently on the IOU's banned list.

In addition to elite level disability sport, there have also been a number of initiatives to support the participation of disabled children in sport. In Britain, for example, the Institute of Youth Sport laun-ched the TOP Sportsability programme in 1998. This was aimed at developing the sports provision for disabled children across the country.

See also: **discrimination**

Further reading: Anderson (2000a), Cashman and Hughes (2000), DePauw and Gavron (1995), Middleton (1999).

DISCRIMINATION

Discrimination is the differentiation between groups or individuals on the basis of race, gender, age, sexual orientation or other factors. Often this is due to prejudice, where an unfavourable and often intolerant attitude is taken against others on the basis of inadequate knowledge. In turn this often stems from the stereotyping of particular groups so that all members of it are identified as having similar traits. Some forms of discrimination are illegal, but not all. Unlawful discrimination in sport covers such matters as means of recruitment, terms of employment, opportunities for training and promotion, and access to benefits and services. Discrimination in sport on the grounds of a person's gender or ethnic origin is illegal under the Sex Discrimination and Race Relations Acts. Indeed, women have successfully challenged sports bodies in the courts over their reluctance to grant them licences to train racehorses and to fight as professional boxers. However, currently the Disability Discrimination Act is not fully applicable to participatory sport because of the physical skills required, though its provisions do apply to other forms of employment offered by a sports club or association. However, private sports clubs can operate discriminatory policies. The Royal and Ancient Golf Club of St Andrews, the ruling body in golf, is still a men-only organisation. Significantly, the Sex Discrimination and Race Relations Acts technically also render it illegal to adopt a policy of positive discrimination so as to deliberately employ more females or ethnic minorities at the expense of males or other racial groups; though this has not yet been challenged within sport.

See also: **affirmative action, racism**

Further reading: McArdle (1999)

DISREPUTE

'Bringing the game into disrepute' is a clause in their regulations that sports authorities invoke to maintain acceptable behaviour by participants in their sport, be they players, officials or administrators. A well drafted disrepute provision gives governing bodies wide latitude to discipline participants, but also a wide margin of discretion as to when to take action. An acceptance by all those involved in the sport of the right of the ruling body to enforce discipline in this way keeps matters such as the taking of recreational drugs, the making of offensive gestures and the wearing of inappropriate clothing out of the courts. Nevertheless, to allow the sports authorities such unfettered power necessitates that they act consistently, in good faith, and with fair procedures. One of the main criticisms is that some authorities use their discretion to ignore incidents on which they do not wish to receive publicity.

DRILL SERGEANTS

The first physical education teachers were drill sergeants, who began to appear in schools following amendments in 1875 to the Forster Education Act of 1870 which allowed payments to be made to them by School Boards. They instructed the pupils in marching, posture exercises and dummy arms drill, with the prime aim of instilling discipline but with the implicit intent to improve the fitness of army recruits. Unfortunately, many of these ex-soldiers were incapable of differentiating between adult military personnel and **state school** pupils. The **public schools**, however, tended to employ a better class of drill instructor, often ex-instructors from the Aldershot military school, who were able to teach other skills such as fencing and gymnastics. Drill sergeants died away as training colleges began to supply qualified personnel.

DRUGS

The issue of drugs in sport has centred on a number of issues including fairness, athletes' rights, dehumanisation and **health** and **safety** concerns. All of these continue to surround sport at the highest levels, such as in Olympic competition, but are also becoming of increasing concern at lower levels and amongst younger athletes, as they see the potential for gaining the wealth, status and recognition of highly successful athletes. If the use of particular drugs can enhance performance through building muscle, increasing oxygen uptake or limiting pain, athletes in search of aids to traditional training techniques only have to look to such drugs for assistance.

The list of banned substances issued by the **International Olympic Committee** (IOC) continues to grow as pharmacological experts discover new performance-enhancing compounds. The IOC and similar sporting bodies are involved in a drug war, which, despite strong efforts to control drug use, they appear to be losing. The stated aims for controlling drug use are, first, to protect the health of athletes because of the possible side effects of drug usage; and second, to maintain fairness in sport since not all athletes have access to such drugs and thus are disadvantaged. Many athletes and sport philosophers have argued for an athlete's right to choose to take drugs and against the control of such behaviour by groups such as the IOC. They have also argued that in cultures where the use of drugs is prevalent for overcoming illness, promoting rehabilitation and providing normality, it is inconsistent to argue against the use of drugs for enhancing athletic performance.

See also: **drug testing, ethics**

Further reading: Beamish and Ritchie (2005), Brown (1980), Burke and Roberts (1997), Dimeo (2006), Lavin (1987), Schneider and Butcher (1993–1994), Simon (1991), Waddington (2005)

DRUG TESTING

Drug testing at an international level was first employed at the 1968 Winter **Olympics** in response to advances in sports medicine and training around the world. There were specific concerns amongst Western nations that Eastern Bloc countries such as East Germany and the USSR were using pharmaceutical expertise to gain an unfair advantage in sports. Over the next twenty years, a variety of athletes were disqualified at the Olympics. However, it was not until the 1988 disqualification of Canadian sprinter Ben Johnson, following a drug test which showed evidence of use of the banned **anabolic steroid** Stanzanol, that those outside sport joined the discussion, and widespread debate about **drugs** and drug testing occurred.

For the Olympic movement, drug testing became a means of promoting an image of true sport, and was used to promote a psychology of fear where potential drug use among Olympic athletes was concerned. Fear psychology has been aided by the impact of the widely publicised side effects of drugs on **health**.

The sports that have been most plagued by drugs, and thus have been in the vanguard of drug testing, are cycling and weightlifting. The death of British cyclist Tommy Simpson first alerted the sporting public to the issue of drug use, and helped foster the long-standing debate over issues of privacy and personal freedom on the one hand,

and pure sport and fair play on the other. Sport philosophers continue to debate these issues, and the Olympic movement continues to try to improve its testing procedures to keep pace with the pharmacological advances in sport performance enhancement.

Drug testing is beset with legal problems regarding civil liberties and procedural disputes, economic problems concerning the costs of administration and enforcement, and political problems of corruption and inconsistency by the sports authorities in many countries.

See also: **drugs**

Further reading: Simon (1991), Williams (1998), Yesalis (2000)

DUTY OF CARE

Participants in competitive sport owe a duty to each other and to spectators and officials to take all reasonable care not to cause injury or distress. Similarly, coaches both of children and adults have a duty of care not to risk injuring their charges by asking them to perform when unfit or not competent. Although occasionally it has been held that higher-level players and highly qualified coaches have a higher duty of care than lesser ones, mainly it has been the standard of ordinary reasonable sportspersons that has been used in legal decisions. Also taken into account are the particular circumstances of the incident and the playing culture of the sport concerned. In the recent case of *Smolden vs. Whitworth*, a referee was held liable for the paralysis of a player injured when a scrum collapsed, something that had already occurred twenty times in the match without the match official taking action to prevent it re-occurring.

See also: **law**

ECONOMIC IMPACT STATEMENTS

Economists often use economic impact statements to analyse the potential effects of a development on a variety of activities. It is similar to **cost-benefit analysis**, but need not take a full overall approach and can focus on specific aspects. Hence, for example, the building of a new sports stadium or even an Olympic Games bid can be looked at in terms of economic regeneration of an area, the short- and longer-term employment demands, the resultant traffic and parking issues, or of the inward investment that might be stimulated.

ECONOMIC RENT

In a free market economy, workers with special or scarce skills can expect to earn above average wages. This additional amount is termed an economic rent. In sport the application of **salary caps** and **maximum wages** has often prevented professional sportspersons from earning their full economic rent.

ECONOMICS

Unless they have a major financial **patron** who will bail them out of any economic difficulties, sports clubs have to balance the books. Hence like any other business they must work within a budget constraint and hire, train and retain labour, market their product, and invest in production facilities. However, whereas in a conventional business an objective might well be to dominate the market and become a monopolist who can set higher prices and make larger profits than a company operating in a more competitive environment, this cannot occur in sport. There is no game without a competitor. Chelsea versus Chelsea Reserves eventually would pall even for diehard fans of the Blues; the economics of sport is peculiar to the extent that rival producers (or teams) must combine together to produce a saleable product (individual matches). Without cooperation between the member clubs of a league, it would not be possible for matches to be played. The product (matches) is therefore produced cooperatively. The same argument can be applied to individual sports: there is no profit in being heavyweight champion of the world if there is no challenger. Some sports are essentially non-viable unless participants regard their activity as being part of their **consumption** pattern. Entrepreneurs do not build factories for fun, but the same is not true of leisure activities where enormous sums can be spent with little financial return. A prime example is game preservation for shooting, which makes the cost of each bird killed far higher than the price in the butcher's shop. Similarly the ownership of a racehorse in many cases is an amalgam of **consumption** and **investment**, with the former more to the fore.

See also: **industry**

Further reading: Dobson (2000), Sloane (1980), Taylor and Gratton (2000)

ELECTRON TRANSPORT CHAIN

The electron transport chain (ETC) is located on the inner membrane of the mitochondria, and is coupled to the process of oxidative phosphorylation (or **ATP** synthesis). This process involves the movement of reducing equivalents (NADH and FADH formed during glycolysis and in the **Krebs cycle**) along the ETC, where electrons are stripped from the high-energy hydrogen and these electrons are then passed to oxygen at the end of the chain to form water. (Campbell 1996: 170) As electrons are transferred at each complex of the chain, the resulting protons (H+) are pumped into the inter-membrane space of the mitochondria, thus creating a gradient of H+ across the membrane. These H+ complete the circuit by flowing down their gradient (known as a proton motive force) back into the mitochondrial matrix through specific portals, and this process in turn provides the energy for the re-phosphorylation of ADP to ATP. The ETC is regulated by the concentrations of adenine nucleotides, with ADP and ATP stimulating and inhibiting the chain respectively.

See also: **Krebs cycle**

Further reading: Brooks et al. (1996), Campbell (1996)

EMOTION

The impact of emotion on performance and learning in sport and physical activity is an understudied phenomenon. We have all experienced the impact of extreme excitement or fear on our heart rate. Researchers are now beginning to look more closely at the importance of emotion on sport performance through assessing its impact on motivation, attention and concentration and looking at how adaptive coping can be used to help re-focus emotion. Hanin (2000) has presented a model entitled Individual Zones of Optimal Functioning (120F) as one possible approach for understanding performance-related emotional states in competitive sports. Much more work needs to be done on Emotion in sport but research in neuroscience and physical activity holds great potential in this area.

Further reading: Hanin (2000), Lavallee et al. (2004)

ENDORSEMENT

Lying somewhere between **sponsorship** and **advertising**, endorsement implies that a team or player recommends the use of a particular product. Whether the public really believe that sporting success can be associated with, and derived from, buying the advertised product is a moot point.

Further reading: Hudson (2000)

ENDURANCE SPORTS

Time and energy are both scarce resources. Endurance sports test an athlete's stamina against the clock. One of the earliest endurance sports involved long-distance athletic feats done for wagers. Famous pedestrians (as they were known) included Foster Powell, who undertook long walks of several days duration; Lieutenant Fairman of the Royal Lancashire Militia, who went sixty miles in 13 hours 33 minutes in 1804; and Captain Barclay, who in 1809 gained fame for winning a challenge to run a thousand miles in a thousand hours. Other endurance sportsmen were the bare-knuckled pugilists who fought to exhaustion, fights often lasting several hours. A round ended only when one combatant was put to the floor; he then had half a minute's respite before placing his toe on a line scratched across the centre of the ring and resuming battle. Not until one fighter failed 'to come up to scratch' was a result declared: there were no wins on points in those days, just the objective test of an inability to continue.

As sports became codified and urbanisation demanded set times for sporting events, such endurance sports became less popular. Only the marathon, run over 26 miles and 385 yards, received the Olympic accolade. In Europe particularly, advantage was taken of new **technology** to inaugurate the long-distance cycle race taking several days to complete. In Britain such mass-start road racing was banned, though time trials were allowed. In many sporting matters, Britain remained isolated from the continent, though channel swimmers such as Captain Matthew Webb, who first accomplished the feat in 1875, attempted to close the gap.

In recent years, however, perhaps as part of the move towards nature and a reaction against the perceived softness of civilisation, sportspersons have again begun to challenge both themselves and the elements. Although these have included long-distance horse-back riding involving travel over varying terrain and in all weathers, most have involved persons solely challenging themselves mentally and physically. A distinction could be drawn between those endurance sports which have emerged out of conventional sports such as the multi-sport triathlon based on running, swimming and cycling and now an Olympic event, and those which are essentially televised circus-style events such as the world's strongest man, where men test their lifting, holding, and carrying powers to the limit. Some of these endurance events merge into **extreme sports**.

See also: **adventure sports**

ENERGY

Energy is the capacity to do work, and is often measured in terms of oxygen consumption. Since sport and physical activity are energetic events, sport scientists have sought to understand what energy is, what the significant sources of energy are, and then how the body uses those sources of energy during specific types of physical activity. These studies are based on the laws of bioenergetics, and are underpinned by two very significant limitations. The first is that energy is not created but rather is acquired in the form of food, etc., and is converted through the processes of **energy metabolism** into another form of energy. The second is that the conversion process itself is not a particularly efficient system and that much of the energy released is released as heat. Athletic activities are often classified as being typical of one of three groups: activities typified by the need for power, speed or endurance. In the **Olympic Games** we see examples of each type in weightlifting, the 100 metre sprint and the marathon, respectively. **Skeletal** muscle is provided with energy for these three different types of activity by three different energy systems: the **ATP-PC** system; the lactic acid system; and the oxygen system.

See also: **energy metabolism, energy systems**

Further reading: Brooks et al. (1996), Fox et al. (1987), Howley and Franks (1997)

ENERGY METABOLISM

Metabolism refers to all of the chemical reactions that occur in the body in the production of energy for work. Since our bodies cannot use foods in the form that we ingest them, they must be broken down into forms usable as **energy** by the cells. In breaking down food, the body manufactures adenosine triphosphate (**ATP**), which is stored in all cells and is the source of energy for all biological functions from muscular contractions to cellular growth. The process of turning food components in a cell into usable energy is described by the **Krebs cycle** or citric acid cycle.

See also: **ATP, Krebs cycle**

Further reading: Brooks et al. (1996), Fox et al. (1987), McArdle et al. (2000)

ENERGY SYSTEMS

The body has three energy systems. Two of the systems, the adenosine triphosphate-phosphocreatine system (**ATP**-PC) and the glycolysis system are anaerobic because they do not require oxygen to sustain the chemical reactions that manufacture ATP. The third or oxidative energy system is aerobic and thus does require oxygen for the transduction of energy. The two anaerobic systems supply only limited amounts of ATP. During high-intensity, short-term exercise typically lasting twenty-seconds or less, energy production is dominated by the ATP-PC system. For intense exercise lasting longer than forty-five seconds all three systems combine to produce the needed ATP to fuel muscular activity. The energy to perform prolonged exercise of more than ten minutes' duration comes primarily from the aerobic system.

Further reading: Brooks et al. (1996), McArdle et al. (2000)

ENGINEERING

The application of science to sport via engineering is a relatively new academic discipline, though it has been practised for a long time in the production and improvement of sports equipment. Examples of the way it has altered sports **technology** include the shifting of the centre of mass of the javelin to restrict the length of its flight so as to lessen the danger to spectators and athletes and the building of all-weather tracks to allow events to proceed.

See also: **technology**

ENVIRONMENT

With the growth of green politics, and increased concerns over the relationship between humankind and the environment, the world of sport has come under pressure to pursue positive policies with respect to the natural world. The central problem has been reconciling the positive benefits that sport and exercise have on the human body, with the often negative impact of sport on the environment. Motor racing is seen as an environmentally challenging sport. While debates within the context of transport policy look towards a reduction of emissions from the combustion engine, motor racing depends on high-powered and high-consumption vehicles, sponsored by multinational petrochemical companies, racing solely for the pleasure of spectators. For many people the activity is therefore a symbol of an environmentally unethical sport. Similarly, there are constant questions asked about the rapid spread of golf courses into the green belts that encircle the major cities of the Western world. While many people, especially golfers, consider a well manicured course a thing of beauty, it is evident that the development of a new golf club has an environmental cost. Part of the natural landscape is lost, as hills, lakes, greens, fairways and bunkers are built. Huge amounts of chemical fertiliser are put into the soil to develop, and then maintain the course to the highest standards. Environmental concerns have also been expressed about the modifications to mountain terrain in the construction of a ski piste, the effect of windsurfing, power boating and jet skiing on the ecosystem of the oceans, and the damage to hills and peaks from mountain bikers.

It is not solely sporting pursuits that have an impact on the environment. Major spectator sports and the associated stadia create problems concerning transport networks, the waste associated with crowd consumption and noise pollution. More recently the planners of stadia for major events, most notably the Homebush site of the 2000 Olympics, have adapted to environmental concerns. 'Greeness' has now to be part of Olympic bids. The development of the Sydney 2000 facilities were used as a way of improving the city's transport network, of promoting urban renewal, and developing, in the case of the athletes' village, environmentally friendly houses.

A poor environment, even though not directly caused by sport, can have a negative impact on competitors. Surfers across the world have been campaigning since the 1960s against pollution in the oceans, while the high levels of roadside pollution in major cities has meant that many joggers now have higher blood lead levels than their non-active counterparts.

See also: **geography, landscape**

Further reading: Bale (1989), Jarvie (2006), Schmidt (2006), Sherry and Wilson (1998), Wheeler and Nauright (2006)

EQUALITY

The concept of equality, and how it might be best achieved, has dominated Western liberal thinking for over three centuries. The desire for equality is based on the simple principle that all people are created equal, and therefore society in its broadest sense should treat all individuals the same. Politically the concept has been difficult to apply, and although most Western democratic states have embraced the base principles of equality and egalitarianism, the dominance of competitive capitalism within market economies prevents any full application of equality. In sport, the idea of equality is even more complex to apply. Whereas many sports administrators and organisations believe in equality, and have put programmes such as **Sport for All** in place, sport by its very nature is not conducive to equality. Competition depends on one athlete being stronger or faster than the other. In sport, people are not created equal, but different in terms of physical and mental ability. Sport measures, times, records and catalogues such differences in its quest to assess winners and losers. In sport the principle of equality underpins ideas relating to access to facilities and opportunity, but does not apply, it could be argued, to the nature of competition.

See also: **discrimination, gender, racism**

EQUALITY OF COMPETITION

Most economists would argue that it is not in the interests of a sports league if one team dominates the competition for too long. If results become too predictable then, it is argued, aggregate attendances will fall and the competition may lose its viability. Static equality of competition refers to a single competitive season, whereas dynamic equality of competition considers several seasons. It is the latter on which economists have based their arguments.

See also: **economics**

Further reading: Borland and McDonald (2003), Symanski (2003)

ETHICS

Sports ethics is the study of right and wrong, good or bad. It involves thinking about the moral issues that occur in sport. Generally it takes three forms. It can be descriptive (outlining what the moral issue is), normative (dealing with how moral decisions should be made), or meta-ethical (looking at how such decisions are made). Increasingly, sports philosophers are becoming more concerned with applied rather than theoretical sports ethics. This has focused on the personal morality of individuals in sport, and on professional conduct within sports organisations.

Further reading: Loland (2005), McNamee and Parry (1998), Stoll (1996)

ETHNICITY

Ethnicity is a term that is commonly used by historians, sociologists and social scientists. It is used to describe those elements that lead to the identification of any given group, and has increasingly come to replace the idea of race as a method of sub-dividing human groups. Sport, it has been argued by many commentators supporting the concept of **functionalism**, has been used by many ethnic groups as a way of integrating and assimilating with the dominant population. Those supportive of **conflict theory** argue that sport has been used as a method of creating a homogeneous identity which largely ignores ethnicity so that existing power structures remain intact. Some of the most useful engagement with the concept of ethnicity has come through those advocating types of **critical theory**, who see sporting forms as a venue for the promotion of group and individual pride in separate ethnicities. Sport clearly aids the production and promotion of ethnic identities. Colonial sports and games, such as cricket, which originally sought to promote a British or English concept of identity and value, were used by Australians, Indians, South Africans and West Indians, among others, to promote a unique national form of ethnicity which was in opposition (in sporting terms at least) to the colonial identity. For migrant groups, sport has been essential in maintaining a sense of ethnicity. Many migrants have chosen to play the sports of the host nation as a method of assimilation, yet have done so organised into their own ethnic teams. Equally, others have chosen to ignore the games of their hosts, and cement their ethnic identity by playing games from 'home'. This has been a common process amongst British Asians, who have successfully kept games such as kabbadi alive in new surroundings.

Especially important in recent debates surrounding the role of ethnicity within sport, have been the identities of professional athletes. Tiger Woods, for example, who has a high media profile, has chosen to side-step the question of identity by stating that he is 'Calbanasian'. He has effectively argued that he is a product of so many identities and cultures that his own ethnicity is irrelevant. The only important issue is his playing ability and his success on the golf course. Such refusal to engage with the question of ethnic identity is in marked contrast to the experience of disgraced 100 metre champion Ben Johnson. In his moment of victory, Johnson was embraced by his national press as the greatest living Canadian. When his drug taking was discovered and he was stripped of his medal, the same press denounced Johnson as a Jamaican immigrant. Sport, because of its high profile, allows for the ready labelling of all involved in ethnic terms. Studies of ethnicity in sport have demonstrated how mobile and complex such identities are.

See also: **nationalism, racism, sociology**

Further reading: Cronin and Mayall (1998), Eisen and Wiggins (1994), Hargreaves (1986), James (1963), MacClancy (1996), Mangan and Ritchie (2005).

ETHNOGRAPHY

The goal of ethnography is 'to communicate understandings about a culture which are held by members of the culture themselves'. (Harris and Park 1983: 10) Ethnographers typically spend a relatively long period of time closely involved with the culture they are studying. This time period may vary from a matter of months to a number of years. During this time, they typically use a variety of techniques and methods, although two major approaches used involve interviewing and participant observation. In using these techniques, the sports ethnographer is attempting to capture the meanings used and made by members of the culture to describe its sporting and physical activity. Interviews involve the direct questioning of members of the culture being studied in order to hear about their sports and physical activities from an insider's (-emic) perspective. As a means of complementing this approach and the information gleaned, ethnographers often employ participant observation techniques, whereby they participate in on-going events of the culture as well as observe what is going on. As such, they adopt an outsider's (-etic) perspective and orientation. In either case they are searching for the meanings and functions of a culture's sporting and physical activities.

Further reading: Harris and Park (1983), Hughson (2001), Marsh (1983)

ETIQUETTE

Many sports have unwritten rules which influence the conduct and behaviour of participants. Some of these are to do with **fair play** or sportsmanship; others are to do with etiquette and deal with customary expectations as to how the game should be played. In golf, however, there is an etiquette section within the published rules that, although unenforceable in terms of penalties, makes it very clear what sort of behaviour will be required. In the professional game fines are exacted for breaches of etiquette, particularly equipment abuse.

EXERCISE

A leisure-time physical activity that people engage in for the purpose of developing physical activity, exercise is 'planned, structured, repetitive bodily movements that someone engages in for the purpose of improving or maintaining physical fitness or health.' (Buckworth and Dishman 2002: 28) There is now a great deal of research evidence to show that regular exercise is associated with a range of physical and mental health benefits. Sadly, despite the compelling nature of this evidence, many people are reluctant to take up exercise and physical activity; similarly many are easily dissuaded from adhering to it. Dishman (2001) has shown that only about 25 per cent of the adult population of most industrialised countries exercise regularly and that only 10 per cent of such populations exercise either sufficiently vigorously or often enough to obtain significant health and fitness benefits.

See also: **exercise adherence**

Further reading: Buckworth and Dishman (2002), Dishman (2001)

EXERCISE ADHERENCE

Commonly cited factors affecting exercise adherence include lack of time, expense, loss of interest, poor instruction, inadequate support, physical discomfort, inconvenience, and even embarrassments. As such, researchers such as Dishman (1994) have recommended that two categories of factors need to be addressed when planning exercise programmes, if the chances of exercise adherence are to be maximized: situation factors and personal factors. Among the critical situation factors which influence adherence are time, money, role conflict, facilities, social support and exercising with others. Among the personal factors which influence adherence are personality, goals and interest. Research suggests that individuals are more likely to make exercise a regular part of their daily routine if these situational and personal factors are appropriately addressed.

Further reading: Dishman (1994)

EXERCISE PHYSIOLOGY

Exercise physiology is that branch of physiology which deals with the functioning of the body during exercise, with the intent of promoting a better understanding of the physical capabilities and limitations of the human body and its underlying physiology. Typically, researchers study functional responses to exercise in terms of a single bout of exercise (acute) or repeated exercise sessions (chronic). The effects of both acute and chronic exercise are also studied at a range of levels from the cellular to the whole body (or integrative level), in an effort to uncover the body's responses and adaptations to exercise. Like its parent discipline of physiology, exercise physiology is dependent on and intersects with other disciplines such as **anatomy**, biochemistry, biophysics and molecular biology.

See also: **anatomy and physiology**

Further reading: Brooks et al. (1996), Foss (1998), McArdle et al. (2000)

EXTERNALITIES

Participation in sport can confer benefits external to those actually involved. If sport keeps people healthier, then available health service resources can be devoted to treating less preventable disease and illness. If fitter workers are more productive employees, then both individual firms and the economic sector as a whole can gain. If sport counteracts delinquency and vandalism, local communities can profit.

Further reading: Gratton and Taylor (1985)

EXTREME SPORTS *see* **adventure sports**

EXTRINSIC MOTIVES

Extrinsic motives are external to an individual and involve seeking the rewards and benefits of performing a task. Trophies, money and praise are all forms of extrinsic motivation. The value of extrinsic motivation to an athlete depends upon the way in which that athlete perceives such motives. If rewards are perceived positively, they can help increase intrinsic motivation, but rewards that are viewed as negative, in that they are designed to control an athlete's behaviour, can decrease intrinsic motivation.

See also: **intrinsic motives**

Further reading: Lepper and Green (1975), Wann (1997)

FACTORS OF PRODUCTION

Economists use land, labour and capital as shorthand terminology for the various economic resources – or factors of production – that are brought together to produce output. Where sporting production is concerned, land includes the fabric of the sports ground as well as the area on which it is situated. Labour obviously includes the participants themselves, but also the backroom staff and those workers who manufacture the match equipment, tailor the team outfits and print the programmes and tickets. Capital in British sport is often a mixture of public and private funds. The motivation of investors can encompass those seeking a speculative gain, others looking for a safe rate of return, and fans simply supporting their team in another way.

See also: **supply**

FAIR PLAY

The concept of fair play is enshrined in the European Charter of Sport for All as involving respect and consideration for opponents and partners, and always playing in the right spirit. In a recent discussion, Loland asked whether fair play was a historical anachronism or a topical ideal. The question is an important one because the fair play ideal in modern sport is built on nineteenth-century class interests where upholding the ideal was seen as depending upon sport being played in a certain manner and with a certain attitude. To follow the ideal meant playing by the rules as much in spirit as in letter. Fair play's 'ideal-type' was the amateur fostered in the **public schools** and by the **Corinthians**. Both fair play and the amateur were very much upper-middle-class ideals in which the gentlemanly virtues and the spirit of **muscular Christianity** were pervasive.

More recently, fair play has come to mean equal starting conditions and equal chances of winning, although in its most general sense it is still thought of as playing according to and in the spirit of the rules. Some philosophers have drawn a distinction between formal and informal fair play. Formal fair play is concerned with the letter of the rules, and informal with the spirit. This distinction between formal and informal fair play is important because it signifies the importance of a central issue in discussions of fair play – the 'logical incompatibility thesis' (Lehman 1981). Proponents of this thesis hold that if we deliberately break the rules of a game and therefore do not play fairly, it is impossible for us to win the game. They argue that logically, we are not playing the game soccer (as defined by its constitutional rules) if we deliberately break those rules. We are in fact playing another game altogether although it may look very much like soccer.

Many consider this view of fair play too narrow and restrictive and lacking the idea of the spirit of fair play. As such, informal fair play is seen as an attitude which players bring both towards the rules of the game and, as importantly, towards their opponents. The argument is made that if we view our opponents with esteem and respect, we should grant them equal starting conditions (such as offered by weight classes in boxing) and an equal chance of winning the game. Opponents are thus viewed as partners in a shared activity rather than obstacles to be overcome.

Fair play needs to reflect both the formal and informal elements, because while each is a necessary condition for understanding fair play, neither is a sufficient condition. In essence, therefore, the ideal of fair play, as promoting the importance of abiding by both the letter and the spirit of the rules, continues.

Further reading: Lehman (1981), Loland (1998), McIntosh (1979), Simon (1991), Steenberger and Tamboer (1998)

FARTLEK

A Swedish term literally meaning 'speed play', fartlek was popularised as an early means of cross-training by Swedish Olympic Coach Gostra Holmer in the 1950s. Holmer was looking for a means of overcoming boredom for his distance runners, and developed a range of workouts involving walking, sprinting, running up and down hills, and retrorunning. He varied the length of the work-out, the terrain over which it was run, and the pace of the activities in tailoring specific regimens for individual athletes. In addition to its use as a training tool for overcoming boredom and the associated problems of **over-training** and **burn-out** – the negative aspects of training – coaches have also used fartlek as a means of enhancing the positive aspects of psychological training, by emphasising the 'play' aspect of 'speed play'.

Further reading: Pate et al. (1984)

FATIGUE

The term fatigue is generally used to describe overall feelings of tiredness and the inability to continue to perform at a particular level. Generally defined as an inability to maintain a power output or force during repeated muscle contractions, fatigue is thought to have four underlying causes and can be manifested in associated sites. These sites include: the central nervous system (CNS) and peripheral systems associated with neural, mechanical and energetic events such as the accumulation of metabolic by-products, the failure of the muscle fibre's contractile mechanisms and depleted or unbalanced energy systems. While fatigue differs for aerobic and anaerobic processes since such activities require different amounts of energy supplied in different ways, fatigue can also be influenced by environmental conditions such as altitude, heat and humidity, and diet. While appropriate training and preparation are important in limiting and even overcoming fatigue, it should be noted that fatigue has a protective function as well as a limiting effect with regard to exercise and sport.

See also: **central nervous system**

Further reading: Powers and Howley (2004)

FEEDBACK

For researchers in motor learning and control, the old adage 'practice makes perfect' is incomplete. Rather, it is practice with appropriate feedback that 'makes perfect', since feedback plays the important roles of motivating, regulating and ultimately reinforcing learning and behaviour. Feedback can come both from within the system (as in any **closed-loop** system) or from outside the system (**open-loop** system).

We tend to use visual feedback as our most important source. Thus when golfers hit a ball, they are more likely to correct their swing on the basis of the fact that they saw where the ball landed (visual feedback) than that they felt (kinesthetic feedback) that they swung the club 'outside-in'. However, both of these sources of feedback are important and are examples of one important type of feedback known as sensory feedback. A second and equally important form of feedback is external feedback. This is feedback gleaned perhaps from another person, typically a teacher or coach, who observes us performing a skill and provides us with information about the production of that skill and/or of its result. Thus researchers have suggested that this non-sensory or 'external' feedback has two components – feedback as knowledge of performance (KP) and feedback as knowledge of results (KR). Teachers and coaches need to bear in mind a number of important factors when providing feedback to performers in the form of KP and KR. First, they must provide appropriate amounts and types of KP that will help direct a performer's attention to aspects of the performance of the task (e.g. hitting a golf ball) which needs to be improved. Second, they must be aware of the possibility of overloading an individual with feedback if they constantly provide KR after each performance. Finally, coaches may use augmented feedback to help a performer. Learning to putt by using a ball with specific markings which highlight how it is rolling, or learning to bowl 'seam-up' in cricket by using a ball with two different colours either side of the seam, would be examples.

Further reading: Gentile (1972), Magill (1998), Schmidt and Lee (1999), Singer (1980)

FEMININITY

A central issue in debates relating to **feminism** and **gender**, femininity can be defined as the measure of being a woman. The application of this definition can be problematic. Medical debates raged at the end of the nineteenth century about whether or not sport was healthy for women, and these were accompanied by social concerns that the playing of sport and games by women would undermine their femininity. Sport, it was believed, was about strength and masculinity. It was not a pursuit designed for women, and their participation would challenge beliefs held about their **gender**. Women have steadily increased their involvement in sport, and the debates connected with femininity have not lessened. Many commentators argue that women should not play sports such as bodybuilding or rugby union, as their participation fundamentally undermines their femininity, and makes them appear, and behave, in a more **masculine** fashion. The same arguments have been made with respect to women's tennis. Players such as the Williams sisters, who are heavily muscled and play a big serving game, are often criticised as being overtly **masculine**. Equally, tennis player Anna Kournikova was challenged by many feminists for pandering to male constructions of femininity by trading on her looks, rather than proving herself as a sportswoman.

See also: **feminism, gender**

FEMINISM

Sport has most often been associated with men. This is due, in large part to the origins of sport in the **public schools** of Victorian Britain, and the overriding associated ideologies of **muscular Christianity** and gentlemanly conduct. Modern sport in the nineteenth century was predominantly organised and played by men. In Victorian society women were conceived of as the weaker sex, whose primary function was the production of healthy children. As such women had no place in the sporting arena. Sports that women did play in the nineteenth century were largely those that were chosen for gentility, such as tennis or golf. In the twentieth century the situation began to change. In general terms the lot of women improved in the wake of the First World War, when they had proved themselves invaluable to the war effort. In 1918 the first women were given the vote in Britain, and by 1928 this had been extended to all women over twenty-eight. Women began to take part in more sports, and organisations such as the Olympics were instrumental in encouraging women's sport as they did not seek to exclude them. Even into the 1930s, bodies such as the Football Association argued against women's participation in the game because of the potential damage that it might do to their health. The most popular sporting pursuits for women in the inter-war years were those that were built around different forms of gymnastics, such as the Women's League of Health and Beauty.

From the 1960s, and with the advance of a general feminist movement, more women became involved in sport and began campaigning for greater levels of access and inclusion. There has always been one dichotomy at the heart of the relationship between feminism and sport. Those women's sports that have been successful in gaining access to the **media** have been those which have been marketed because of the sexuality of the competitors. In this, it is sports such as women's tennis, ice skating and beach volleyball that can be seen to have captured the imagination. At the heart of the matter is the question of whether someone like Anna Kournikova is celebrated because of her sporting ability or her photogenic good looks. Why has it been that feminine sports have largely succeeded in gaining entry to the mainstream, whereas less glamorous women's sports such as football or rugby have struggled?

Feminism, as a political movement within sport, still has a long way to travel. The majority of sports administrators remain men, and the bulk of prize money in any given tournament is preserved for the male competition. At the centre of the debate is the issue of the body: should the female sporting body be made masculine to compete, or be kept beautiful to preserve **femininity**?

See also: **discrimination, femininity, gender**

Further reading: Fletcher (1984), Hargreaves (1994)

FIELD SPORTS DEBATE

The field sports debate, which has centred to a significant degree on the sport of hunting, has focused on two issues: **animal rights** and ecocentrism. Those who support animal rights argue that animals deserve the same moral concern as humans and thus should not be hunted for sport. This argument is buttressed by the idea that, in hunting animals hunters are guilty of speciesism – a form of inequality considered a parallel to racism and sexism. In its most fundamental form, then, the animal rights argument involves animal liberation, and those holding this view condemn field sports on the grounds that treating animals as objects for the sporting amusement of humans is morally repugnant. Animals, they argue, not only deserve to be treated humanely (as the equals of humans) but also should never be used as a sporting resource. For those in favour of field sports, animals do not command the same moral standing as humans, and those classified as vermin – such as foxes and rats – certainly do not. Thus in answering the animal liberationists, field sports proponents have suggested that killing game, and particularly killing vermin such as foxes, is not a moral issue at all. Rather they have argued that it is amoral in that the desire to hunt is the modern vestige of an evolutionary trait: that of supporting human existence.

Ecocentrists take a rather different view, suggesting that the morality of field sports, and particularly fox hunting, is ultimately a function of the needs of the natural environment. As such, the issue of the moral standing of animals is not something that is granted by humans, but rather is derived from and dependent on the greater good of the global ecosystem of which we are all a part. Only if it can be determined that field sports help balance our ecosystem will ecocentrists be in favour of it. In trying to attract the ecocentrists to their cause, the proponents of field sports have suggested that they are helping to maintain the ecosystem because it is in their interests to maintain the countryside that supports field sports and the habitat for the animals that they pursue.

In this debate, the strength of the animal liberation cause is to be found in the decline in the hunting of animals and the growth of such activities as drag-hunting and blood-hounding. These preserve important aspects of hunting without using animals as a sporting resource, or of doing damage to the countryside since in these activities trails can be planned to limit such concerns.

See also: **animal rights, animal sports**

Further reading: Causey (1989), Singer (1975), Wade (1996)

FIGURATIONAL THESIS

The figurational thesis has most commonly been associated with Eric Dunning and the University of Leicester. The intellectual basis for such work was the writings of Norbert Elias, a German sociologist. Elias argued, most notably in his work on the civilising process, that social life, and this included sporting pursuits, was based on complex interrelationships and dependencies between individuals. Figurational **sociology** undertook to understand and analyse these relationships and dependencies as a method of understanding sport.

See also: **sociology**

Further reading: Dunning et al. (2004), Elias and Dunning (1986)

FINANCE

Sport in Britain has been financed by a combination of private and public funds; the latter mainly concentrated in the educational and martial sectors. Traditionally the major source of funding for most sports was gate money, supplemented in more recent times by media payments for broadcasts and **merchandising** sales. These have not always proved sufficient to cover outgoings, and many clubs have relied on external funding to keep them afloat. These have included donations from fans, **patronage** from the more affluent, **subsidies** from local and national government, and, increasingly, **sponsorship**.

FITNESS

Scientists view fitness as being specific, and thus ask the question 'fitness for what?' They contend that one can be fit for some activities and not for others. Fitness, like the training that develops it, is specific. However, most experts agree that there are two general categories of physical fitness: health-related physical fitness and motor-performance physical fitness.

Health-related physical fitness is generally assumed to be fitness related to some aspect of health characteristics and behaviours, and is concerned with the quality of function of the fundamental organ systems that constitute human physiology, and most particularly the muscular, nervous, cardiovascular and respiratory systems. Thus measures of health-related fitness include strength and endurance of skeletal muscles, joint flexibility, cardiovascular endurance, and body composition. Measures of these indicators of fitness used by scientists are dependent upon the question 'fitness for what?' Thus the health-related fitness requirements for a nine year old are significantly different from those of a ninety year old. Activities of daily living have become one source of measurement for scientists, and most definitions of fitness include, as a significant element, the ability to perform daily tasks efficiently without fatigue.

Cardio-respiratory or aerobic fitness is what most people think of when the word fitness is mentioned. Aerobic fitness refers to the functional capacity of the cardiovascular and respiratory systems to enable the skeletal muscles to expend **energy** and thus perform work. Since aerobic fitness is negatively correlated with such ailments as heart disease and hypertension, it has become an important benchmark for health-related fitness. By contrast, motor-performance physical fitness is defined as the ability of the neuromuscular system to perform specific tasks.

Thus, while cardio-respiratory endurance, muscular strength and endurance, body composition and flexibility are important aspects of both types of fitness, factors such as agility, power, speed and balance become far more important in determining an individual's motor-performance fitness. And while training can enhance an individual's agility, speed or balance, to an extent, these aspects of fitness are more dependent upon genetic potential in that they appear to be less easily influenced by training.

Further reading: Corbin and Lindsey (1997), Howley and Franks (1997), McArdle et al. (2000), Miller and Allen (1995), Williams (1996)

FITNESS ADAPTATIONS

The aim of any fitness training is to bring about improvements or adaptations to one or more of the body's systems. This requires stressing the system or systems adequately, to ensure that by employing the overload principle, we elicit an adaptive response from that system. Physiological adaptations occur when training principles such as progressive resistance, specificity, frequency, duration and intensity of exercise are followed.

FITNESS EDUCATION

Fitness education is a central part of the British national curriculum at school level, and runs through levels one to eight. The overall aim is to introduce pupils to a knowledge and understanding of fitness and its relationship to health. Over the various stages of the curriculum students are encouraged to understand what effect fitness will have on their bodies and how this will improve their health. By engaging with the different sports and activities that they undertake they seek to understand how fitness plays an important part in their health and well-being, and specifically how each type of physical activity impacts on their body. The curriculum also encourages students to understand how their levels of fitness relate to the quality of their sporting performance, and those they are playing with and competing against. In its entirety, fitness education is concerned with making students realise that regular, planned activity will have a lasting impact on their personal levels of health and fitness, and encourage them to plan their own appropriate exercise and activity programme.

FITNESS HISTORY

One of the key motivations for many people who play sport or go to the gym, is to keep their body fit. There is clear evidence that the ancient sports and games promoted by the Greeks and Romans, and those martial arts that existed across Asia, were part of a culture that promoted and championed the cause of physical fitness.

An awareness of the importance of fitness, as a way of ensuring quality of life and longevity, and of avoiding illness, began to develop in the nineteenth century in Europe. Fitness was keenly promoted by the Protestant and Methodist Churches of that period, who argued that the simple dictum, 'a healthy mind and a healthy body', was an ideal model for living. In Germany, Denmark, Sweden and Finland, amongst others, various forms of gymnastics were promoted, and these formed the bedrock of a fitness culture. During that time, and especially within the confines of British **public schools**, the pursuit of fitness was seen as an essential part of instilling order within society and as a means of preparing young men for war. With the **diffusion** of modern sport and **exercise** across the globe during the second half of the nineteenth century, fitness became a watchword in most modern nations. In most countries, men and women entering the army, especially those who were conscripted, were put through a range of medical tests to make sure that they were fit to fight. The pursuit of a society where everyone could be defined as A1 fit became highly important. Where nations were seen to fail on the battlefield, or when army recruits were being shown to be unfit, a sense of crisis ensued. In Britain, in the wake of defeats during the Boer War, and as a result of the poor health and fitness standards of First World War recruits, central government encouraged plans that would introduce physical exercise to the school curriculum, thereby improving the fitness levels within society.

During the inter-war period, the enthusiasm for fitness was readily apparent. While the belief that a fit body was one ready for war, it became increasingly apparent to many observers and interested members of the medical profession, that fitness was a benefit to those in the workplace, and for women of all ages. In Britain, for example, the inter-war years witnessed the explosive growth of the Women's League for Health and Beauty. Across the modern world, similar movements blossomed, and all forms of physical activity that induced fitness were readily embraced by individuals, communities and poli-tical regimes. In the new suburban towns of Europe and America, tennis clubs, swimming pools and other venues for fitness became a central part of everyday life.

In the post-war years medical investigations demonstrated that those who regularly took exercise, and promoted their own personal fitness, would significantly reduce their risk of coronary disease. As society became more aware of the threat of poor diet and lack of exercise, so fitness became ever more important as a remedy. From the 1970s onwards, the need to achieve a level of personal fitness encouraged the boom in activities such as jogging and aerobics, and led to the construction of private gym clubs in towns and cities across many parts of Europe, America and beyond.

As modern society has changed, and working practices have transformed, so fitness has become an active choice. In the past, when most work involved physical exertion, and motor transport was a rarity, fitness was easier to come by. With the advent of a post-industrial service society in the Western world, being fit is not a given part of living, it is something that has to be actively pursued. Constant government and media surveys demonstrate that all modern societies are becoming increasingly unfit, obese and prone to serious illness. All medical evidence has demonstrated that a physical exercise programme that develops cardio-respiratory fitness, muscular fitness and flexibility, while controlling the portion of body weight, will lead to a reduced risk from a range of serious illness, will keep weight down and lead to an all round fitter body. To achieve such levels of fitness a range of activities, including weight training, cycling, walking and swimming, must be regularly undertaken. It is currently estimated that over 40 million Americans currently undertake regular exercise in an attempt to keep fit. Of these, over 20 million regularly take part in an aerobics class. In addition to those who seek fitness through organised clubs and classes, are the many millions that purchase home gyms and other keep fit equipment, books or videos. In its entirety the fitness industry is worth in excess of £500 million in Britain alone.

While it is clear that the pursuit of fitness is a worthwhile enterprise, it is not one without its problems. The fitness industry is one that is closely linked to the dieting industry, and both of these, accompanied by the media, have created images of the ideally fit body that many people find difficult to live up to. In addition to sporting injuries caused by the pursuit of fitness, many others have suffered psychological damage in their attempts to match the image of what society often understands a fit person should look like.

See also: **exercise, health**

Further reading: Cooper (1968), Gavin (1992)

FITNESS METHODS

Since fitness is composed of a number of components, including cardio-respiratory fitness, muscular strength, muscular endurance, flexibility, nutrition and body composition, all fitness methods need to address these factors. With significant emphasis being placed by doctors and other health and fitness professionals on being fit to counteract heart disease, activities which stress cardio-respiratory or aerobic fitness have been the most widely practised method of promoting general fitness. Weight training has been the preferred method of producing gains in muscular strength and endurance, while dieting has been the most widely used approach to addressing nutrition and body composition concerns. Perhaps the least practised element of fitness is flexibility. The ideal fitness method or approach will employ activities to promote fitness in all of these areas.

Further reading: Fox et al. (1987)

FITNESS TESTING

When trying to maximise performance, it is important that athletes establish their strengths and weaknesses in relation to the demands of the activity in which they are involved. For endurance activities that require cardiovascular endurance and thus aerobic fitness, maximal tests such as **VO$_2$ Max** are considered preferable. In such tests the body is exercised to exhaustion and thus no extrapolation, based on sub-maximal test results, is necessary to predict fitness level. This is not the case with sub-maximal tests, such as the Harvard Step Test or the Astrand bicycle ergometer test, which are predictive tests. For strength and power tests, pull-ups, push-ups, vertical jump, standing long jump and 30-second Wingate cycle-ergometer test are all used. Tests of health-related fitness include heart rate, blood pressure and lung function, and are factors we are more likely to associate with a visit to a doctor's surgery than to our local sports or health club.

Further reading: Fox et al. (1987), Howley and Franks (1997)

FOOTBALL IN THE COMMUNITY

In 1978 the government provided over £1 million to football clubs to begin community-based projects, preferably in areas of economic and social deprivation. The hope was that the clubs might gain local supporters and the community might benefit from having role models for children and activities that offered an alternative to anti-social behaviour. Although there were initial instances of the resources being used to improve club facilities without the knock-on effect for the community, the intervention of the Professional Footballers' Association – who saw employment opportunities for ex-players – in the mid-1980s rejuvenated the idea. Today all professional and some semi-professional clubs in England have a Football in the Community Officer operating the scheme, which is now run by the PFA, the Football Association and the Football League.

Further reading: Mellor (2001)

FOOTBALL SPORTS

Football in its various guises emerged out of the folk games where one village might be arraigned against another with the objective of getting a ball or other trophy back to their home. It contrasts with organised games of football with their specified numbers of players, fixed time limits and marked-out pitches. Football games were found in most cultures but the modern game is a British invention of the late nineteenth century. It was in Britain that the rules were codified, the first clubs established, and organised competitive fixtures begun. Much credit is given to the **public schools** for first codifying the games of soccer (from association football) and rugger (rugby union) as part of their games cult and the drive for school discipline. Each school, however, tended to produce its own variant of football, and inter-school and university fixtures required the development of a single set of rules. This came with the formation of the Football Association in 1863, though there was still dispute about whether or not the ball could be handled. The adherents of this approach eventually formed the Rugby Football Union in 1871. This was the same year that the FA Cup competition commenced.

A football league in which leading clubs in the North and the Midlands played each other on a home and away basis was established in 1888. Soccer remains the only football variant that expressly forbids the handling of the ball by outfield players.

Rugby itself split in 1895 when what became the sport of rugby league broke away from the established union game, ostensibly on the grounds of broken-time payments to players. The RFU feared that the working-class players and spectators in the north would swamp 'their' game. The new organisation abolished the line-out in 1897, allowed open professionalism in 1898, and fundamentally changed the nature of the game in 1906 when it reduced the number of players to thirteen per side and introduced the play-the-ball rule after a tackle.

Gaelic football is the most popular sport in Ireland, and offers an important social and cultural activity to emigrant Irish in Britain who dominate the competitions held on the mainland. Gaelic football's first rules were published in December 1884 at the second convention of the Gaelic Athletic Association. The codification of its rules was a response by Irish nationalists to the growth of 'English' football, and the game became identified with the assertion of Irish national culture and opposition to British rule. Played by teams of fifteen players each, the goals resemble rugby goalposts. Three points are scored by kicking the ball between the posts and under the bar and one point if it is kicked above the bar. Throwing the ball is outlawed but it can be carried provided that it is bounced every four steps.

Britain exported most codes of football to the rest of the world: in return it received two variants, neither of which has achieved anywhere near the popularity gained in the exporting country. American football, commonly referred to in Britain as gridiron (from the markings on the field of play) was adapted from British rugby in the late nineteenth century and has recently returned both as an amateur participatory sport and a commercial enterprise at the professional level. There are eleven players per side with unlimited substitutions allowed. The scrum of rugby has been replaced by a 'snap'. Four attempts are allowed to carry the ball forward ten yards and, unlike in rugby, passing the ball forwards is permissible. Australian rules football was devised in Melbourne to keep cricketers fit during the winter. It predates both rugby and soccer in its codification and is based on neither. Two of its unique features are that the playing area is oval in shape and there are eighteen players a side. There are four goal posts with six points scored for kicking the ball through the centre two posts and one point for between the outer posts. Carrying the ball is allowed provided it is bounced every five yards, and the ball can be kicked or hand passed. A player catching a kicked ball can claim a mark and an unimpeded kick.

Recent decades have seen the development of touch football, a non-contact version of rugby suitable for mixed-gender teams, and the expansion of mini-versions of soccer and rugby, the former often taking place indoors.

Further reading: Collins (2001), Harvey (2005)

FORCE

Possessing both magnitude and direction, force is a vector quantity, and is 'the effect that one body has on another'. (Wells and Luttgens 1976: 291) All motion is derived from the application of force, be it force from muscular contractions, force from **gravity** or force from friction. The major concern for those involved in sport and physical activity is in changing the state of motion of athletes and their implements, be they javelins, tennis rackets, soccer balls, etc. In addition to direction and magnitude, critical to any analysis of force is its point of application. The effect of force varies with its point of application, as we see when we hit a tennis ball closer to the top or bottom, thereby providing topspin or backspin with resultant changes in trajectory and flight. We measure force as the product of mass and acceleration, using the unit weight as the measure of magnitude. The direction of force is along its action line. Gravity exerts a downward vertical force, while muscular force is represented by the direction of a muscle's line of pull.

Further reading: Dyson (1986), Hay (1993), Wells and Luttgens (1976)

FRANCHISES

Most common in American sport, franchises are the granting of the right to play in a particular tournament to the owners of a team. These owners can, and do, take the franchise with them to another city or sell to another aspiring owner elsewhere. In Britain such transferable private ownership of sports teams is rare, though it occurs in ice-hockey and speedway. In rugby league the right to compete has been withdrawn from several teams in an effort by the league organisers to assure quality control.

FREE AGENTS

When professional sportspeople complete their contract with a club they are regarded as free agents and are legally entitled to negotiate another contract with any potential employer without any transfer fee having to be paid to their former club. Free agency allows players to secure higher wages than if a transfer had to be paid; in effect they secure the fee, in whole or in part, for themselves.

See also: **transfers**

FUNCTIONALISM

The study of sport through a functionalist approach presumes that society is a well ordered structure that consists of many interrelated constituents, all of which are united in their belief in common values and processes. The three major forms of functionalism identified by Abrahamson (1973) are individualistic (society responding to the needs of the individual), interpersonal (communications between people aimed at minimising social strains) and societal (practices, such as the law, which satisfy the needs of the social system). The study of functionalism in sport is effectively concerned with the role of sporting activity in creating balance within the wider society. The main concerns of research into sport, which adopts the functionalist approach, is to assess whether sport creates good character, how it brings about the coherence and solidarity of the communities within which it functions, whether it creates good citizens who are supportive of the existing social order, and how sport instils a positive work ethic into people (adapted from Coakley 1998: 33). Functionalism has been embraced by many sports sociologists as it views sport as essentially positive.

Further reading: Abrahamson (1973), Booth and Loy (2000), Coakley (1998)

GAMBLING

Gambling has become a regular and well publicised recreation provided by business organisations and taxed by governments. It involves betting on the outcome of an event. Sport lends itself to gambling because of its competitive character with winners and losers. Gambling can take one of three forms: remote speculation, as with lotteries; incidental, where the gambling is perhaps subservient to other social purposes, such as bingo; and judgemental, which applies to most sports betting.

Competitive sport has winners and losers, the basic element required for betting. Today most people associate gambling on sport with horse racing, dog racing, or, via the pools, with football. Yet many other sports have a long association with gambling and, as **internet** betting develops, few sports will be left untouched. Historically there was petty wagering on many brutal **animal sports**, but cock-fighting often involved significant betting. The press often featured sporting challenges in which an endurance athlete would pit his ability and purse against those prepared to bet that a certain feat was impossible. From the eighteenth century both horse racing and pugilism became the major vehicles for gamblers, the former being greatly assisted by the emergence of the bookmaker willing to take bets from all comers rather than the traditional betting of individuals with each other. In the inter-war years football pools became popular and offered small-scale gamblers the chance of a huge return for a little outlay. In recent years the pools have been undermined by the development of the **National Lottery**, in which the exercise of judgement on the ability of teams has been replaced by simply choosing numbers. The last few years have also seen the emergence of **spread betting**, in which neither winnings nor losses are predetermined at the time of the bet.

The **law** has played a major role in the relationship between sport and gambling. For many years ready-money betting away from the sports event itself was illegal as betting shops were not legalised until 1961. Once betting became accepted by the government as a normal part of consumer spending, it was open to taxation. Unlike income tax, the tax on betting is not progressive in that large winnings have the same percentage deduction as small ones, though, of course, gambling taxes, like most ones on recreational activities, are voluntary, as only people who choose to bet need to pay them.

The size of the gambling industry is often exaggerated by a failure to distinguish between gross and net expenditure, the former including re-bet winnings and laid-off bets from one bookmaker to another. Anti-gambling advocates emphasise the unproductive nature of gambling, but economists would draw attention to the employment that is created and the investment that is generated.

See also: **spread betting**

Further reading: Munting (1996)

GAMES

Games are a form of organised recreational activity, characterised by competition and criteria for determining a winner. Unlike **play**, in games the goals for participation originate outside the game in that people participate not just for fun but also for prestige, recognition or status. Generally games have **rules**, either formal or informal, specifically as regards the termination and result of the game. Often these rules are deliberately inefficient in that the objective of the game could be achieved more easily were it not for their imposition: physically carrying the ball to the hole and dropping it in is a more effective way of holing out than resorting to the vagaries of the putter; but it is not golf.

GAS EXCHANGE

The efficient exchange of oxygen and carbon dioxide (O_2) between the air and the blood is necessary to ensure that oxygen is delivered to the working muscles and that CO_2 is removed from the working muscles. Contact between air and blood is necessary for this to happen, and this contact takes place in the alveoli, the tiny air sacs located deep within the lungs. Contact between the alveoli and the pulmonary capillaries allows for diffusion of oxygen and carbon dioxide across the permeable alveoli capillary membrane.

Further reading: Brooks et al. (1996), McArdle et al. (2000)

GAY GAMES

The Gay Games were inspired by Dr Tom Waddell, who organised the first in San Francisco in 1982. The Gay Games are held every four years and are open to all gay men and women. They have only ever been staged in North America, with the exception of the 1998 games in Amsterdam. The overall number of competitors has grown from the inaugural 1,300 to over 11,000. The games are based on the Olympic model, and as they have grown in size, have had to become increasingly commercialised. The budget for the 1998 games was estimated at US$9.3 million. The Gay Games have served to highlight the cause of gay rights, and have also heightened awareness of the issues surrounding AIDS and HIV. Events such as the Gay Games are the embodiment of many of the arguments put forward by the proponents of **critical theory**.

See also: **discrimination, gender**

Further reading: Elling et al. (2003), Townes (1996)

GENDER

The concept of gender is a popular means of discussing the similarities, differences and conflicts that exist between the sexes. It has
emerged as a more favourable vehicle for discussing sex relations and
the context within which they exist, as the concepts of **masculinity**
and **femininity** were often viewed in isolation from each other. By
using gender as a method of investigation, a wider and more useful
context is provided that includes both sexes. Sport is an arena where
gender is of the utmost importance, and one where, because of **history**,
the different sexes have gendered roles. Sport helps to construct gender,
and affords a venue for the maintenance of the ideology of gender
difference.

The origins of modern sport in the nineteenth century separated
the genders along clear masculine and feminine lines. Institutions
such as the **public schools**, that were so important to the establishment of team sports, were exclusively male institutions. The ethos
that accompanied sports such as rugby, cricket and football was concerned with the ideological creation of manliness, gentlemanly conduct and **muscular Christianity**, all of which were explicitly male-
centred. It was not solely the **public schools** that separated women
from sport, but also the clubs and associations that were established to
oversee the running of sport. Bodies such as the Rugby Football
Union, the Football Association and the MCC, all explicitly excluded
women from their structures and disqualified them from taking part
on the playing field. The only perceived place for women in sport
was as spectators in the stands, or in the kitchens preparing teas. Such
exclusion was aided by the medical profession, which argued, well
into the early twentieth century, that excessive exercise or exertion
was bad for women. Sport was suspected as having a potentially
damaging effect on women's reproductive systems. The situation
changed rapidly during the first half of the twentieth century, in part
because of the role that women played in the war effort between
1914 and 1918. In the 1920s and 1930s, sport and exercise for
women became increasingly popular, and they were granted increasing access to major sporting events such as the **Olympic Games**.
Attitudes towards gender, despite changing, were not completely
transformed. In 1948, when Fanny Blankers-Koen won four gold
medals at the **Olympics**, she was still castigated by the press. Many
male correspondents argued that women, and especially those like
Blankers-Koen who were mothers, had no place in the Olympics.
The feminist movement which rose to prominence in the 1960s and

1970s, was especially important in challenging the accepted gendered roles within society, and used sport, amongst other things, to project strong and positive images of women.

Despite such advances, there are still arguments that surround the accepted gender roles within society, and how far equality between genders has actually been achieved. In the contemporary period some sports continue to exclude women, there are institutional bars on women competing in sports such as boxing, many religions disqualify women from competing in sport because of cultural arguments, and some countries still frown on women's sports because of domestic traditions. For those sports which women do take part in, there are continuing debates about their representation and their rates of pay. Women's basketball in the United States, staged under the auspices of the WNBA, has been particularly criticised for promoting sexualised rather than sporting images of its star players, and failing to pay the salaries of the game's male counterparts.

There are a host of other issues that have come to the fore as part of the gender debate in sport. These include the levels of violence amongst sportsmen and supporters which are replicated in wider society, questions relating to the place of gay and lesbian athletes, and the medical issue of gender tests for sportswomen. Studying gender is essential in understanding many of the sexualised and power domi-nant roles in sport, and ideal for highlighting the issues of **femininity** and **masculinity**.

See also: **discrimination, feminism, femininity, masculinity**

Further reading: Birrell and Cole (1994), Cahn (1994), Coakley (1998), Hall (1996), Hargreaves (1994), Mesmer and Sabo (1992)

GEOGRAPHY

The study of sports geography is, by comparison with other areas of academic investigation, surprisingly underdeveloped. Consider-ing the impact that sport has had on the **landscape**, and given the arguments that have surrounded the siting and environmental impact of major sporting venues, an understanding of sports geo-graphy should be essential for those involved in the business of sport.

Bale (2000) identified three major approaches to the study of geo-graphy. These are the study of regional variations, the **landscape** of geography, and the welfare of geography. The study of regional variations has been driven by a need to understand the uneven spread of sports types and talents across any given country. It is clear that few sports are evenly spread, and that all have particular areas where they are strongest and most frequently played. In Britain the concentration of rugby league in the northern counties of England, or in Australia the dominance of Australian rules football in Victoria, would be prime examples of regional variation. By combining a process of mapping, with an understanding of both **history** and contemporary developments such as business pressures, the geographer can explain why sports have succeeded or failed in different areas. The same process is true of the production of sports players. In Britain the majority of professional football players have emerged in the Northeast. By mapping the origins of sports players, the geographer can demonstrate where talent emerges from in any given sport. Such information is invaluable to those who are charged by professional associations or work in education with developing and identifying new talent.

The study of **landscape** has been at the heart of much geographical study. This area of investigation can examine micro–issues, such as the siting and construction of football stadia, as well as macro–issues, for example the dominance of golf courses in areas of east central Scotland and their effect on local surroundings. In studying the landscape geographers have had to be aware of both technological and societal changes that affect sport. **Technology** has played an important part in taking sport to areas where previously natural elements had conspired against them. Modern watering technology has allowed for the construction of grass racecourses in desert countries such as Dubai, while indoor stadium technology and the advent of astroturf meant that cold, snowbound cities such as Toronto could play a full season of American football without hindrance from the weather.

Sports venues undoubtedly create problems and frustrations for those people who live in the adjacent area. Such problems include traffic, noise, the litter from temporary catering outlets, and in the case of football, the violence and disruption associated with **hooliganism**. The appliance of welfare geographers has attempted to overcome these difficulties, by planning out new stadia in an informed manner that is sympathetic to the surrounding area and population. The post-Taylor Report building of new grounds for British football, has seen the construction of out-of-town stadia in industrial or commercial areas. These grounds, such as those of Derby

County, Bolton Wanderers or Millwall offer better facilities for supporters, and reduce the impact felt by the local community.

See also: **environment, landscape**

Further reading: Bale (1981; 1992; 1993a; 1993b; 2000), Hall and Page
(2005), Patmore (1983), Vertinsky and Bale (2004)

GLOBALISATION

In the years since the Second World War, with the ending of many
formal imperial links and the advent of new technological media and
business markets, it has been argued by many academics, especially
those in **sociology**, that globalisation is now a major force in the
world. There do appear to be many themes that are now common
throughout the whole world, and the majority of these pertain
to global cultures and markets. Easily recognisable symbols of
the globalised world would include the omnipresence of brands
such as McDonalds, Burger King, Coca-Cola and Nike. The strength
of these products has been their high profile, their ability to break
into and dominate new markets, and the strength of the ethos –
predominantly American, capitalist and profit-driven – that accom-
panies them. Beyond globalised products that are available on any
high street, there has been an accompanying advance of other
products and tools of globalisation. The global dominance of
high finance and the steady alignment of all the major money and
stock markets has led to a globalisation of capital, while the steady
spread of major media companies, such those owned by Rupert
Murdoch or Ted Turner, has brought about an homogenising of what
is shown on **television** sets across the world. Sport has not been
immune from the forces of globalisation, and can in fact be seen to
be one of the most visible and commonly understood forms of this
phenomenon.

Cashmore (2000) has identified three major levels of globalisation.
These include the creation of global sporting competitions, the
development of satellite communications and the growth of a sporting goods market. The International Olympic Committee was the
first global sports organisation that sought to include all nations as
members. Other sporting organisations, such as the MCC in cricket
or FIFA in football, have had a large geographical spread, but this has
not been as extensive as the Olympics. It is not solely the large-scale

international membership of the **Olympics** which makes it a force of globalisation. The IOC has been very astute in its dealings with the **media**, and its television rights sale to NBC ensured that events such as the opening ceremony or the 100 metres final achieve the largest viewing audiences of any sporting event. The development of satellite communications has meant that televised sporting events are now seen across the world both live, and as part of edited highlights programmes. British Premier League football is shown in most countries across the world. The success and appeal of the Premier League is evidenced by the globalised nature of what are essentially local teams. Manchester United's following, for example, largely as a result of satellite television coverage, now relies on a global network of merchandise sales and supporters' clubs. Similarly the NBA and NFL, although promoting specifically American-based sports, successfully used the global television market to ensure that the names of Michael Jordan and Magic Johnson were as well known in Europe as they were in North America. The marketing of sporting teams, stars and merchandise has been one of the most successful strands of the globalisation of sport. Companies such as Nike, Reebok and Ellesse have built on the global fascination for sport, and sporting professionals as marketing tools, to construct a global market for training shoes, tracksuits and other sports related merchandise. Equally, the market for replica team shirts has extended far beyond the domestic shores of teams such as Arsenal, the New York Yankees or Knicks, or the Dallas Cowboys.

Beyond Cashmore's useful definition of globalisation, two other themes should be considered. First is the globalised market for sporting stars. Since the nineteenth century, top sportsmen and women have moved around the world in pursuit of the best wages and opportunities. What began with Scottish footballers moving to England and Welsh rugby players moving to play rugby league for cash, has now blossomed into a truly global market. All sporting forms across the world now recruit players from other countries. The second globalising force is the celebrity nature of the **sporting hero**. With the growth of global **television** coverage and the marketing of sporting goods, sports stars have been sold around the world. Professionals such as Muhammad Ali, Pele, Bjorn Borg or Tiger Woods have almost ceased to be national figures, and have instead become globalised.

See also: **colonialism, colonisation, cultural imperialism**

Further reading: Cashmore (2000), Dunning (2000), Lanfranchi and Taylor (2001), Maguire (2000), Rowe (2000)

GOAL ORIENTATION

In a scenario that is entirely outcome-driven (e.g. the achievement of a new personal best performance) the aims of a training programme would be focused heavily on specific aims or targets. The process by which such targets (goals) are achieved would be important, but only because they are a means to an end. It is important therefore to differentiate between performance goals and process-orientated goals.

See also: **process orientation**

GOVERNMENT POLICY

It has often been argued by British governments, most notably during the period of Margaret Thatcher's time as Prime Minister, that sport and politics are separate entities. This is not however, the case. Governments across the world, of all different political persuasions, have to intervene in sporting matters and evolve policy so that sport is given a clear agenda for its role within society. There are two main types of government policy. The first, which is when government is in reactive mode, produces policies which respond to any given crisis or emergent issue in the political arena. Examples of the reactive mode would be the decision to implement the terms of the Taylor Report after the Hillsborough tragedy, or the British government's decision not to enforce a boycott of the 1980 **Olympics** in Moscow despite the Soviet invasion of Afghanistan. The second major type of government policy is that which actively seeks to involve central government in sport, thereby shaping the future provision of facilities, the success of the nation's elite athletes, the improved health of the people, and so on. Examples of this approach would be the decision to establish the Sports Councils, support and funding for initiatives such as the **Sport for All** campaign, and government backing for host cities bidding for the Olympic or **Commonwealth Games**. One of the most public government policy initiatives of recent times was the decision to support, at great expense, London's bid to host the 2012 Olympic Games. Equally complex was the government's policy decision to back the demolition of Wembley

Stadium, and to argue in favour of a new national stadium. The controversy surrounding these two issues, and others emerging from the reactive mode, provoke difficult questions about the actual role of government within the sporting arena. Government policies and funding initiatives need to be clearly spelt out, and should be long-term if they are to succeed. It is clear however, that many knee jerk decisions made by government, in an attempt to capitalise on the popularity of sport, create problems rather than offer solutions.

Government policy in Britain has largely been concerned with issues of access to sporting provision, and improvements in the health of the nation. The emergence in 1935 of the Central Council of Physical Recreation, from within the Ministry of Education, is symbolic of this trend, as was the establishment of the **Sports Council** in the 1970s. It is only since the mid-1960s that policy has focused on the performance of elite athletes and the benefits that good performances on the world stage bring to the nation. The funding of elite athletes improved dramatically in the 1990s with the government's decision to instigate a national lottery and to allow the bulk of its proceeds to fund the sports area. The success of this policy was evidenced by the positive performance of British athletes at the 2000 Sydney Olympics. Elsewhere in the world, other governments, most notably in Australia and the United States, have been far more proactive in pursuing policies to improve sporting performance and accessibility. Many of the lessons regarding a centrally planned sporting policy for government were learnt from the decisions made by the former Soviet bloc nations during the 1960s and 1970s. By allowing government policy to directly intervene in sports, nations such as the Soviet Union, East Germany and Czechoslovakia improved their sporting performance on the world stage, and brought great glory to their countries.

See also: **politics**

Further reading: Allison (1993), Coghlan (1990), Houlihan (1991)

GRAVITY

As a force, gravity causes an equal downward acceleration in all objects, regardless of their mass, at a rate of 32 feet per second per second. This downward pull is obviously a major factor affecting all sporting and physical activity, applying equally to performers and to the sporting implements that they might wield, hit, throw or strike.

Likewise, since the pull of gravity influences the stability of the body during the performance of physical activity, the balance or appropriate distribution of those gravitational forces upon the body is essential to promoting stability or 'balance'. The location of the centre of gravity, or the point around which the mass or sum of gravitational forces is equally distributed or 'balanced', is thus of vital import in the performance of physical skills. We know that the lower the centre of gravity and the closer it is to the base of support, the more stable an object. Thus when rugby players scrummage they attempt to get their body weight as low as possible to avoid being pushed backwards. Likewise, when those involved in a tug-of-war pull on the rope they try to lower their centre of gravity by leaning backwards and planting their feet well in front of them to increase stability and decrease their chances of being pulled forward by their opponents.

Further reading: Dyson (1986), Hay (1993)

GYMNASTICS

The term gymnastics is often applied to the use of movement to sustain, develop and exercise control of the body in an athletic or aesthetic context. Historically the term has frequently been linked with others such as 'gymnastic training' or 'gymnastic exercise', which could be militaristic or therapeutic in motivation. Two major European schools of thought have influenced British gymnastics. In competitive gymnastics the German system became dominant, with its rings, high bar, horse and parallel bars, but in the educational sphere the Swedish system became the most influential, partly because its beams, ropes and vaulting box were more easily financed than the swings, slides, pulley systems, ropes and rigging, climbing frames and vaulting pits of the German variety.

See also: **physical education**

Further reading: Bailey and Vamplew (1999)

HAEMOGLOBIN

The iron-containing pigment and buffer in red blood cells, haemoglobin is the protein that builds oxygen and is responsible for transporting oxygen to tissues. Each molecule of haemoglobin can carry four molecules of oxygen. Normal haemoglobin concentration is about 150 grams per litre of blood for healthy males and 130 grams per litre of blood for healthy females.

HEALTH

Improved health is one of the major benefits posited for participation in sport and physical activity. Principles of general health and well-being, including prevention of illness as well as health promotion, are widely touted as laudable outcomes of such participation. However, there is concern that many groups are not achieving appropriate levels of physical activity to obtain these posited health benefits. Thus we find that some young athletes are being overstressed and subjected to excessive amounts of 'unhealthy' competition. By contrast, many other young people are not enjoying the health benefits which participation in sport and physical activity can confer because they are inactive, and not involved in sport or regular physical activity. For example, obesity is a growing problem amongst the young in the Western world. It is also clear that participation in sport and physical activity can delay the onset and speed of physical decline associated with aging, and thus can help maintain higher levels of health for older adults. However, as yet, we offer little incentive and few opportunities for such individuals to be involved in sport. Despite advances in **disability sport** and sport for the elderly, sport and physical activity are still thought to be primarily for the young and the able-bodied.

See also: **exercise, fitness**

Further reading: DePauw and Gavron (1995), Rowland (1996), Wann (1997)

HEALTH-RELATED EXERCISE

In addition to competing is actual sports, sports educators have also championed a general understanding, especially amongst children, of the benefits of health related exercise. In Britain this has become part of the National Curriculum. Classes are used that introduce children to basic benefits of being healthy, and teach them about their bodies. Key areas of study include understanding and identifying fitness components, namely, flexibility, cardio-respiratory endurance, muscular endurance, strength and body composition. Students are introduced to ways in which general health related exercise can increase the well-being of the individual and increase the levels of their social, emotional, and physical health. Classes are also used to explain what can happen if general health is not cared for, namely poor cardio-respiratory health and weak physical performance. Students are encouraged to improve their cardio-respiratory endurance, strength, muscular endurance and flexibility by taking part in regular health related exercise, and to understand that such exercise should be part of a lifetime commitment to their well-being.

Further reading: Harris (2000)

HEART RATE

Heart Rate (HR) is both a very simple and a very informative measure of cardiovascular function. Measured in beats per minute (bpm), heart rate reflects the number of contractions or 'beats' of the heart. Resting heart rate averages 60 to 80 BPm, with rates exceeding 100 BPm in sedentary and obese individuals, and as low as 28 to 40 BPm for highly-trained endurance athletes. In addition to being affected by exercise, heart rate is also affected by age, as well as by environmental factors such as temperature and altitude. Heart rate reflects the amount of work the heart must do to meet the demands of the body when engaged in activity, as it is controlled by the SA node and involves both the sympathetic and parasympathetic nervous systems.

HEGEMONY

Originally a concept utilised by Marxists to describe the predominance of one social class over others, hegemony is now often used to describe any social grouping that dominates or holds power over another. The idea of hegemonic power is broad, and extends beyond the concept merely of political power, also to encompass the victory of the ideological and social vision of the dominant social group over others. It follows from such thinking that for any change in the status quo or other structures to be achieved, hegemony must be transferred from one group to the next. In sports studies, the concept of hegemony and hegemonic power has been used to explore the dominance of men over women within sporting **gender** battles, the strength of the white racial groups over others, and the control exerted by certain classes over others in sporting institutions and organisations.

See also: **control, gender, politics**

HERITAGE

Looking backwards at sport has become an industry as sports marketers offer memories for sale. Seniors' tournaments allow fans to watch the sports stars of their youth continuing to demonstrate their skills; retro-heritage events such as playing golf with old-fashioned hickory-shafted clubs go back even further in time; and stadium tour operators and sports museums charge enthusiasts for worshipping at the shrine of individual and collective memory. More commonly street names commemorate stars of the past: Newmarket, the centre of British horseracing, has them named after jockeys, horses, owners, trainers and administrators. Another form of sporting heritage lies in the fact that some sporting terminologies have become part of our everyday language. How many of us realise that 'coming up to scratch' and 'having bottle' emanate from prize-fighting or that 'fast and loose' was originally a term in archery?

A word of warning. Nostalgia does not always infer a true recollection of the past. Memory can be edited and gilded. Each generation juxtaposes a re-constructed past with an 'inferior' present and often even poorer future; sport back in 'the good old days' was perceived as being played differently. History can also be perverted as with **invented traditions** which deliberately offer a false perception of continuity.

Further reading: Vamplew (2004)

HIGH CULTURE

A definition of high culture is the training, development and refinement of mind, taste and manners in a society. In Britain it tends to be based on affluence, intellect and class position. Despite claims that football is the 'beautiful game', generally sport is regarded as being part of **mass**- rather than high culture. One reason is that the grace and beauty of sport is transitory. Nevertheless sporting art, poetry, and sculpture are associated with high culture, particularly at the cultural festivals linked with the **Olympic Games**.

HISTORY

The study of the history of sport, as a serious academic undertaking, emerged during the 1960s as part of the broader study of social history. In moving away from the history of kings and queens, politicians and other social elites, social historians embraced the study of history from below. They argued, in key journals such as *History Workshop*, that an understanding of how the working classes had lived was vital to the study of history. It was stressed that the study of the lower social orders should not be restricted to research into areas of political interaction, such as the trade unions or the labour movement, but should embrace all aspects of life, including sporting and leisure activities. The move of academics into the fertile area of sports history in the 1960s and 1970s, although important for professional historians and those working in universities, did not signal the invention of a new subject. Throughout the nineteenth and twentieth centuries there have been countless amateur historians who have catalogued many events from sporting history. However, such history is predominantly reliant on what Vamplew (1998) has described as 'sportifacts'. These are lists of winners, game scores and scorers, season and career averages, and chronological accounts, often blow-by-blow, of club and team performances. Histories that are based on sportifacts are invaluable records of what happened, but they do not allow for much interpretation of the significance and relevance of any given sport or event to the history of wider society.

Historical work that has examined the importance of sport beyond the collection of sportifacts, has taken a wide range of approaches. Issues such as the economic history of sport, the part sport played in imperialism, the social impact of sport and the history of sporting cultures have been key amongst the main approaches. Most chronological and geographical areas are now well covered by history, although there has been an over-concentration on the period from the mid-nineteenth century and the emergence of 'modern' sport. Theoretical approaches have become increasingly important in studying sport, and this development has been heavily influenced by the historical approach taken by those whose primary interest has been in **sociology**.

The first academic sports history organisation was established in 1972. The North American Society for Sport History meets annually in conference, and has since 1974 published the *Journal of Sports History*. The British Society for Sports History was founded in 1981, and has published its own journal from 1983. The Australian Society for Sports History was formed in 1983, and has produced *Sporting Traditions* since 1984. Beyond the national, the International Society for the History of Physical Education and Sport emerged in 1989, and the European Committee for Sport History in 1996. The largest commercially produced journal, which grew out of the British Society for Sports History, is the *International Journal of Sports History*, which has been in print since 1987. The range and scope of academic interest in the subject of sports history has been reflected in the growing number of dedicated research centres across the world, and the large number of courses, at undergraduate and postgraduate level, that teach sports history.

Outside the universities and colleges, sports history is finding a ready outlet in the growing number of **museums** and sporting 'halls of fame' that are being established. Also important in promoting interest in sporting history and heritage has been the engagement of the **media** with the subject. In Britain, for example, the BBC has produced landmark **television** histories of football ('The People's Game') and rugby union ('The Union Game'). Sports-specific programmes, such as 'TransWorld Sport', now regularly incorporate a history feature in their weekly output.

See also: **archives, museums, sporting associations**

Further reading: Booth (2005) Guttmann (2004), Holt (1989), Kyle and Storks (1990), Mason (1989)

HOOLIGANISM

Crowd violence at sporting venues has a long **history**, and can be found in reports of rugby and football matches in the late nineteenth century. Hooliganism, although most commonly associated with European football, is now spread across the world and a feature of many sports including baseball in the United States, cricket matches in Asia and football in Japan. Many studies of hooliganism have been conducted, and these have concentrated on violence connected with football in Britain and Europe. Such studies have been dominated by the work of **sociologists** at Leicester University in England, and have taken a variety of theoretical approaches, especially those based on **figurational theory**.

Hooliganism was rife in British football during the 1970s and 1980s. Many explanations for its rise focused on the economic recessions of the period that affected heavy industry, a dominant and violent masculine culture, the impact of racism and far-right politics, and the terrace culture of stadia. Better policing methods and greater intelligence had an impact on the levels of hooligan behaviour, but the greatest shift in attitudes was as a result of the Taylor Report. All-seater stadia have dramatically reduced levels of hooliganism, although the experiences of the World Cup final in 1998 and the European Championships in 2000 demonstrate that hooligan elements now attach themselves to the English national football team.

See also: **government policy, politics, sociology, violence**

Further reading: Williams et al. (1984)

HORMONES

Regulation of the body to achieve homeostasis is accomplished largely by two systems: the nervous system and the endocrine system. The endocrine system exerts its control through the release and use of hormones into the blood to circulate to tissues. Hormones are chemical messengers which bind to a specific protein acting in a lock-and-key manner and are divided into two basic types: steroid and non-steroid hormones, with chemical structure and solubility level being the distinguishing features of the two types. The effect that a hormone exerts is directly related to its concentration in the blood and the number of active receptors to which it can bind.

See also: **anatomy and physiology**

INCLUSION

The spirit of inclusion has been mainly driven by the inclusive education movement. The principle is that all children, irrespective of ability, race or gender, be included in all the activities of a school. The inclusive education movement opposed the idea of selection or streaming.

Inclusion is therefore underpinned by the idea that everyone can become part of the community of the school and create new visions for it. The spirit of inclusion has been broadened to embrace a general idea that no individual or groups should be excluded from society, and that the aim of any state should be the pursuit of policies that promote social inclusion.

Sport has become an important part of this campaign. The belief is that sport, as a potentially friendly and positive activity, can be used to integrate marginalised or excluded groups into the wider society. In Britain, bodies such as the Central Council for Physical Recreation, the Commission for Racial Equality and even central government have all identified sport as a vehicle for promoting inclusion. More broadly, the issue of inclusion was central to the European Union's promotion of sport during its 2004 year of Education through Sport. Inclusion has also been a key policy with respect of children with disability, and various campaigns, such as those by the Youth Sport Trust, to include those with physical disabilities in mainstream education classes.

Further reading: CCPR. (2002), DCMS. (2004)

INDUSTRIALISATION

Industrialisation and the associated urbanisation have had a major influence on the development of sport. Historically there was not the strict demarcation between work and leisure that exists today. Many seventeenth- and eighteenth-century sports were based on occupational skills, so that agricultural workers demonstrated their expertise in ploughing contests and watermen raced each other in rowing matches. Even the martial abilities of part-time soldiery were turned into sports via archery, cudgelling and fights using staves which provided tests of skill and courage. Events frequently took place on sites used for other activities, such as roads, rivers and open fields. With industrialisation and urbanisation, leisure and work became more distinct, and by the end of the nineteenth century the only work aspect of most sport was that of the professional sportsman, venues were in fixed locations, and sports were often held within specified time frames. All this resulted from the needs of industry for long and regular hours of work, the shortage of leisure space in an urban–industrialised environment, and the specialisation of tasks within industrial occupations.

Further reading: Brailsford (1991), Struna (1996), Vamplew (1988)

INDUSTRY

Sport as an industry contributes to the economy in several ways, not least in the employment that it generates. This is not just the professional sportspersons but also the sports-related occupations such as ground staff and equipment manufacturers as well the less sports-specific ones of clerks, receptionists and salespersons, all of which are needed to keep the sports business afloat. In turn the spending of these employees can boost other sectors of the economy. The existence of a major sports club can assist economic growth in a particular locality via spending, sponsorship and attracting inward investment by putting the area 'on the map'. It has been estimated that in 2000 employment in England attributable to sport totalled 400,000, just under 2.0 per cent of all employment. In terms of value added to the economy, sports-related activity in England generated £9.8 billion in 2000, around 1.5 per cent of England's total value-added.

See also: **economics**

Further reading: Cambridge Econometrics (2003), Gratton (1998)

INFORMATION PROCESSING

The development of the field of psychology from its origins in philosophy of mind through behaviouristic theories of learning (in which the learner was viewed as essentially passive), to current cognitive theories of learning in which the learner is viewed as an active meaning-maker, mirror the development of our thinking about information processing. Advances in areas such as cognitive science, artificial intelligence and cybernetics have also greatly impacted our views of motor learning, motor control and motor skill development. The metaphor of the 'brain as computer', and of information processing being comprised of specific sub-routines which organise, sequence and integrate our movements, currently holds sway in sport and physical activity research. As such, the most common variable used to assess the effectiveness of our mental processes has been time. However, although information processing models create a framework which is apparently compatible with our current understanding of the structure and function of the nervous system, it is quite clear that this linear information processing theory alone cannot account for all of the complex processes which underlie the learning and production of human movement skills. As such, it offers but a partial explanation for the extraordinary capacity of humans to learn and perform sport skills, and needs to be supplemented by other approaches, such as those involving hierarchical processing.

Further reading: Franks and Goodman (1992), Kelso (1982), Magill (1998), Schmidt and Lee (1999)

INJURIES/TREATMENT

A variety of medical and paramedical personnel are involved in the prevention, management, treatment and rehabilitation of athletic injuries, including physicians, exercise physiologists, athletic trainers, physiotherapists, nurses, coaches and physical educators. Concern over injuries and their treatment has grown as the numbers of individuals of all ages participating in all types of sporting and physical activity has increased over recent years. The types of injury which athletes experience are largely physical and involve breaking bones, damaging soft tissue, straining joints, or suffering concussions, all of which are forms of impact or overuse trauma. Increasingly, psychological and emotional trauma are also being identified as 'injuries' that may need treatment (by sport psychologists or even psychiatrists), and certainly athletes with drug problems often seek professional psychiatric treatment.

It is in the area of injury prevention that those involved in sports medicine have been placing the greatest emphasis. Thus increased use of training and conditioning programmes, warm-up and stretching activities, and the wearing of appropriate clothing and **protective equipment** have been stressed as vital elements in the management of sport. A range of treatment approaches or therapeutic modalities have been developed, including the use of electrical stimulation, heat, cold, massage, manipulation and exercise to deal with the range of injuries which athletes suffer. Particular sub-populations are susceptible to certain types of injury. Thus the young are susceptible to problems relating to bone growth and development, just as the elderly are also at risk from bone problems caused by osteoporosis. All athletes are susceptible to over-use injuries, for which the treatment is invariably rest and reduced participation and training.

See also: **sports medicine, training principles**

Further reading: Hillman (2000), Howe (2004), McLatchie (2000), Peterson and Renstrom (2001)

INSTITUTIONALISATION

Sport is an institutionalised activity. This is a sociological term which relates to the processes through which conduct and organisation are standardised over time. As sport is an activity that is governed by rules and regulations, relating, for example, to the number of players on the field, the size of the pitch or the weight of the ball, it is therefore subject to institutionalisation. Coakley (1998) has argued that the process of institutionalisation, in the context of sport, results in the following: the rules of the activity become standardised; official regulatory agencies take over rule enforcement; the organisational and technical aspects of the activity become important; and the learning of games skills becomes formalised.

As international organisations such as the IOC and FIFA become more powerful and globalised, so the force of institutionalisation becomes stronger, and sporting activity is ever more controlled.

Further reading: Coakley (1998), Coakley and Dunning (2000), Wilson (1994)

INSTRUMENTALITY

In studying **aggression** and **violence**, researchers have attempted to clarify an important distinction between acts of aggression and violence that are means to an end (instrumental aggression) and acts that are ends in themselves (hostile aggression). The concept of instrumentality refers to those acts that are means (or instruments) to an end. So while in cases of both instrumental and hostile aggression, the intent is to inflict physical and/or psychological harm to another person or persons, acts of instrumental aggression are performed in order to elicit external positive reinforcement from coaches, fans and/or teammates. It is hardly surprising, therefore, that we witness such behaviour when we hear coaches imploring players to 'be more aggressive'.

See also: **aggression, violence**

Further reading: Wann (1997)

111

INTERNET *see* **World Wide Web**

INTERVAL TRAINING

Interval training involves interspersing periods of strenuous activity with periods of low-intensity active recovery. By strenuous activity, physiologists mean working at a heart rate of between 75 and 85 per cent of a maximum safe heart rate. By low-intensity recovery, physiologists mean working at a heart rate of between 50 and 60 per cent of maximum. The advantage of interval training is that it allows the athlete to increase the intensity at which an activity is performed, thereby producing an increase in work perhaps by as much as two anda half times over performances of continuous work. This means that the hours necessary to produce training benefits can be reduced, which has also been found to have a positive motivational impact on athletes.

Two further benefits have been noted for interval training. The first is that it is adaptable, and may be used effectively in training for a wide variety of activities such as cycling, swimming, track and weight training, as well as aerobics and general physical fitness. A second is that because of the use of rest intervals which enable body temperature to drop, interval training can help avoid some of the environmental heat problems associated with continuous activity.

Further reading: Brooks et al. (1996), Fox and Mathews (1974), Pate and Hohn (1984)

INTERVENTION PROCESSES

Since one of the major goals of sport psychology is to improve or enhance athletic performance, performance-enhancing interventions and strategies are used by sport psychologists as means of helping athletes perform better. They are also used as a means of fostering psychological well-being amongst athletes. Typically, intervention processes are targeted at reducing factors which might inhibit athletic performance, such as anxiety, arousal and stress, and enhance factors which might assist athletic performance, such as self-confidence, attention and concentration.

For those athletes suffering from detrimental levels of anxiety, arousal or stress, sport psychologists use intervention processes which foster personal coping strategies such as seeking social support, relaxation procedures such as progressive relaxation, meditation or biofeedback, and stress management training. All of these strategies are used as a means of reducing high levels of anxiety and trying to enable athletes to 'get in the zone' for optimal performance.

For those athletes for whom increased levels of anxiety and arousal are necessary in order to enhance performance, sport psychologists employ a range of psyching-up strategies and techniques. These techniques range from increasing attentional focus through psyching-up activities, to the use of visualisation and imaging techniques in which athletes visualise successful performance as they prepare for their activity. Thus we may see downhill skiers visualising a successful run as they stand in the starting gate. They also include the use of inspirational music and, of course, the motivational speech prior to the beginning of a contest. The most significant element in this area of sport psychology is that interventions need to be individually tailored for each athlete and each activity. Thus sport psychologists develop individualised psychological skills training programmes based on an assessment of an athlete's psychological skills, and the activity in which they will be involved.

Further reading: Anshel (2004), Murphy (1995), Wann (1997)

INTRINSIC MOTIVES

Intrinsic motives are internal to an individual and 'involve that individual's interest in and enjoyment of a task'. A child who plays tennis because he or she likes the sport is intrinsically motivated. This is an important factor in developing an enthusiasm for sport amongst children in educational settings. The aim of any sports programme, if it is to succeed, is to foster the intrinsic motives for participation.

Further reading: Anshel (2004), Deci (1975), Wann (1997)

INVENTED TRADITION

Invented tradition involves the creation of a false continuity with the past which, by constant repetition, eventually becomes accepted as conventional wisdom. For example, many people believe that the torch relay which culminates in the opening ceremony has always been associated with the modern **Olympics** but in fact it was devised for the Berlin Games of 1936. Another major example is the belief that William Webb Ellis invented rugby in the 1820s when he picked up the ball and ran with it. There is no evidence that this ever occurred but the myth was propounded seventy years later when Rugby School wished to establish that the game was developed under its auspices and had nothing to do with plebeian folk football. So much has the invented tradition succeeded in becoming established that the average British sports fan now almost invariably associates Webb Ellis with the development of rugby.

Further reading: Collins (2005)

INVESTMENT

In strict economic terms, investment means the use of funds for the provision of production or service facilities such as the building of a stadium that will host sports events, but it is also often used in lay terms to infer the purchase of shares in a company which may not necessarily lead to any increase in output.

JAHN

Friedrich Ludwig Jahn (1778–1852) is generally credited with the development of Turnen or German gymnastics, but, although he added to the range of exercises undertaken and equipment used, it is clear that he borrowed many ideas from others, especially Johann Friedrich Guts Muth (1759–1839). His immediate objective was to end the Napoleonic occupation of Germany, and the anti-French element of his political agenda eventually widened into a rejection of all things not German. He was not supported by his own government, which felt that his abrasive nationalism was too uncompromising, and indeed in 1818 Turnen was banned and not legalised again till 1842. A fanatical nationalist who saw physical fitness as a basis for moral development, his name became indelibly linked with Turnen following the political unification of Germany in 1871. Although his work had these political overtones, generally in Britain his name has been associated with the actual gymnastic activities rather than the nationalistic philosophy attached to it.

Competitive gymnastics is still based on the rings, horizontal and parallel bars, and the pommel horse first widely used by Jahn and his followers.

See also: **gymnastics, physical education**

Further reading: Ueberhorst (1996)

JOURNALISM

As much of modern organised sport depended on paying spectators to keep it in business, so sports journalism needed its readers. The reporting of sport in newspapers began in the eighteenth century. In those early days it was mainly racing results and cricket scores that made it into the paper. As newspapers were originally the preserve of the literate, and therefore predominantly the well off, the sports that were reported on were those that interested the gentry. Despite the basic coverage that was offered in the early years, sporting journalists did come to the fore. Pierce Egan, who was on the staff of the *Weekly Dispatch* during the first two decades of the nineteenth century, became popular as its boxing reporter. A trend that Egan began, that of the expert and well known sports reporter or correspondent, would become a central theme in sports journalism in later years. The first British sports-dedicated newspaper emerged in 1822, with the publication of *Bell's Life*. In 1859 it was joined on the shelves by the daily *Sporting Life* – a paper that would be published for the next century and a half. Other titles followed, namely the *Sportsman* from 1865, and the *Sporting Chronicle* from 1871.

In the second half of the nineteenth century, as popular interest in sport soared, newspapers began devoting increasing amounts of space to sports coverage. It was not solely the sports of the gentry that were reported on, but increasingly comment on the football and rugby seasons was to be found. In response to the growth of football, *Athletic News* devoted the bulk of its pages to the game, and was duly rewarded with impressive circulation figures.

Daily newspapers had to respond to the growing interest in, and demand for reporting on, sports events. From the 1860s the business of reporting on sport was made easier with the opening of the first press boxes, and in 1883 the Press Association began a sports service. These factors, plus ever improving communications technology, allowed results and stories to be filed quickly. From the mid-1880s the first Saturday evening editions began to appear in Britain's major cities.

In 1896 the *Daily Mail* was launched, and included from the outset a page dedicated to sport. This was a new phenomenon for national newspapers. Although all the dailies had carried sports stories, the idea of a dedicated space had never evolved. In the post-war years the success of the daily newspapers in following the lead of the *Daily Mail*, and producing dedicated sports pages, and the steady growth of radio broadcasting, killed off the majority of Britain's sports-specific newspapers. Those that survived, such as the Sporting Life, did so on a diet of horse racing news.

Britain has failed to develop a permanent dedicated sporting press. Although France has *L'Equipe*, Italy the *Gazzetta*, and *America Sports Illustrated*, British sports reporting has relied on the national dailies for its outlet. In the 1980s, as newspapers fought for sales, and interest in sport grew on the back of investment from satellite television, the newspapers all began dedicated sports pull-out sections through the weekends and on Mondays. In these sections, all the elements of the history of British sporting journalism can be found. Mixed in with the results are match reports, special features by sport-specific correspondents, and guest pieces by former or current players giving the 'inside' story.

See also: **media**

Further reading: Harris (1998), Mason (1986)

KEY STAGES

The introduction of the concept of a **national curriculum** for physical education was associated with the idea of benchmarking achievement levels at certain key stages of schooling.

For physical education a brief overview is: key stage 1 (students aged 5–7 years) includes dance activities, games activities, gymnastic activities, swimming activities and water safety. Key stage 2 (students aged 7–11 years) includes activities from stage 1 plus: athletic activities and outdoor adventurous activities. Key stage 3 (students aged 11–14 years) includes activities as for stage 2 but at a more advanced level. Key stage 4 (students aged 14–16 years) includes activities as for stages 2 and 3 but at a more advanced level. Those students taking examination courses in physical education at GCSE satisfy the criteria for key stage 4.

Anomalies exist in that although swimming activities and outdoor adventurous activities appear in the National Curriculum, they are in many cases not practical realities for many students, owing to difficulty of access and/or lack of funding.

See also: **national curriculum**

Further reading: Department for Education (2001)

KICK IT CAMPAIGN

This campaign is part of the attempt to rid professional football of racism. Initially launched as 'Kick racism out of football' by the Commission for Racial Equality and the Professional Footballers' Association in August 1993, its organisation was taken over by an independent body, 'Kick it Out', which undertakes outreach work with clubs, local authorities, ethnic minority communities and supporters' groups. It has received the support of the Football Association and most clubs.

KREBS CYCLE

The Krebs cycle (named after Sir Hans Krebs who did much of the work elaborating the pathway) is also known as the citric acid cycle (the first constituent in the cycle is citric acid) or the tricarboxylic acid cycle (TCA, the initial constituents have three carboxyl groups). This cycle and its associated enzymes are located in the mitochondria matrix, either free or attached to the inner mitochondria membrane. The major function of this cycle is to act as the final common pathway for the oxidation of carbohydrates, lipids and proteins which in turn result in the production of ATP and high energy reducing equivalents, NADH and FADH2.

Acetyl CoA is the entry substance in the TCA cycle and is the product of carbohydrate, protein and lipid metabolism. Acetyl CoA enters the cycle and in the presence of citrate synthase, combines with oxaloacetate to form citrate. Citrate then follows a series of reactions involving specific dehydrogenase enzymes that result in the production of reducing equivalents, the release of two molecules of

CO_2 and the regeneration of oxaloacetate. As a result of one acetyl CoA entering and traversing through the cycle, one GTP (guanosine triphosphate, energetically equivalent to an ATP), one $FADH_2$ and three NADH are formed. These reducing equivalents then enter the respiratory chain (or **electron transport chain**) where **ATP**s are generated through the process of oxidative phosphorylation (each NADH results in the generation of three ATPs, and each FADHZ generates two ATPs). Thus twelve ATP molecules are generated for each molecule of acetyl CoA that traverses through the cycle.

Several factors can be rate limiting to the TCA cycle. This cycle can only function under aerobic conditions, as oxygen serves as the final oxidant of the reducing equivalents. Thus the cycle can be partially or totally inhibited if oxygen availability is reduced (hypoxic conditions) or totally absent (anoxic conditions) respectively. The dehydrogenase enzymes of the TCA cycle are also sensitive to the redox (reduction-oxidation) potential in the cell i.e. NADH/NAD+ ratio. If this redox potential is high, the dehydrogenases will be inhibited and likewise are stimulated by a decrease in the redox potential.

Further reading: Brooks et al. (1996), McArdle et al. (2000)

LACTATE THRESHOLD

A point during an exercise bout of increasing intensity when the blood lactate concentration increases abruptly above resting levels. It is thought to reflect the interaction of the aerobic and anaerobic energy systems, and is usually expressed in terms of the percentage of maximal oxygen uptake (per cent **VO_2 Max**). Many researchers consider lactate threshold to be a good indicator of an athlete's potential for endurance exercise.

LANDSCAPE

For those studying sports **geography**, the question of landscapes, their impact on sport and the impact of sport upon them, has been a key area of research. Landscapes can take a variety of forms, for example physical, social, political and virtual and are a combination of what can be seen (the assemblage of objects that make up a landscape) and a way of seeing (from the outside, and from a number of different viewpoints). Sport geographical study has considered the physical landscape at a number of scales from micro (local) to macro (global) level.

Initially much sport was determined by the physical landscapes within which it took place. For example mountaineering and skiing made use of natural landscapes and real tennis was played in human-constructed landscapes of courtyards. Bale has identified two key points that transform this relationship between sport and landscapes. First, the increasingly spatial confinement of the sites within which sport is practised and second the gradual artificialisation of the sports environment make great impacts on landscapes. With the advent of modern sport, the staging of events and the need to construct pitches and venues of standard measurements, landscapes began to be changed by sport. That is not to say that all pre-modern sport had no impact: the Mayan ball courts of ancient Mexico are a classic example of a structure built for sport which transformed the landscape. Many **traditional** games, such as folk football, had used the existing landscape, but modern rules demanded standardised playing surfaces. This development led to the construction of permanent landscape changes. Golf courses, football stadia, baseball pitches and race tracks all altered the terrain in which they were set. As sport has grown in its commercial scale, so the demands for sporting complexes, which serve a set of different purposes, not solely the staging of the game, have increased. The hosting of a major event such as the Olympics, can transform the landscape of an entire city.

In the **post-modern** era, landscapes have again begun to influence sport, and new **adventure sports** such as eco-challenge depend heavily on the natural environment rather than requiring any altered or specific sport landscapes. Spatial confinement and artificialisation however have begun to occur in some of those **adventure sports** and they have been transformed by **modernising** processes. For example snowboarding, that began as an alternative to rule-bound, competitive sports, has become formalised and in some places artificial tracks and courses have been constructed to enable judging or racing and it has even become part of the Winter **Olympics**.

Globalisation continues to influence the relationship between sport and landscapes. While the impacts of landscapes on sport may be decreasing, with **standardisation** of sport facilities, the impact of sport on landscapes may be increasing as artificial facilities are created. In the future, other aspects of landscape including social and cultural landscapes may become more important in sport studies.

See also: **geography**

Further reading: Bale (1989), Eichberg (1986)

LANGUAGE

Most sports have their specific terminologies which are forms of shorthand language used by participants and observers to communicate with each other. So a rifleman will appreciate that his shot is not the same as the cricketer's, and others that a tennis stroke is different from the rower who sets the pace for the crew Over the years sporting terminology has infiltrated the nation's language so that most of us are now conversant with such English expressions concerning fair play as 'it's not cricket', 'a level playing field' and 'moving the goalposts'. Others which come readily to mind include golf's 'stymied', 'bunkered', 'par for the course' and 'the rub of the green'; cricket's 'playing with a straight bat'; 'game, set and match' from tennis; 'snookered' and 'caught behind the eight ball' from the green baize games; as well as 'jumping the gun' from athletics. More historical, and often with their original meaning forgotten, are 'crestfallen', for when a fighting cock disappoints, and 'playing fast and loose', as dangerous in one's love life as in unregulated archery.

Such use of language, and the meanings attached to it, has been at the root of some of the most intense academic arguments during the twentieth century, and has given birth to a host of theoretical approaches. At its most basic level, the purpose of language is to allow the communication of thoughts and observations between people. Commentaries during sports programmes on either **television** or through the radio use language to describe the scene, and convey details, facts and images to the watcher and listeners.

The study of language, and its analysis, is not straightforward. Theorists have argued that the use of language does not simply impart information, but develops meaning as a result of choosing given words within a cultural setting. Meaning can be understood as the product of the intentions of the speaker, but this is challenged by theories of **post-modernism**, **structuralism** and post-structuralism. All these theories argue that speakers and their intentions are not value-free, but are controlled by the simple fact of the prior existence of language. More broadly, the existence of language, and its usage, have sparked debates that question whether language represents or constructs the world around us. Construction is especially important in the language of sport. Such language has traditionally been seen as predominantly masculine, and constructs sports as male, violent and warlike. Sporting contests are described as 'clashes', a 'head-to-head', the 'decider', and so on. The choice of such words imparts a belief that sport is about a struggle, where only the fittest survive and win. Those failing in such contests are described as 'weak', 'soft', or in the case of the England football team that was defeated by the Irish in 1948, as like 'a girls' house hockey team'. Especially important for the use of language in sport has been the development of advertising and sponsorship, where words become signifiers and dreams are constructed. Nike's appeal for us all to 'just do it', encouraged us to embrace sport and competitiveness, become a winner, and most importantly, to wear the correct footwear.

Further reading: Baker and Boyd (1997), Beard (1998), Haldane and Wright (1993)

LAW

Grayson has noted that there are four levels of laws that apply in sport. First there are the basic playing laws – the rules of the game. When these are broken, the playing penal laws come into operation, these being the penalties imposed such as free kicks, yellow cards and sendings-off. The third level is the administrative laws such as disciplinary tribunals and suspensions. All these are within the confines of the game itself and its administrators, unlike the fourth level which concerns the law of the land.

At this level sports law involves the application of legal principles to problems arising in sport. Indeed, there is no such phenomenon as sports law recognised by the legal system. What exists are branches of law which can be applied to sporting institutions and unsporting situations. In many ways sporting bodies operate like conventional businesses. They have to recruit, train and retain a work force; secure revenue from a paying clientele; and pay out operating expenses. In all such matters they are subject to the same laws of contract as any other enterprise.

Then there is the question of assault and injury. Although in principle sportspersons are not immune from prosecution for illegal violent acts that they commit during games, in practice blind eyes appear to be turned at most incidents of participatory violence, with more reliance being placed on **civil law** to compensate those injured than on

criminal law to prosecute those responsible. Much legal debate has occurred over the issue of players consenting to be the subject of **violence** in the sports that they play. Generally if the rules of the game sanction certain forms of violence such as a tackle in rugby or a punch in boxing, then anyone injured as a result of these occurring is seen as being the unfortunate victim of hard but fair play. The legal problem arises if the tackle was high or the punch below the belt. Although theoretically the **law** does not distinguish between an assault on the playing field and one in the street, in practice sentences for the former are more lenient than for other offenders. Rationales for the lesser sentences are that sports violence is often heat-of-the moment rather than premeditated, and that the seriousness of the injuries was not foreseen or intended. Sports authorities would in most cases prefer to keep the law out of sport and run their own disciplinary bodies. However, such self-regulation has come under increasing scrutiny as sport has become more professional and more commercial. Participants have too much to lose, and will challenge the legality of the rule book. It is thus vitally important that disciplinary bodies, at club or associate level, act in accordance with the principles of natural justice.

Nevertheless it should be stressed that there is a legal responsibility on all those who organise, officiate or participate in sport to exercise a **duty of care** to those whom they can foresee could be damaged by their failure to act reasonably. One area of increasing importance is the liability of the organisers of sports events for injury to spectators. The current position is that they are not expected to ensure the safety of all spectators from all contingencies, only from reasonably foreseeable dangers. Spectators themselves have been subject to law specifically enacted for consumers of sport. In particular the Football (Offences) Act of 1991 sought to regulate fan behaviour in terms of racist chanting, throwing missiles and pitch invasion.

Ultimately, the law can determine whether a sport can exist. Historically it has been used to ban sporting activities which interfered with war effort via playing football rather than practising archery, as in the days of James I, or attracted too many spectators to matches, as in the First World War, or which were considered morally reprehensible, as with cockfighting in the nineteenth century, pistol shooting in the twentieth, and hunting with dogs in the twenty-first.

See also: **duty of care, safety**

Further reading: Brackenbridge (1997), Gardiner (2006), Grayson (1999b), Greenfield and Osborn (2000a), Lewis and Taylor (2003), McArdle (2000)

LEADERSHIP

Sport leadership is to be found at all organisational levels, from the President of the IOC to the captain of a junior club team. Sport leaders may or may not hold an official position within a team or sport, but they fulfil a role in which they influence other members of their sporting organisation regarding the selection and attainment of that group's goals.

Leadership theory and research in sport have generally reflected the major perspectives of leadership theorists working in other academic disciplines. Thus early work on leadership and the leadership process tended to be focused on the traits of successful leaders. However, when this line of research proved to be relatively unsuccessful, theorists turned to leadership behaviours and developed a variety of continuums to reflect observed ranges of leadership behaviour. These included continuums regarding decision-making style (autocratic vs. democratic), interaction styles (directive vs. permissive) and leadership orientation (task-oriented vs. person-oriented).

While a range of other theories have been applied to sport leadership, such as contingency theory, attributional theory, and transactional and transformational theories, the single most important sport-specific theory is the multi-dimensional theory of leadership proposed by Chelladurai. In this model, Chelladurai predicts that as the congruence between the required, the actual and the preferred leadership behavioural stakes increases, so group performance and satisfaction will improve. The important antecedents to this model are the characteristics of the members (are they Olympic or junior club team athletes?), the leader's characteristics (autocratic or consultative) and the situational characteristics.

See also: **administration, bureaucracy**

Further reading: Anshel (2004), Chelladurai (1993), McConnell and McConnell (1996), Stogdill (1974)

LEISURE

An understanding of leisure must take into account the dimensions of time, activity and experience. Clearly, leisure time is the discretionary residual time that an individual has free from work and other duties that may be used for relaxation, diversion, social interaction or personal development. However, it is not simply 'free' time, as many unemployed persons might argue that such enforced time free from work does not provide them with true leisure, which many believe should encompass activities characterised by a feeling of comparative freedom. When thinking about leisure as activity, we often list 'hobbies' or pastimes that we choose to be involved in because we value and enjoy them. They may offer a means of diversion from non-leisure activities, such as work, or an opportunity for self-expression or self-development. To that degree, leisure is not a purposeless activity. However, it is often difficult on the basis of naming an activity as leisure – for example swimming – when we know that swimming in the role of lifeguard is not the same as swimming for pleasure. Thus one activity can be viewed in a number of different ways. In our example, swimming as a lifeguard may in fact be considered a work, rather than a leisure activity.

The concept of leisure as time has been helpful for researchers in sport and physical activity because it is both a useful and simple measure of leisure. However, it cannot be used to address questions of meaning nor quality of leisure. It is to confront such issues that people are asked to define leisure as experience. In this definition, leisure is a state of mind or mental condition in which we find freedom in a freely chosen activity that we undertake for its own intrinsic reasons. In other words, as Kelly has suggested, leisure is in the mind of the participant, and is activity that is chosen primarily for its own sake.

Further reading: Brightbill (1960), deGrazia (1964), Dumazedier (1967), Kelly (1996)

LEVERS

All levers (human or otherwise) are rigid bars which rotate around a fixed point, known as a fulcrum, for the purpose of using a relatively small force to overcome a relatively large resistance. In the body, the bone is the rigid bar, the joint the fulcrum, and the contracting muscles provide the force. When analysing movement in sport and physical activity, it is often convenient to regard segments of an athlete such as an arm, leg or trunk as a simple lever.

Levers are classified into three types or classes according to the arrangement of the fulcrum, the force and the resistance. First-class levers have the fulcrum situated between the effort and resistance points, an example being a 'see-saw'. Second-class levers have the resistance point situated between the fulcrum and the effort point, an example being a wheelbarrow. Third-class levers have the effort point between the fulcrum and the resistance point and are the most common of body levers. Thus any throwing activity uses the arm as a third-class lever.

The lever arm or moment arm is defined as that portion of the lever between the fulcrum and the force points. The effort arm is the distance between the fulcrum and the effort point. The resistance arm is the distance between the fulcrum and the resistance point. The principle of levers states that 'a lever of any class will balance when the product of the effort and the effort arm equals the product of the resistance and the resistance arm'. With few exceptions, the effort arm in skeletal levers is shorter than the resistance arm, and thus tends to favour speed and range of movement over effort. Sports implements such as golf clubs or tennis rackets tend to magnify these effects.

Further reading: Dyson (1986), Hay (1993), Wells and Luttgens (1976)

LIMITED CHANNEL CAPACITY

In applying the general principles of cognitive **psychology** to information processing related to motor skills, a number of basic tenets apply. Perhaps the most important is that the human **information processing** system has a limited capacity. Thus the amount of information that can be processed at any one time is limited because of specific constraints at work in the cognitive stage of **skill acquisition**. When learning a new motor skill, and even when performing a well learnt skill in a novel environment, or under conditions of extreme stress, we require more processing power. Cognitive psychologists suggest that this is due to the needs of the executive function that oversees the human information processing system. Limited channel capacity has significant impact on factors such as attention and memory. What is clear is that effective practice of motor skills helps reduce attentional requirements, thus providing additional capacity for other aspects of information processing in the performance of motor skills.

Further reading: Kahneman (1973), Magill (1998), Schmidt and Lee (1999)

LING

Per Henrik Ling (1776–1839) devised a system of gymnastics that became adopted by the Swedish government and was developed into an educational tool for schoolchildren by his son, Hjalmar (1820–1886). It was introduced into Britain in the mid-nineteenth century, but had made little encroachment until the appointment of Miss Concorde Löfring to the London School Board in 1878 and Martina Österberg similarly three years later. Its essential features were a specific starting position for each exercise; every movement then had to be precise and accurate and completed to a command, before finishing in a predetermined position; each part of the body was worked equally and exercises increased in difficulty and exertion. There was no free expression, and little continuous movement save for short bouts of skipping, marching and running. This Swedish system was taught in the early women's training colleges, and by 1909 had become accepted as the recommended form of physical education by the Board of Education. Indeed it gained widespread acceptance throughout British **gymnastics** except in the competitive area, where the German version dominated.

See also: **gymnastics, physical education**

Further reading: Bailey and Vamplew (1999)

LISTED EVENTS

In the early years of televised sport in Britain, the BBC had a monopoly, and as the respected national provider, had an easy relationship with the majority of sporting organisations. With the opening of Britain's first commercial station, ITV, in 1955, the BBC's stranglehold on sports coverage was challenged. In response to increasingly bitter battles over the rights to cover sporting events, the government, sports organisations and television companies accepted a list of ten events which, from 1954, would not be subject to exclusive rights agreements. This meant that all such events would remain freely available. The listed events include: the English and Scottish FA Cup finals, test cricket, Wimbledon, the Boat Race, the Grand National and Derby, the football World Cup finals, the Commonwealth Games and the Olympics. The listed events system has so far withstood most pressure from satellite and cable providers of television coverage, and the legislation controlling it was updated in the 1990s to strengthen the position of terrestrial television. However, it is likely that the **globalisation** of television rights for events such as the World Cup finals or the Olympics, will make it increasingly difficult for the listed events system to remain in place and cricket test matches have already succumbed as the England and Wales Cricket Board persuaded the government to allow them to take a lucrative financial offer from Sky Television.

See also: **media, television**

Further reading: Barnett (1990), Gearing and McNeil (1999)

MACLAREN

Archibald Maclaren (1820–1884), a pioneer of gymnastics in England, was influenced by continental methods but felt that apparatus work should be supplemented with other physical activities such as walking, riding and swimming. In the 1860s he was called upon to re-organise physical training in the British Army. He did so using the German system of gymnastics following the principles of **Jahn**. Although the Navy adopted the Swedish system of **Ling** when the Naval Gymnastic School was founded at Portsmouth in 1902, the Army did not switch from the German-based exercises until 1907.

MANAGEMENT

Sports management has traditionally been of two types, depending on whether the manager worked in the **public** or **private** sector. Those in the latter have always been concerned with seeking profits in order to ensure a return on the capital invested in the enterprise, be it a sports store or a commercially run fitness gymnasium. In that sense they are no different from managers elsewhere in the private sector, except that a knowledge of the sports industry rather than, say, transport or banking was relevant to their occupation. In the public, not-for-profit sports sector, clubs and governing bodies traditionally were run by volunteers who filled coaching and administrative positions. These people operated relatively informally, with minimal policies and procedures to guide their operations. Their main responsibilities were to ensure the enforcement of the amateur code, run national championships, and where appropriate send representative teams to international competitions. Nevertheless, although such voluntary clubs and their governing bodies still form the central means of delivering 'amateur' sport in Britain, the structure and management of these organisations has become increasingly more sophisticated.

In recent years these organisations have become more commercial and more 'business like' in their operations and management. Many are no longer run solely by volunteers, but employ paid professional coaches and administrators to help oversee their operations. Funding bodies such as the Sports Council and the growing number of commercial sponsors involved in sport have demanded more financial and operating accountability, and this has resulted in an increase in formal policies and procedures. In addition, the volunteer managers, who traditionally required only enthusiasm and a knowledge of the sport to do their job, are now having to possess a more sophisticated set of management skills as clubs and governing bodies engage in such complex activities as applying for lottery funding, creating partnerships with local authorities, and brokering television and sponsorship agreements.

Further reading: Slack (1996)

MANLINESS

Manliness was a catch-all term used by those who attributed positive values to sport in Victorian Britain. It embraced courage, physical prowess and loyalty to one's team, all virtues preached by proponents of muscular Christianity.

See also: **gender, public schools**

MARKETING

Marketing is the management process responsible for identifying, anticipating and satisfying customer requirements profitably, or more applicable to non-profit organisations, as are many sports organisations, efficiently. Basically, marketing involves researching the potential demand for the product at particular prices in particular venues and, in the light of that information, considering how to promote the product. There are two distinct but complementary elements to any definition of sport marketing. First, there is the marketing of sport which involves sports leagues, associations, clubs and individuals marketing their events, products and services directly to sport consumers. Second, there is marketing through sport which involves the activities of consumer and industrial organisations that use sport as a vehicle to market their products and services to sport consumers. At the cutting edge, sports marketing involves the introduction of customer research programmes, development of ancillary products and services such as merchandise, and the provision of ticket booking facilities, flexible pricing packages, all-seater stadia, quality catering facilities, prematch entertainment and high levels of customer service, all with considerable emphasis on promotion, branding and public relations.

The sports industry is just one part of the service sector, and as a result marketing a sports event or club is in many ways similar to marketing other leisure utilities and services such as the theatre, cinema and concerts. However, the unique characteristics of the sport product and the unusual market conditions have required marketing personnel to adopt different marketing strategies from those used in other service sectors. Unlike other industries, the sports market is characterised by joint interdependence in that the clubs together provide the core product, e.g. the game. Sports organisations therefore simultaneously compete and cooperate. It is therefore not possible to consider the marketing of individual sports clubs in isolation from the marketing of the sport as a whole.

At club level, sports consumers are often considered to be different from consumers in other industry sectors in that they have an emotional attachment to the sport or club and see themselves as 'fans' rather than customers. Because of this emotional attachment they rarely switch to a competing 'brand' even if their team is not performing well. This unique characteristic can be a double-edged sword for sports marketers. On the one hand this fan loyalty provides commercial opportunities for product and service extensions in areas such as merchandising. However, it can also leave sports marketers open to accusations of exploitation if not handled with care and sensitivity.

See also: **endorsement, sponsorship**

Further reading: Mullin et al. (1993), Shank (1999)

MARTIAL ARTS

Martial arts include a wide range of fighting skills, arts or sports, most of which are of East Asian origin. These arts are typically categorised as being with or without weapons, and thus their practitioners as being either armed or unarmed. Martial arts are also categorised by their basic physical technique – striking or grappling – and by their function and philosophy – typically self-improvement or self-defence, physical fitness or competitive sport. Donohue has suggested that the martial arts offer a unique approach to mind/body unity, are significant sources of both personal and cultural identity, and provide important symbols and rituals to enhance those identities.

In their development, many of the East Asian martial arts were strongly influenced by Taoism and Zen Buddhism. As such, these activities give specific attention to developing both mind and body, and have been adopted in many Western cultures as means of promoting social, philosophical and spiritual goals such as etiquette, and spiritual as well as physical development, in addition to self-protection. These are known as the budo-oriented arts since they encompass and meld the warrior arts of ancient Japan with the Zen Buddist ideals of do – self-mastery, harmony and balance. Thus the most popular martial arts, karatedo, judo, kendo, aikido and tae kwan do all have the do element as an integral part of their **philosophy**. Additionally, practitioners wear particular coloured belts to denote rank or level of advancement in the art, ranging from a white belt for novices to a black belt for experts. Practitioners must pass through increasingly difficult tests of competence in order to reach black belt status. Having done so they can then achieve various levels or degrees of black belt, known as first through tenth dan, where first through fifth dan signifies a junior master, and sixth through tenth dan are reserved as honorary ranks for those who have reached 'master' status.

Karate (meaning 'empty hand') is now the world's most popular martial art. It is an unarmed method of self-defence involving punching, striking, kicking and blocking. Karate is thought to have originated on the island of Okinawa in the seventeenth century, probably bearing some relation to kung fu, although karate employs a closed-fist technique whereas kung fu uses an open-hand style. Modern karate was introduced to Japan in 1922 by the Okinawan school teacher Gichin Funakashi, who added the philosophical component to this ancient martial art. Training is conducted in a dojo or training hall, requires the traditional uniform developed by Funakashi of white trousers and jacket fastened with the appropriate belt, and focuses on developing proficiency in three areas: basic movements, formal exercises (kata) and freestyle sparring. And in the same way that particular movements or 'stunts' in gymnastics bear the style and often the name of the gymnasts who developed them, so in karate each of the stylised kata embodies the stylistic contributions of the master or masters of that style.

The rapid spread and wide appeal of karate led to the development of the first world championships in 1970. However, despite its widespread appeal and its impact on popular culture as evidenced by the success of films such as *The Karate Kid*, karate has yet to become an Olympic sport.

By comparison, judo and tae kwan do have both been adopted as Olympic sports. Judo first appeared in the Tokyo Olympics in 1964 and tae kwan do in the Seoul Olympics of 1988. Judo was developed by Dr Jigaro Kano in 1882 and (despite its name which means gentle, flexible or yielding way) involves throwing an opponent, applying an effective stranglehold or pinning the opponent. The techniques of judo have been taken from a variety of other martial arts, but like karate, judo is an attempt to combine mind and body in healthy activity. Tae kwan do, literally 'way of hands and feet' is the national sport of Korea and has been used as a means of promoting national and cultural identity following the Japanese occupation of Korea in the first half of the twentieth century. Following the liberation of Korea after the Second World War, a group of leading Korean martial artists tried to unify their various martial art forms in one style of hands and feet sparring. In the late 1950s this style of martial art was systematised and formalised, and became a part of the training of both the military and the police. Bearing many of the trademarks of amateur boxing, with headgear, three-minute rounds, mandatory 'eight counts' and a ring, tae kwan do held its first world championships in 1973. Having been a demonstration sport at both the Seoul and Barcelona Olympics, it became a full Olympic sport in Sydney in 2000, Korea leading the medal table with three gold and one silver medal. However, the challenge to Korean dominance is already apparent, with seventeen other countries winning medals. With 50 million practitioners in over 150 countries around the world, the sport is proving extremely popular.

There is little doubt that the broad cultural appeal of many of the martial arts, the exposure offered by the Olympics and world championships, and the effects of **globalisation** on sporting forms and contests, have had a significant impact on martial arts around the world. And while the emphasis on sportsmanship and self-mastery is still strong, the fact that ultimate or **extreme** contests have developed suggests that the action and violence of these 'no-holds-barred' forms of the martial arts have significant spectator appeal. The cult status accorded Bruce Lee and the impact of his film *Enter the Dragon* and its successors, have also helped popularise the martial arts around the world, and particularly kung fu and t'ai-chi, two martial arts which are of Chinese origin.

While there are a number of other martial art forms which have East Asian and particularly Japanese roots, such as kendo (the way of the sword) and jujutsu (the art of gentleness), martial arts are also to be found in the Philippines and in South Asia, and particularly South India.

Further reading: Donohue (1994), Finn (1988), Wiley (1996), Zarrilli (1996)

MASCULINITY

As sport has traditionally been so male dominated, studies of masculinity have been important within sports studies. The study of masculinity is centrally concerned with the roles and activities of men within society, and has been especially favoured by sociologists. Research into the area of masculinity has often concentrated on negative aspects of men and sport, and as a result issues such as **hooliganism, discrimination** and sexual abuse have dominated the agenda. Also of importance have been those studies of sporting **language** which have identified the overriding masculine nature of sport commentary and comment. In language, as in the **media** and through **sponsorship**, the virtues of masculinity, and the associated imagery of strength and power, have dominated the sports-related agenda. Despite the dominant position that men have held within the sporting world, masculinity has been little studied in comparison with that work that has focused on **femininity**. Studies of masculinity have become increasingly important as part of the wider research into the broad area of **gender**. The importance of the link between sport and masculinity should not be understated. Connell (1987: 85) has argued that 'images of ideal masculinity are constructed and promoted most systematically through competitive sport'.

One of the key areas for recent research has been an assessment of the body, and the attempts of men to take control of their own. Work has concentrated on the role of sport in empowering men within society, as a result of shows of strength and the development of an aesthetically pleasing body that demonstrates physical prowess. Messner (1992) and Connell (1990) have both demonstrated how notions of masculinity are linked with the creation of a 'strong' body. Men in team sports have always been seen as creating and sustaining hegemonic ideas of masculinity, especially through the 'locker-room' culture. Curry (1991) has shown how the 'locker-room' aids not only a culture of masculinity, but also one that is hostile to positive or empowering images of women.

Although studies of masculinity are often concerned with dominant ideologies of power, the concept has been problematised in the context of non-white and non-heterosexual males. Ideas of masculinity have had to be reappraised in light of images of strong black men, such as Michael Jordan, and elite gay sportsmen such as Justin Fashanu.

See also: **discrimination, femininity, gender, manliness**

Further reading: Connell (1987, 1990), Curry (1991), Messner (1992), Plummer (2006)

MASS CULTURE

In a sporting sense, mass culture usually refers to the activities and attitudes of large population groups within modern industrialised urban societies. It postulates that those in these groups have common unifying values and share similar emotions in the sporting arena. Some critics argue that the behaviour of such groups is dominated by immediate excitement and instant gratification rather than by any intellectual expression or exercise. In this it is differentiated from **high culture**.

Further reading: Hughson et al. (2005)

MATERIAL CULTURE

The study of material culture has been a growing area of academic research in recent decades. Material culture relates to the study of objects and artefacts within society. The objects that make up the material culture of a society are important in many ways. They can be studied in isolation by assessing their decorative value or function, but can also be viewed in a wider context. All objects of material culture are powerful symbols of the age in which they were created and used. The study of sporting items of material culture is still largely under-developed. However, it is an important part of sport. Items of material culture in sport include trophies, the tools of the athletes (footballs, golf clubs, tennis racquets and so on), the dress of athletes and the ephemera of match programmes and tickets. All these items would provide evidence for changing technologies (the development of the golf ball), fashions (the clothes worn by tennis players) and taste (the link between sport and advertising).

Further reading: Cronin (2005)

MAXIMUM WAGE

Setting a maximum wage that any player can receive is one method of attempting to equalise playing strength between clubs, as it offers little incentive for a player to switch teams in the hope of gaining a pay rise. Historically, its main impact was in English football between its introduction in 1901 and its abolition in 1961. It led to a levelling of wages among the top professional players and, even with some increases, also served to limit the payments to players compared to unregulated occupations. Whereas in 1939 the footballers' £8 was approximately double the average industrial wage, by 1960 the gap was only 25 per cent, with relative earnings being £20 and £15. These days overall club **salary caps** tend to be imposed to serve the same objectives, leaving star players the opportunity to earn nearer their **economic rent**.

MEDIA

The relationship between the media and sport is one that has been referred to as 'a match made in heaven' (Cashmore 1990: 193). The media have been instrumental in the success of modern sport. Whether through newspapers, magazines, radio or television, the audience for sport has always extended far beyond the minority that attended the game or event as a spectator. The spread of sport across the globe, its cultural impact and business success, have mirrored the expansion of media technology and the globalisation of its practices and institutions. The close relationship between sport and the media, that has spanned over two centuries, has meant that the latter has not solely reported on and analysed sporting events, but has shaped the debates that surround the actual development and conduct of sport generally. In the contemporary world, all sporting events, from the football World Cup finals and the **Olympics**, to national and regional championships, rely on successful media coverage for income and exposure. Rowe (2000) has demonstrated how important the links between the two are, and how central the mutual relationship is to the business and financial success of both. The increasing amounts of money that television companies are prepared to pay for the exclusive rights to sports events, amounting to many millions of pounds for prestige sports such as football, baseball and basketball, demonstrate how central sport is to the commercial success of television companies. The advertising rates charged by television companies during an event such as the American football Superbowl final, will annually be higher than for any commercial break during the remainder of the year.

Media interest in sport began in earnest in the nineteenth century with sports-specific newspaper titles such as *Bell's Life*, *Sporting Magazine* and *Athletic News*. In the early twentieth century, improved communications technology allowed for the production of Saturday evening results newspapers, and the growing concentration across all newspaper titles on sports issues. In the 1920s, the advent of photo-graphs in the pages of the newspapers added an extra dimension to the reader's pleasure. The photographs enabled those readers who were not present at an event or match to better understand the action, and to see pictures of the stars of the day. The production of such pictures, which helped give a clearer identity to sportsmen, meant that **sporting heroes** were more readily produced and more commonly shared. The place of the sports star in the newspapers became more firmly fixed from the 1960s as leading players began writing their own columns. This added to their stardom, while making the relationship between sport and the media ever closer. News items increasingly emerged from the 'back pages' of news-papers as interest in sport and fascination with its stars grew

Radio broadcasting began in April 1914 when the innings-by-innings scores of an exhibition baseball game between the New York Giants and the Memphis Turtles, playing at the Red Elm Bottoms in Memphis, were sent from the Falls Building to the steamboat G. W. Robertson. Information was telephoned from the ball park to the Falls Building, and then sent by Victor H. Laughter's voice transmitter to the Robertson. As technology improved, so did the number and type of broadcasts. In 1921, the first baseball game with a play-by-play description was broadcast in Pittsburgh. The first national coverage of a sporting event on the radio was when the Irish station 2RN covered the all-Ireland football final in 1928. As radios were comparatively cheap to buy, the take-up in ownership grew rapidly. By 1940, 44 million Americans owned a radio. With each new radio set, a new sports fan emerged. The dominance of radio grew through the 1930s as the coverage of sport stretched beyond actual games, and began to include discussion programmes and results bulletins. After the Second World War, a new medium, **television**, would become dominant. By 1950, 9 per cent of American homes owned a television; by 1972 that figure had leapt to 64 per cent. The relationship between sport and television has been a close one, but one that has often been fraught, due to disputes over exclusive rights and the cost of buying coverage. Live coverage of games, and the global spread of television, have helped create a new type of sports fan. Many people's experience of sport is restricted to watching big events or live games at home or in bars with friends and family. New stations dedicated to sport, such as Sky in Britain or ESPN in America, have fed the hunger for sport. In an attempt to beat off their rivals, such stations have constantly introduced new **technology** as a method of keeping their viewers hooked. Media coverage of sport is important for the business of sport, for creating and sustaining its cultural relevance, and as a symbol of globalisation.

See also: **television**

Further reading: Cashmore (1990), Chandler (1988), Koppett (1981), Larson and Heung-Soo (1993), Oriard (1993), Rader (1984), Rowe (2000), Whannel (1992)

MERCHANDISING

Sports clubs have always been involved in sales of products other than match tickets, though primarily this has been programmes and refreshments. In the past two decades or so, however, there has been a move into merchandising goods branded with the logo or name of the team. For some clubs, such as Manchester United in football, this has become a major source of revenue, with club shops being opened in locations well away from the club's ground, sometimes even in other countries. There has been little move in Britain to adopt the American system of marketing official club products through approved league outlets that sell items for all member clubs.

See also: **branding**

METABOLISM

Metabolism is defined as the total of all cellular reactions that occur in the body including both the synthesis of molecules (anabolism) and the breakdown of molecules (catabolism). Metabolism usually consists of sequences of enzymatic steps or metabolic pathways that are capable of converting foodstuffs (carbohydrates, fats, proteins) into usable energy, and is regulated by enzymatic activity.

See also: **energy metabolism**

MILITARISM

Early physical education in state schools was dominated by militarism, not just in the use of **drill sergeants**, but also in the first **model course** of 1902 that was produced at the behest of militarists who were concerned about the fitness of army recruits.

MOBILITY

As well as its conventional meaning relating to the physical attribute of being able to move easily in the gym or on the playing field, mobility also refers to the ease with which players can change clubs. Generally this is not a problem in the lower echelons of amateur sport where, apart from players not being able to represent different sides in the same cup competition or even in a league competition after a certain cut-off date within a season, players are generally free to change clubs. At the elite level, however, a **transfer** payment might have to be made between clubs to secure the services of any player who is not a **free agent**. Historically, residential or birth qualifications have been used to impede the mobility of players.

MODEL COURSE OF 1902

The syllabus for this course was based on the 'red book' of instructions for soldiers, and essentially looked to produce children who could march, shoulder arms, instantly obey commands, and perform exercises to improve their physique. It lacked real educational purpose. Its introduction stemmed from political dismay at the standard of recruits during the Boer War (1899–1902) and a view in some influential quarters that the Swedish drill being taught in elementary schools was ill suited to the needs of the military. The course came under sustained attack from teachers, and in 1904 a Board of Education Committee recommended that a new syllabus be produced that would take account of age and gender.

Further reading: Bailey and Vamplew (1999)

MODERNISATION

A blanket term used by many social scientists to describe the process that follows in the wake of industrialisation and mechanisation. For most of Europe and North America, the period of modernisation can be located in the late nineteenth- and early twentieth centuries. Modernisation has many effects, but these include the freeing-up of strict divisions between social classes, an increase in social mobility, the growth in access to education, extensions to the political franchise, and the development of social welfare. The period of modernisation was accompanied by the development, in artistic and intellectual circles, of modernism.

The process of modernisation, and the changes that it effected on society, had a profound influence on, and were also reflected in, sport. As the lines between social classes blurred, so the distinction between amateur and professional ceased to be as important a class marker as it had once been. The opening up of education not only increased the number of children who attended school, but exposed many people to organised sport. In Britain, the 1919 physical education syllabus made allowance for the provision of playing fields and school baths, and made exercise a compulsory part of a 'child-centred' range of activities. The later Acts of 1933 and 1944 furthered the provisions that had been made in 1919. Sport has also served as a useful marker of social mobility. As the effects of modernisation were felt across society, so access to sporting facilities and venues grew. More people went to watch professional sport than ever before during the inter-war years, and the rise of the middle classes gave an extra impetus to the rapidly spreading network of private sports clubs, especially those catering for golf and tennis, that was part of the fabric of the suburbs. It is questionable whether the period of modernisation has actually ended, although many commentators contend that society has now entered a period of **post-modernism**.

See also: **post-modernism**

MODERN SPORT

Allen Guttmann has provided a seven-category model with which to distinguish modern sport from that of previous eras. First comes **secularism**, by which any religious connotations of sport have been jettisoned and sport is played not to make the earth more fertile but for more personal and social reasons. Second, he postulates that another characteristic of modern sport is **equality**. This is in two senses: that theoretically everyone should have the opportunity to compete, and that the conditions of competition should be the same for all contestants. Third is **specialisation**, in which players within teams have sharply defined roles unlike in, say, folk football, where there were no specific defenders or attackers. This specialisation emanates from the modern emphasis on achievement in sport. Fourth, sport has become **rationalised**, with rules rather than customs and with the use of sports science to improve performance. Fifth, there has been the development of extensive, bureaucratic organisations to establish universal rules and oversee their implementation. The sixth aspect is that of an obsession with quantification and a detailing of statistical information. Finally, and following on from quantification, is the quest for records within sport so that athletes can aim to be faster, higher and stronger.

Further reading: Guttmann (2004)

MOMENTS

When equal, oppositely directed, and parallel forces are exerted on a body, these forces (or 'couple') tend to cause the body to rotate. The extent of this tendency depends on two factors related to the nature of those forces – the magnitude of the forces and the distance between the lines of action of the two forces. The greater the magnitude, the greater the tendency to **rotation**; and the greater the distance between the lines of action, the greater the tendency to rotation. The moment is the product of the factors' magnitude and distance, and is sometimes known as torque.

Further reading: Dyson (1986), Hay (1993)

MOMENTUM

Momentum is the product of an object's mass and its velocity. The greater the momentum of an object, the greater the effect it can produce upon impact with another object. We know that the impact of a train travelling at thirty miles an hour is far greater than a bicycle travelling at the same speed. In such a collision situation, momentum is actually conceived so that the momentum of the train or the bicycle is transferred to the object with which it collides, with the momentum of the whole system remaining constant. This is an important principle in sport and physical activity, because since momentum remains constant within a system, it is possible to transfer momentum from one body segment to another as well as from one object to another. Thus in striking a golf ball, the speed of the clubhead is a result of the summation of forces internally produced by trunk rotation, leg drive, arm swing, etc. and culminating in the wrist speed used to generate club-head speed to provide impulse to the ball. 'Long hitters', such as Tiger Woods, have developed the ability to effectively and efficiently transfer momentum through segmented body movements, to enable them to hit the ball long distances.

Further reading: Dyson (1986), Hay (1993), Wells and Luttgens (1976)

MONOPOLY

A monopoly exists when there is only one seller in a market. This enables that seller to charge a higher price than would be the case if there was a degree of competition. For example, most buyers of a particular club's endorsed products would not consider purchasing a similar item carrying the logo of another club. Thus official club products usually carry a mark-up as well as a brand logo, as fans and those who wish to be identified with a team are exploited in a monopoly market.

MOTION

Motion, usually defined as the act or process of changing position with respect to point of reference, is of three types: linear or translatory, angular or rotary, and a combination of these two types known as general motion. Linear motion occurs when a body or object moves from one location to another with all its parts moving in the same direction, the same distance and at the same speed. There are very few examples of pure linear motion in sport (which can occur in a straight line or in a curvilinear pattern) because even in activities such as bobsledding, various body parts change their relative position during movement as the sled gains speed during the run.

Angular motion occurs when one portion of an object or body is stationary and the rest moves about this given point, known as the axis. Again, pure angular motion is not common, although a 'giant swing' in a gymnastic routine on the horizontal bar closely approximates pure angular motion since all parts of the body travel through the same angle in the same direction in the same amount of time, in a circular path. More typical in sport and physical activity is a combination of linear and angular motion, and as such, is the type of motion most commonly analysed. Kinematics is the descriptive analysis of motion, and involves factors such as velocity speed, acceleration and distance without reference to the forces responsible for the motion. Teachers and coaches tend to focus their efforts on optimising these aspects of students' or athletes' performances. Kinetics is the analysis of motion with respect to the forces initiating and altering motion, and is based on Newton's three laws of motion, regarding inertia, acceleration and reaction. Forces that affect motion are gravity and friction or resistance, and are important elements in any kinetic analysis, whether such forces be assessed in relation to the analysis of breast stroke, high jump or kicking a football, or in the design of running shoes or racing bikes. The development of high-speed computers, 3-D camera systems, EMG technology and telemetry systems has advanced the study of biomechanics and provided sport scientists and coaches with important information to enhance athletic performance.

Further reading: Hay (1993), Roy (1992)

MOTIVATION

Motivation is the term used to explain the causes of an individual's initiating and sustaining a particular action and has always been at the heart of psychology because it is concerned with why people think and behave as they do. Theories of motivation ask why people initiate and sustain such actions. Maehr and Braskamp (1986: 3) suggest that 'most motivational talk arises from observations about variation in five behavioural patterns: direction, persistence, continuing motivation, intensity and performance'. In the context of sport and physical activity, direction refers to whether an individual participates in a particular activity; persistence refers to continued attention to that activity or duration of activity; continuing motivation refers to the extent to which an individual returns on a regular basis to an activity (see **exercise adherence**); intensity refers to how much effort an individual puts forth in a particular situation; and finally inferences about motivation can also be made from performance.

Motivation has been seen as an outcome variable, as well as the product of an interaction between an individual and the physical/social environment in which the activity is performed. It has also been viewed as an individual difference factor used to explain the differing behaviour of individuals in sporting or athletic situations. Historically, human motivation has been viewed from a range of theoretical perspectives. However, there have been three major theoretical approaches to motivation. The first were instinctual approaches that were based on the premise that motivation is inherited or innate. The second were drive theories that represented the belief that human behaviour is motivated by drives which are designed to reduce biological needs: we still ask what 'drives' certain athletes to try as hard as they do, suggesting that the athlete has a need which is reduced by attaining a particular sporting goal. The most recent approaches to motivation have focused more on explaining why human behaviour is motivated by future events, and are termed expectancy theories.

We are rarely motivated by a single factor at any one time, and in fact are often motivated by a number of factors, some of which may even be in conflict with one another. Thus a player might want to be a member of the soccer team but not want to be the goalkeeper. Expectancy theories are founded on a social-cognitive approach to motivation and behaviour, and focus on the **cognition** and thought processes as governing action. These approaches have focused on such constricts as self-efficacy, goal-setting, and achievement motivation. Nevertheless, as Vealey (1996: 776) points out, all theories about motivation have 'one common thread that they all share [which] is that people are motivated to feel competent, worthy and self-determining'.

Most current theories fit into one of three general orientations that parallel the approaches to **personality** theory: the trait (or participant-centred) view, the state (or situation-centred) view, and the interactional view. In the trait-centred approach, motivation is a function of the personality, needs and goals of the performer. In the state-centred approach, the situation is the determining factor in motivation, so that an individual can be highly motivated in one physical activity such as football but not in another such as swimming. However, the viewpoint that is becoming most widely accepted is the interactional view, in that it is in the interaction between the participant and the situation that we will discover the root of motivation.

The major theory of motivation employing an interactional approach to achievement motivation is need-achievement theory, from which have developed: attribution theory, which focuses on how people explain their (athletic) successes and failures; achievement goal theory, which asks what success and failure mean to an athlete; and competence motivation theory, which looks at how feelings of competence and self-worth influence motivation. All of these theories predict high and low achievers on the basis of their motivational orientation. It appears, therefore, that a critical element affecting our motivation to be involved in sport and physical activity is our motivational orientation. An **intrinsic** or mastery-oriented individual looks for challenges to help promote personal mastery of a task, leading to feelings of competence, and the promotion of persistence, intensity and continuing motivation. The **extrinsic** or outcome-oriented individual selects less-than-optimal challenges and focuses on outcome (winning) as a means of judging capability. Unless successful outcomes are achieved, this orientation will tend to diminish persistence, intensity and continued motivation.

As such, the fostering of **intrinsic motives** is essential if we want to promote lifelong sport and physical activity among all individuals, especially for recreational purposes. High and low achievers can be distinguished by their motives, the tasks they select to be evaluated on, the effort they exert during competition, their persistence, and their performance. High achievers usually adopt mastery (tasks) goals and have high perceptions of their ability and control. Low achievers usually have low perceived ability and control, judge themselves more on outcome goals, and attribute successes to luck or ease of the task; they attribute failure to low ability.

Finally, much of the research on motivation in sport and physical activity has been biased towards the younger end of the age scale. We now need to know more about motivation of older adults and the changes in motivation that occur across the life-span if we are to foster continued physical activity for people of all ages. Further research on interventions to promote physical activity and lifestyle change is also necessary if we are to understand how best to help people make physical activity part of their daily lives.

Further reading: Biddle (1995), Deci (1975), Horn (1992), Lepper and Green (1975), Maehr and Braskamp (1986), Marcus and Forsyth (2004), Vealey (1996), Wann (1997), Weinberg and Gould (1999)

MOTOR SKILL

The acquisition of perceptual-motor skills is fundamental to human existence. At each stage within the cycle of life, humans continuously strive to acquire new skills or to refine existing ones in the hope that productivity and quality of life is enhanced. This is particularly the case within the domain of sport where individuals are judged almost exclusively by their ability to reproduce such skills, often in a diverse range of performance settings.

See also: **skill, skill acquisition.**

Further reading: Williams and Hodges (2004)

MOTOR UNITS

A single motor nerve cell in the spinal cord, together with its nerve fibre and the muscle fibres emanating from its branches, make up a single motor unit. Motor units abide by the 'all-or-nothing' law so that when nervous stimulation received by the motor unit is of sufficient intensity and duration, the muscle fibres of that motor unit all contract. This all-or-nothing response does not apply to an entire muscle, however. Only the number of muscle fibres required to pick up a book or close a door are activated, and thus only a specific number of motor units are active. During prolonged activity, motor units actually take turns. It is only for activities requiring maximal effort that all motor units operate at the same time.

Further reading: Magill (1998), Schmidt and Lee (1999)

MULTICULTURAL

The pursuit of a multicultural society has been a key aim of most Western nations since the 1960s. The aim is to produce a society in which all cultural or ethnic groups are equal, and all have the same access to that society through the law, education, sporting opportunity and so on. Multiculturalism is a liberal agenda that seeks to embrace and respect difference, especially in relation to race and religion, so long as each distinct group also defers to the laws of the nation. Britain in a prime example of a nation that has pursued a policy of multiculturalism. Since the first wave of new Commonwealth immigration in the 1950s, all groups have been respected for their race and any decisions that they might make regarding their religious affiliation. Multicultural societies abhor racism, and the rights of different racial and ethnic groups to exist free from the fear of either verbal or physical attack are protected by law.

A policy of multiculturalism has been pursued by all the main sporting bodies in Britain, and from school level a policy of sport for all has been followed. At the European level, policy documents such as the 2005 report on sport and multiculturalism, pledged the European Union to the pursuit of multiculturalism through sport. The report concluded that sport should be used by the Commission as a communication tool to promote anti-racism messages. The report also argued that there was a need to unleash the positive potential of sport, both inside and outside the EU. However, critics of the policy state that while the intentions are good (and the anti–racism message has been clearly vocalised by most sports organisations), many sports are failing in advancing the cause of multiculturalism. Critics question how far ethnic minorities have been integrated into the sporting world, and cite the small number of black managers and officials in football, the absence of Asians in rugby and football, and the near failure of most sports to cater for the Muslim population. Such criticism are not unique to Britain, and similar complaints have been made about the pursuit of sporting multiculturalism in Australia, France, and the United States. The problem seems to be that while organisations such as FIFA can actively pursue a high profile anti-racism campaign to good effect, this does not necessarily equate to members of different ethnic groups actually taking part in football. Therefore while the sporting world can be seen as one that promotes multiculturalism, the question remains as to how effective it has been in bringing different groups together on the field of play, on the terraces and in the boardroom.

Further reading: European Commission DG Education and Culture (2004), Karlis (2003)

MUSCULAR CHRISTIANITY

Coined by T. C. Sandars in a review of Charles Kingsley's *Two Years Ago* (1857) for the *Saturday Review*, the term muscular Christianity highlights and celebrates the association between physical strength and resilience, religious certainty, and successful struggles 'against the odds', which the Victorians (and particularly Victorian males) found so appealing. In an age that was 'deeply troubled with religious doubt [and] acutely aware of weakness and frustration' (Houghton 1957: 216), muscular Christianity found a ready and enthusiastic audience.

Kingsley's muscular Christian ideal – of a man who feared God and could walk a thousand miles in a thousand hours – was widely revered. It was popularised by a range of authors, including Thomas Hughes in *Tom Brown's Schooldays*, in which the muscular Christian Old Brooke was portrayed as a typical blend of piety and physical talent, guts and gusto. Hughes' association with Rugby School, the impact of Thomas Arnold and the Rugby School model on the **public school** system and its links to health, nationalism and Empire, all led to the growth, development and diffusion of the muscular Christian ideology within the education of white, upper-middle-class English males in mid-to-late nineteenth-century Victorian England. The English middle classes, influenced by the Evangelical movement in the first half of the nineteenth century, were religious. Their aim in education was exemplified, as Newsome has shown, in the ideal of 'godliness and good learning'. It was to this ideal that the public schools, headed by Arnold's Rugby, were responding. The increased emphasis on character training, the inculcation of strong moral principles in the school chapel, and the desire for healthy activity and the development of strong bodies on the playing fields, reflected the muscular Christian ideology and placed the public schools at the centre of the development of this ideology. By the 1860s a public school education had become virtually mandatory for the upper middle classes, thus ensuring the widespread acceptance and influence of muscular Christianity. The English public school system drew comfort and confidence from this ideology, which also helped ensure its future. The ideology was to become an inoculation against potential threats to religious belief, bodily health, social stability and national prestige. Within muscular Christian discourse, the male body is often used as a metaphor for social, national and religious bodies, with the underlying frame of reference of a body's constitution, adding to the depth of metaphor.

In a world where the certainties of creationism were challenged by the writings of Charles Darwin, where the technological advances of the industrial revolution undermined the bucolic beauties of an agrarian society, and the development of cities led to the loneliness of the crowd and the disruption of the traditional ties of the rural community, the search for a strong muscular Christian hero who could display Christian manliness in the face of such onslaughts was perhaps inevitable. Victorian patriarchy ensured that the hero would be male; concerns about class and ruling-class power ensured that the hero would be a 'gentleman'; the need to sustain an imperial identity ensured that the hero would be British. The public schools ensured the supply of a stream of muscular Christians to carry the ideology abroad.

See also: **athleticism, public schools**

Further reading: Chandler (1998), Hall (1994), Houghton (1957), Hughes (1964), Kingsley (1921), MacAloon (2006), Mangan and Walvin (1987), Newsome (1961), Vance (1985)

MUSCULAR SYSTEM *see* **anatomy and physiology**

MUSEUMS

In the light of how passionate sports fans are for their teams and players, it is perhaps surprising how few sports museums actually exist. A great deal of nostalgia surrounds sport, and while high prices are paid for items of memorabilia, individual sports associations and clubs have often been hesitant to invest the large sums of money necessary to build a museum. Those museums that do exist are usually based around one of three themes: the player, the stadium or the sporting association. In North America it is the sporting hall of fame, based around the careers of sporting heroes, that dominate. The museum that is built in, and based around the stadium, has been most successful. Collections of memorabilia and accounts of key events in a stadium museum have usually been associated with a tour around the stadium itself. In Britain, football clubs such as Manchester United have built museums that form a stop-off point on the Old Trafford tour. This is similar to the cricket museum at the Melbourne Cricket Ground, which is accessed on the tour around this legendary cricket venue. Such museums have usually been the most successful, as they are part of a broader sporting tourism visit, and rely on the need of fans to visit their favourite stadium. Museums, such as those at Cheltenham for National Hunt racing and at Preston for association football, based around the history of individual sports, although the most serious and employing professional curators, have been slow to emerge. The advent of lottery money in Britain has assisted the growth and spread of the sporting museum, but while individual fans remain willing to pay vast sums of money for memorabilia, it seems unlikely that many museums will be able to compete financially.

See also: **archives, history**

Further reading: Cox (1996), Johnes and Mason (2003), Vamplew (1998), Vamplew (2004)

NATIONAL COACHING FOUNDATION

Founded in 1983, the National Coaching Foundation with its motto 'Better Coaching ... Better Sport' is based in Leeds and is a charitable company. It is funded largely by grant aid from Sport UK and Sport England, is overseen by a board of directors and run by a corporate management team consisting of a chief executive and the executive directors of six 'teams'. These take responsibility for: high performance coaching; local coaching development; research and development; communications; management services and coach education; and standards and structures. In order to fulfil its mission of improving the quality of coaching, NCF provides consulting, assessment and funding for efforts by institutions of further and higher education to provide training for coaches at all levels, and provide national standards for coaches in line with the National Occupational Standards for Sport, Recreation and Allied Occupations.

NATIONAL CURRICULUM

The introduction of the National Curriculum was intended to raise standards, and thus included assessment tests to evaluate whether those desired levels were being attained. The National Curriculum was created as a result of the 1988 educational reforms, and directs what should be taught to children between the ages of 5 and 16 years in **state schools** in England. Northern Ireland, Scotland and Wales now have their own legislation governing such matters. Attainment targets are specified, and the degree to which schools are successful in delivering the National Curriculum is monitored by the Office for Standards in Education (OFSTED) and takes the form of periodic visits to schools by teams of registered inspectors who are empowered to scrutinise all aspects of curriculum management and delivery. Public and independent schools are not subject to the requirements of the National Curriculum, but an increasing number now do so voluntarily.

The National Curriculum for Physical Education in Britain teaches and monitors children throughout their schooling. Based around a series of different levels, and with clear attainment targets, the curriculum works from the basics of understanding simple movement skills through to a knowledge of health and fitness plans.

See also: **key stages**

Further reading: Department for Education (2001), DfEE/QCA (1999)

NATIONALISM

Since the formation of national sporting federations and associations, the foundation of the modern Olympics, and the emergence of international fixtures, all of which happened in the second half of the nineteenth century, sport has been inseparable from nationalism. International rivalries, that had previously been played out on the battlefield, in the race for empire or through industrial output, found a new outlet. Sport allowed nations to compete against each other, and to measure performance. It meant that 'our' nation could beat 'them', which demonstrated that we were better, stronger and superior. Of course, much of this was hidden beneath the late nineteenth-century attachment to fair play and gentlemanly conduct, but press interest in, and attendance at, international fixtures demonstrates that the potential victory of the nation over another was an appealing prospect.

Throughout the twentieth century, links between the forces of sport and nationalism continued to develop. In nations such as Ireland, which wished to stress its independence from Britain, sport was used as a vehicle for nationalism. The promotion of Gaelic games, steeped as they were in Irish history, language and culture, offered a counterweight to the **cultural imperialism** of Britain. Similarly, those nations who were colonised, and who subsequently entered a stage of **decolonisation**, used sport as a method of demonstrating their nationalism. Their players could wear national shirts, would stand under the nation's flag and listen to their own anthem. If they could then successfully defeat the 'mother' nation, the victory of the new nation over its imperial overlord would be complete.

International competition has acted as a conduit for nationalism. The Olympics, the **Commonwealth Games**, and the football, rugby and cricket world cups, all allow for competition between nations. By staging a major international event, the hosts are afforded the opportunity of displaying their nation to the world. The 1936 Olympics in Berlin were a showcase for the power of Nazi Germany's nationalism, while the 1995 rugby union World Cup victory allowed post-apartheid South Africa to emerge on to the global stage proudly displaying its new flag and anthem, and proving itself strongest on the field of play.

International sporting organisations are important measures of national status. For many of the 'new' nations that emerged because of the collapse of the former Soviet Union, the process of gaining recognition from the IOC or FIFA was an important part of nation building. While economic reconstruction or political stability were difficult to achieve quickly, the presence of the national team on the world stage allowed everyone, home and abroad, to know that the new nation had been formalised.

Nationalism, it is clear, is a central part of sport, and the excitement that the 'them' against 'us' competition affords is a vital ingredient in the success of many sporting competitions. However, the nationalism created by sport should be seen as neither permanent, nor necessarily a force for good. It has been convincingly argued by Jarvie and Walker (1994) that the nationalism associated with sport is a 'ninety minute patriotism'. Thus, rather than being a permanent force, sports nationalism should be understood as temporary and transitory, lasting in the hearts and minds of players and supporters only as long as the game itself. Equally, nationalism, it should be remembered, is not always a positive force. Many football hooligans claim that they are 'fighting' for the pride of their country against the ranks of foreign supporters.

When considering the links between sport and nationalism we should remember that, while highly visible and with a long history, the links are many and varied.

See also: **boycotts, colonialism, decolonisation, politics**

Further reading: Bairner (2001), Billig (1995), Cashman (1995), Cronin (1999), Houlihan (1991), Jarvie and Walker (1994), Wigglesworth (1996)

NATIONAL LOTTERY

The National Lottery began in 1994, and by 2006 had given or committed almost £3 billion to sport in Britain, ranging from small-scale local projects, through grants to high-performance athletes, to multi-million capital investment in stadia and other national facilities. In 1997 the distribution of funds was delegated to the Sports Council. Unfortunately for some sports which relied on the Football Trust and the Foundation for Sports and Arts, both financed by the football pools companies, the popularity of the National Lottery has undermined this source of funding.

Further reading: Cox et al. (2000)

NERVOUS SYSTEM *see* anatomy and physiology

NUTRITION

Nutrition is the study of the process by which the human body takes in and uses food. It is central to our understanding of how we convert what we eat into a source of **energy** to enable us to be physically active and build body tissues. In terms of sport and physical activity, nutrition is a significant factor in **fitness**, both health-related and performance-related, since type and quantity of food ingested has an impact on health and athletic performance.

Nutritional fitness involves selecting foods according to their caloric and nutritive values. There are three fundamental classes of food nutrients: energy nutrients, vitamins and minerals, and water. Energy nutrients are fats, proteins and carbohydrates, and are the basic sources of fuel that provide **ATP**. Vitamins and minerals are inorganic compounds, which are necessary for building and repairing body tissue as well as for proper body function. Thus we need such minerals as calcium for teeth and bone, iron for preventing anaemia, and potassium for efficient functioning of muscle cells. We need vitamins to ensure the appropriate metabolism of fats and carbohydrates. Finally, we need water. Water is perhaps the most essential of all nutrients for human life. We can survive for many weeks without food, but only a matter of days without water. Water is necessary to control body temperature, for energy production, and for waste elimination. In deciding what our food requirements are, we need to take account of both our overall nutritional needs and our caloric needs, as the type of exercise we are involved in determines the type of energy source we will utilise.

Fats make the greater contribution to energy provision when the body is at rest or performing low levels of exercise. Carbohydrates become a more significant source as exercise intensity increases. Thus, for those wishing to lose weight (by reducing fat), low-intensity exercise of sufficient duration is the recommended method.

Athletes have attempted to improve performance by employing specific diets such as 'carbohydrate loading', as well as the use of drinks that contain caffeine, sugar to enhance blood glucose, or electrolyte preparations to help in maintaining mineral levels. Research in this area of sport science and human performance continues as commercial companies look to market such products.

Further reading: Gibney et al. (2002), Howley and Franks (1997), Williams (2005)

OBESITY

Obesity has emerged as one of the great health challenges of the late twentieth and early twenty-first centuries. As diets have changed, and the populations of many Western nations have become more sedentary, so the average weight of people has increased. The issue of obesity is of special concern with respect of children. According to recent American statistics, obesity prevalence doubled in adults between the years 1980 to 2002. In the same period overweight prevalence has tripled in children and adolescents. Between 2003–2004,

17.1 per cent of children and adolescents aged 2 to 19 years were over-weight, and 32.2 per cent of adults aged 20 years or older were classed as obese.

The steady rise in rates of obesity has been attributed to environ-mental factors (lack of activity, greater availability of fast food and so on) and population factors (greater urban areas with higher car usage, two income families and concomitant change in meal patterns and so on). This has given rise to the growth in the number of overweight and obese individuals. Essentially, people in the Western world are decreasing their levels of physical activity and increasing their calorie consumption. The growth in calorie consumption has been aided by the rise in the number of fast food outlets and the culture or super-sizing. For example, a portion of McDonalds fries in 1960 contained 200 calories, whereas now the standard serving contains some 600 calories.

One of the ways of tackling obesity, especially among children, has been through the promotion of sport and healthy activity. In 2003 a major campaign was launched in Britain to get all schoolchildren exercising or taking part in sport for a minimum of two hours per week. Despite the campaign, which was supported by leading sports stars and a national newspaper, figures in 2006 showed that only one third of school children were actually doing two hours of exercise. Campaigns headed by sports stars to encourage physical activity amongst children as a way of combating obesity have also been launched in Australia (the 1Seven Programme) and in the United States.

Further reading: Kirk (2006)

OLYMPIC GAMES *see* **Olympics (ancient), Olympics (modern), Olympism**

OLYMPICS (ANCIENT)

The ancient Olympic Games were part of a very important religious festival held in honour of the god Zeus. This festival, held every four years at Olympia, was the most important and oldest of the gather-ings for athletic competition in antiquity. Olympia was important in that it provided a unique and significant religious context (the sanc-tuary of Zeus) for these games and contests. The fact that the games lasted for over a thousand years and formed a common cultural bond amongst the independent city states that made up ancient Greece, is indicative of the status which the games came to hold in Greek society.

Traditionally dating from 776 BC, the original contests, which were held as sacred rituals, were developed over time to become a five-day-long festival. It is unclear as to how the programme of events was expanded from the stadium (a sprint of approximately 200 metres) to the range of events which included other foot races, wrestling, long jump, discus, javelin, boxing, pentathlon, chariot racing and pankration, the latter a free-for-all activity in which all was legitimate except gouging of the eyes and biting. All athletes competed nude, and women, except for a priestess of Demeter, were barred from the games. Athletes competed for their city state, although they could declare themselves as representing other states if they so wished or if they were paid to do so. They swore an oath to abide by the rules and were expected to be in training for up to ten months before the festival. Not unlike today's athletes, successful Olympians were treated as heroes. They were also not unlike today's athletes in that they employed professional coaches, followed specialised training regimens and received material rewards for their efforts. Again, like their modern equivalents, the ancient games were not without their critics, who worried that athletes were more revered than intellectuals, and that brawn was more admired than brain by the Greeks. Unlike modern Olympians, all participants in the ancient games had to be at Olympia one month before the beginning of the games for final preparation under the supervision of the hellanodikae or judges.

Historians have offered a range of theories to explain the development of sport in Ancient Greece and specifically the Olympic Games. These include the games as: funeral celebrations honouring the dead; part of the cult of fertility associated with the goddess Demeter; a means of military training; and as a ritual sacrifice of human energy. It seems likely that all of these may have contributed to the remarkable longevity of the games as different eras found different rationales for their continuity.

Three major theorems have been offered by historians to explain the decline of the games. The first is the professionalisation of the games, the second is the increasing influence of the Roman Empire, and the third is the rise of Christianity. While the first two may have had limited impact on the decline of the games, it seems more likely that Christianity, which viewed the worship of pagan gods such as

Zeus as sacrilegious, would have been a more decisive factor in the demise of the Olympics.

Further reading: Kyle (1996), Sansone (1988), Young (1984)

OLYMPICS (MODERN)

As the architect of the modern Olympics, Pierre de Coubertin was convinced that the demise of the ancient games had been the result of influences outside the games themselves – influences that had undermined both the spirit and the status of the games. In order to prevent this from happening to the modern Olympics, de Coubertin tried to ensure limited outside influence by making International Olympic Committee (IOC) members independent of influence. As such, they took on the position of ambassadors for Olympism to their national sporting organisations, and are independent of any national government. The IOC elects its own members, and is run by an elected president and an executive board from its headquarters in Lausanne, Switzerland. de Coubertin's vision was of sport, and particularly Olympic sport, as a religion, a secular faith based on good sportsmanship and **fair play**. However, his motives for reviving the games were broader than this. In ideal form he saw the games as being for health and cultural progress; education and character building; international understanding and peace; equal opportunity; fair and equal competition; cultural expression; beauty and excellence; and for sport's independence as an instrument of social reform rather than government legislation. de Coubertin's ideals have proven to be very naive. Thus the organisation of the games as contests between individuals representing specific countries or nations has often fostered intense nationalism, nullifying de Coubertin's goal of internationalism. That the games were originally for men only, and in most cases middle-class white men, has meant that class, race and gender have been issues that have restricted access to the benefits of Olympic competition and **Olympism** to a few. That issues of politics, professionalism and commercialisation have continued to plague the modern games is indicative of the fact that, no matter what de Coubertin's intentions, the unintended consequences of his philosophy have led to as many failures as successes in the achievement of his goals for the games and for Olympism. The recent corruption scandal surrounding the 2002 Winter Olympics in Salt Lake City, Utah, the continuing problem of drugs and drug regulation, and the growth of the games as a mass media 'event' all suggest that the games' future is likely to look no less chequered than its past. In 2012 London will host the Summer Olympics. The benefits of the games are huge as it will allow London to regenerate the east end of the city, transform its transport infrastructure and, if the games perform profitably, leave the city with a financial legacy estimated at £82 million.

Further reading: Barney (1996), Barney et al. (2002), Girginov and Parry (2004), Guttmann (1992), MacAloon (1981), Miller (2003), Segrave and Chu (1988), Simson and Jennings (1992)

OLYMPISM

According to the International Olympic Committee,

> Olympism is a state of mind, a philosophy even, encompassing a particular concept of modern sport, according to which sport can, through an extension of its practice, play a part in the development of the individual, and of humankind in general. . . . and to strengthen understanding and friendship among peoples.

The **Olympic Games** were reformulated by Pierre de Coubertin as a means of fostering social improvement and contributing to the general welfare and betterment of humanity. This emphasis on the pursuit of social values and moral and ethical goals distinguishes the Olympic Games from all other international sporting festivals and institutions, and provides the basis for the games' philosophy of Olympism. We find important elements of Olympism contained in the Olympic Creed, the Olympic Motto and the Olympic Oath.

The modern **Olympics** are perhaps best exemplified by the pursuit of excellence – a key element of Olympism. The comparative nature of the Olympic Motto, 'citius, altius, fortius', (faster, higher, stronger) suggests the goal of trying to do better than one's opponent. At the same time the games are a means of celebrating physical and sporting excellence. For de Coubertin, there was also the pursuit of spiritual excellence. In recent times, the pursuit of excellence (and winning a medal) has often come into conflict with spiritual and moral excellence so that issues of drug taking and **drug testing** have detracted from the ideals of Olympism. Similarly, the commercialisation of the games and the possibility of commercial gain which athletic success can bring have also sullied, in the minds of many, the spirit of

Olympism and the underlying social and moral values which the philosophy of Olympism implies.

de Coubertin considered the Olympic Games as having an educational purpose, and Olympism underpins that purpose in promoting sport in general and the Olympic Games in particular as a platform for popularising the educational value of sport for youth. The Olympic Creed highlights this value in suggesting that the most important aspect of the games is not in winning but in taking part, not in the triumph but in the struggle. 'The essential thing is not to have conquered but to have fought well.' Again, the inherent contradictions evident in this statement when compared to the Olympic Motto, provides one of the great paradoxes of Olympism, and contributes to our continuing ambivalence about the games and the feelings of fascination and disappointment which accompany the festival every four years.

A third element of Olympism has always been the promotion of peace and increased international understanding. de Coubertin firmly believed that in order to promote understanding among individuals and nations, it was necessary to know each other's history and culture, and respect it. It is for this reason that the host nation opens each Olympiad with a display of its own unique cultural heritage in order to promote such understanding. The long-term goal of Olympism, in this regard, is 'internationalism', whereby mutual respect amongst individuals and nations can be fostered. Again, inherent in this philosophy are the problems of patriotism and nationalism. The Olympic Games have been used to promote patriotism and nationalism, as in Berlin in 1936, at the expense of internationalism. This inherent contradiction has never been fully resolved, and provides an additional source of on-going tension in the Olympic philosophy.

Equally important to de Coubertin and his philosophy of Olympism was the emphasis on **fair play**. Since he had always advocated for the moral and ethical grounds of sport's importance, he followed the nineteenth-century English **public school** model of fair play, with its amateur (i.e. non-professional) ethic. Sport was to be conducted in an honest, honourable and chivalrous fashion, by honest, honourable, chivalrous athletes, pursuing a more scrupulous and generous humanity. The Olympic Oath, with its emphasis on the true spirit of sportsmanship, the glory of sport and the honour of each team, highlights this concern. However, although anomalies do exist, it is generally recognised that success in the Olympic Games is far more readily achieved by athletes from the developed countries, and that there is a strong correlation between a country's gross domestic product and the number of medals it wins. Such an advantage for the economically developed countries continues to cause concern amongst many who value the positive aspects of Olympism.

Olympism is not without its critics, who argue that it is a naive philosophy and that its inherent contradictions undermine its ideological force. While de Coubertin recognised that sport could be both positive and negative in its effects, he believed that by continuing to bring the youth of the world together every four years, the positive aspects of Olympism could be promoted and achieved.

Further reading: Gruneau and Cantelon (1988), Guttmann (1992), MacAloon (1981), Segrave (1988), Senn (1999)

OPEN LOOP

The idea of an open loop mode of movement control is that a movement is 'pre-programmed' and executed without on-going correction (or feedback). Proponents of this idea acknowledge that this model probably only applies to certain types of movement performed in certain contexts. Thus Schmidt believes that in a fast movement, such as throwing a ball as far as possible, an open loop mode is employed using generalised motor programmes. And while selection of a new movement can only occur after the movement is completed, there is evidence that corrections in movement execution can be performed. The determining factor is time available, along with level of skill learning of the performer, the difficulty of the task being performed and the type of response required.

Further reading: Magill (1998), Schmidt and Lee (1999)

ORIGINS OF SPORT

As the definition of sport is so contested, it is therefore problematic to clearly point to the exact origins of sport. There is a wealth of archaeological evidence to demonstrate that many ancient cultures, including the Mayans of Central America, and the Greeks and Romans of Europe, venerated athletic competition of various kinds, and that some of these contests, such as the **Olympics (ancient)**, were organised into sporting festivals. However, many of these contests were based around skills that were necessary for success in other spheres of life. Such physical activities, including fighting, javelin or spear throwing, target practice and so on, all belonged to broader habits of survival or military preparation and activity. Essentially ancient physical activities, even when arranged around the celebration of a festival, were primarily concerned with the training for war. In the medieval period, physical events and contests became seen as an essential attraction at fairs and other gatherings. As a result, certain events were encouraged, by different social classes, that share many features with modern sport. One of the key areas in the development of sport was the promotion of sporting events involving animals solely for pleasure and the promotion of gambling. Such blood sports, including bear- and bull baiting, horse racing and hunting, drew large crowds and were enjoyed by different people from across the classes.

It was the nineteenth century that was the key period for the evolution of modern sports. In Western Europe, the century was one of rapid industrialisation and urbanisation, and also a revolutionary period in transportation. Many traditional games and physical contests that had been focused on fairs and other gatherings died out, while others were adapted to the new urban setting and grew in popularity. In an attempt to control the rowdy behaviour that accompanied many events that used animals, such as bear baiting, laws were introduced to outlaw them. This legal control of sporting events placed the middle and upper classes, as well as institutions such as the Church, in a position where they controlled and mediated what sports would be allowed. Those sports that the elites championed, such as horse racing, cricket, boxing or pedestrianism, were controlled by rules that were drawn up by committees of influential men. This was the start of a process of codification, or the formalisation of rules, which would define modern sport. As the whole of industrial society became increasingly controlled by the rule of law, it was profoundly affected by the impact of new transportation opportunities and dominated by the ethos of Christian living, and so sport was modernised. The main development was the advance of **rational** sports with formalised rules and codes of behaviour. This shift defined modern sport and marks a watershed in the origins of sport. As the nineteenth century progressed, the success of games such as football in gaining a paying audience, and the advent of the professional player, marked out a new phase in the **history** of sport.

See also: **modern sport**

Further reading: Brailsford (1992), Holt (1989), Lowerson (1993), Tranter (1998), Vamplew (2005b), Wigglesworth (1996)

OUTCOMES

Outcomes can be specifically identified goals within a sporting context, or the desired outcomes of a programme of study which of itself may be either summative or formative. **Curriculum design** identifies desired 'learning outcomes' as the focus of teaching programmes which influence both the nature of programme content and teaching method(s) which may be deployed. An outcome is the end result of a (teaching/coaching) process that may or may not be either desirable or achieve intended or desired aims.

OVER-TRAINING

There is no one widely accepted definition of over-training, just as there is no agreement that there is a limit to the positive effects of continued training. However, there is some consensus that continuous use of a planned, systematic and progressive increase in training (overload) with inadequate rest can lead to chronic decreases in performance and impaired ability to train, known as over-training syndrome (OS). OS typically takes the form of 'staleness' and an inability to train and perform to capacity, and is often only recognised by an unexpected drop in performance that cannot be attributed to illness or injury. Other symptoms of OS include: mood disturbances such as depression, anger or anxiety; general fatigue induced by loss of energy, and feelings of heaviness in the arms and legs; changes in sleep patterns; and changes in appetite, usually in the form of reduced appetite.

In all cases, researchers suggest that rest is vital in order to overcome the problems of over-training, although total inactivity is not usually warranted. Rather, reduction of stress, which might include other factors such as travel, nutrition, environmental and psychosocial elements, needs to be taken into account. Thus heavy travel schedules, inadequate or poor diet, altitude, heat and humidity, and even adjustments because of changed school, work, or interpersonal situations need to be addressed. Most sport scientists believe that the chief cause of OS is poor coaching and ill conceived training. However, even the most carefully planned training regimen can cause problems for some athletes, since research has shown that athletes with similar fitness levels respond quite differently to the same training programme. In order to increase their physical capabilities and improve their performance, athletes must train under conditions of adaptive stress. Typically, over-training is manifested in a number of ways related to declines in the level of performance in terms of movement skill and coordination, psychological readiness and focus, and/or physical condition.

While the causes of over-training are many and varied, its effects are often the result of inappropriate frequency, duration and/or intensity of training, inappropriate recovery, or excessive competitive stress on athletes. Such issues are obviously of critical import in the training of young athletes, for whom over-training can quickly lead both to physical and psychological injury and even **burn-out**.

See also: **burn-out**

Further reading: Kreider et al. (1998), Kuipers and Keizer (1988), Raglin and Wilson (2000)

OWNERSHIP

Traditionally, people have owned sports clubs and teams in Britain primarily for non-economic reasons. They have been less concerned with profits and more with status, particularly in the local community, or with supporting financially a side that they have supported emotionally. However, as teams have become public, quoted companies on the stock exchange, company regulations mean that the financial aspects of ownership have to be given greater priority. Nevertheless this still involves only a minority of clubs, mainly in the football industry.

PATRIOTISM

A love of one's country is most commonly understood as the emotion lying at the heart of patriotism. This is different from **nationalism**, which is seen as an ideology that is linked with the policies and politics of governments and regimes, rather than the feelings of the individual athlete or the collective sporting crowd. For the sporting patriot the pride in national representative teams and players for their endeavours and victories is important, but so are the emotional ties of sporting venues and traditions. For example, the cricket fan will feel patriotic about the symbolism and imagery of a game being played in the midsummer evening sun on a village green as being representative of England and Englishness. In this format, sport summons up that emotional link to the idea of a national identity, which is not necessarily being played out on the world stage in international competition. Sport can be used, in the patriotic sense, to symbolise national characteristics and stereotypes which evoke love and pride, rather than aggression and competition. Each nation will have a sporting imagery which evokes feelings of patriotism: for the Australian it might be the Melbourne Cricket Ground full to capacity in the build-up to an Australian rules grand final, for the French the image may be the pedethon of the Tour de France surging through fields of sunflowers, while for the Canadian it might be the sports connected with logging festivals. Sporting patriotism is a snapshot of who and what we are in any given country, and allows us to love our homeland.

Further reading: Cronin (1999), Pope (1997)

PATRONAGE

Patronage can be either of a financial or figurehead variety. The former involves altruistic activity by benefactors, usually for reasons of public pride or civic responsibility. The latter generally involves clubs and associations seeking to utilise the name and title of their patron to demonstrate their position in the social hierarchy of sport. In the nineteenth century patrons often sponsored professional sportsmen, particularly pugilists and pedestrians, as part of their gambling activities.

PEDAGOGY

Pedagogy refers to the study of learning and instruction with a particular but not exclusive focus upon the learning process, curriculum design and broader social issues which may pertain to health and physical education. This is sometimes referred to as 'learning theory', and embraces such philosophies as behaviourism, constructivism and humanism, each of which has contributed much to the development of physical education theory and the manner of its application.

Pedagogic theory brings the work of such renowned individuals as Skinner, Piaget, Dewey and Maslow within the remit of physical educationalists, and represents a significant departure from physical training in that the development of the whole person is acknowledged as important, rather than simply a series of competent physical responses.

Further reading: Capel and Piotrowski (2000)

PERIODISATION

If it is to be effective, any training programme needs to be based on sound physical and psychological principles. The 'periodisation of training' is a means of employing systematic and progressive increases in workloads, both physical and psychological, thereby promoting the optimal adaptation to training. According to Dick (2002) such adaptive processes should emphasise the following ordering of emphasis in training: general endurance, **aerobic** endurance, **anaerobic** endurance, strength, **speed**, and **skill**. Further work needs to be done in matching psychological training principles to these physical training principles in order to ensure optimal effectiveness.

Further reading: Dick (2002), Fleck and Kraemer (1997)

PHILOSOPHY

The philosophical study of sport and physical activity is a relatively young field. It has emerged largely as the result of efforts by two groups of individuals: those in physical education and sport studies who have been interested in analysing their field from a philosophical perspective; and, those trained in philosophy who have shown interest in subjecting sport, human movement, games and play, as significant and meaningful human activities, to philosophical analysis. The first major contribution to the area was Paul Weiss' *Sport: A Philosophic Inquiry* (1969). In December 1972, a small number of individuals representing these two groups met and formed the Philosophic Society for the Study of Sport. Since 1974, the society has published the *Journal of the Philosophy of Sport*, which is one of the most important sources for those interested in the philosophical study of sport and physical activity.

According to Pearson, philosophers of sport and physical education tend to use one or more ways of doing philosophical inquiry within four general headings: first, identifying concept-unifying agents which would include such questions as 'what activities might be intuitively considered sport?'; second, working from models or paradigms in which philosophers test a case (e.g. the athletic contest) against each of the components of a paradigm (e.g. Aristotle's paradigm for tragic drama); third, language analysis – where terms such as sport or physical education are analysed in order to detect contradictory or confusing uses of such terms; and fourth, phenomenology, which is a form of inquiry that tries to describe consciousness of experience, and thus show how athletes' 'peak experiences' might have certain common elements.

For the philosophers of physical education, one of the major recurring themes has been to use philosophical analysis as a means of identifying, clarifying and problematising the aims and objectives of physical education. Various rationales have been put forward in support of physical education. Among those rationales have been those that justify physical education as a means of promoting education of the physical, through the physical, and in the physical. With the recent development of the academic study of physical education in schools, some have suggested the additional objective of promoting education about the physical.

For those more concerned with philosophic analysis of sport and physical activity, Morgan has identified three major areas for questions which have drawn attention, mirroring the three major branches of philosophical inquiry: metaphysics, epistemology and axiology. The major metaphysical questions which have been addressed have been regarding the basic features of sport that mark it off from other forms of human activity. This, in turn, leads to definitional efforts so that distinctions can be drawn between related concepts such as **play**, **recreation** and **games**. Morgan identifies the major epistemological questions as being concerned with how we gain knowledge of sport, and thus whether first-hand experience is necessary in order to be able to claim knowledge. In practical terms, we can ask how important it is in terms of **coaching** expertise for a Premier League football coach to have played Premier League football. For the philosopher of sport and physical activity, the question is one of knowledge, knowledge gained from first-hand experience. This question obviously has significance for physical education, the physical education curriculum and the idea of **key stages**, as well as for the education of coaches by the **National Coaching Foundation**. The third arena for questions relates to issues of **value**, and has been dominated by questions of ethics. Thus questions about how we ought to treat one another in sport and how we should pursue athletic excellence in sports have led to some of the most significant and far-reaching debates in sport philosophy. Debates and discussion over such issues as sportsmanship, **fair play**, cheating and winning, and issues concerning performance-enhancing **drugs** and **drug testing**, have been particularly important in demonstrating the practical importance of philosophical inquiry in sport and physical activity. And whereas issues of value relating to the aesthetic aspects of sport and physical activity have been raised by philosophers such as Best, who are interested in qualitative aspects of sport performance such as grace and style, and whether forms of sport qualify as works of art, it has been the ethical issues that have dominated axiological analysis of sport and physical education.

The development of the field of sport philosophy, and the corpus of work that has been produced in the past thirty years, mirrors the increasing interest in and concern about sport and physical activity as significant and meaningful human activities, worthy of philosophic analysis.

Further reading: Arnold (1988), Best (1978), McNamee and Parry (1998), Pearson (1990), Weiss (1969)

PHYSICAL CAPACITY

Physical or functional capacity is the ability to perform work including typical activities of daily living as well as exercise and sporting activities. It is an important measure of both physical fitness and health.

See also: **VO$_2$ Max**

PHYSICAL CULTURE

Interest in physical culture generally developed in the mid-nineteenth century as a response to what was perceived as a weakened urban population with no access to the healthy activities of rural life. It had various guises, but all shared the feature of making use of indoor facilities or of limited outdoor space. It found adherents among the

English **public schools**, who used it to promote leadership and team-building qualities; among the Church, who saw the value of **muscular Christianity**; and among the various eugenics movements, who saw in it a way of improving the breed.

PHYSICAL EDUCATION

Essentially, physical education is the formal inculcation of knowledge and values through physical activity. A more wide-ranging definition of physical education would encompass instruction in the development and care of the body, from simple callisthenic exercises to training in hygiene, gymnastics, and the performance and management of athletic games. Historically, it has focused on diet, exercise and hygiene, as well as musculo-skeletal and psycho-social development. Several areas constitute its sub-disciplines: these include **biomechanics**, exercise physiology, sports **sociology**, **history**, **philosophy** and **psychology**.

Further reading: Baily and Vamplew (1999)

PHYSICAL LITERACY

The term 'physical literacy' refers to the degree to which an individual demonstrates competency in a range of movement forms and proficiency in various forms of physical activity. It also has a cognitive component in that competent or proficient movement, either alone or within a group, constitutes an intellectual as well as a physical response to a given situation or circumstance. In the current environment of student profiling and assessment, physical literacy might be said to be measurable against broadly framed sets of statements that enable qualitative/quantitative measures to be recorded. For it to be meaningful, the term must be inclusive – that is of all groups within communities – and should acknowledge the competence with which individuals master their interaction with their own particular environment. At a basic level, physical education attempts to develop physical literacy in both natural and artificial environments in a way that also builds social skills and confidence, and encourages emotional expression and control.

Further reading: Whitehead (2001)

PHYSICAL TRAINING

Physical training programmes have purely physical rather than cognitive aims. Physical training is often associated with military purpose, where developing physical fitness for a specific purpose is of primary importance and cognitive/intellectual development is of little significance. Early 'PT' programmes in schools were decried as having little or no educational value or purpose, and were gradually replaced with programmes of physical education, which address the all-round development of the individual through the medium of physical activity. This is commonly referred to as 'education through the physical'. In programmes of physical training the outcome or end product is all-important, whereas in programmes of **physical education** the process itself has **intrinsic** value.

PLAY

Three characteristics of play can be stressed: it is a voluntary activity, it is separate from real life, and it is fun. Play is a voluntary activity characterised by minimal **rules**, spontaneity and fantasy, and is viewed by participants as non-work. Among young animals play is generally regarded as being a way in which survival activities such as fighting, fleeing and mating are learnt. In humans, play is any non-utilitarian activity pursued for its own sake. Meanings for the word 'play' abound and are very broad-ranging. Play is often used to refer to a wide variety of activities engaged in voluntarily, and includes such things as **games**, sports, creative activities, and make-believe. It is also a psychological projection or a cognitive process underlying particular types of behaviour (such as 'playing the fool' in order to attract attention to oneself). A third view is of play as a state of mind, or an attitude or disposition brought to a particular activity. Such an approach suggests that a person can play almost anywhere, anytime, and that they can move in and out of a state of playfulness during the course of any activity.

One of the most influential books on play is Homo Ludens (Man the Player) by Dutch historian Johann Huizinga, in which he examines play as a cultural phenomenon, noting that it is an irrational, voluntary activity, characterised by freedom. To Huizinga, play is a free activity standing quite consciously outside 'ordinary' life as being 'not serious', but at the same time absorbing the player intensely and utterly. It is an activity connected with no material interest, and no

profit can be gained by it. It proceeds within its own boundaries of **time** and space. Huizinga states that the function of play can be derived from the two basic aspects under which we meet it: as a contest for something or as a representation of something. These two functions can unite in such a way that the game 'represents' a contest, or else becomes a contest for the best representation of something.

As such, **games** are more formalised forms of play and are characterised by explicit rules, but they are not necessarily characterised by the production of a different outcome, which is why we are able to talk about playing games. However, Schwartzman has suggested that in order to fully understand play, we will have to separate it from games because games 'rule out the ambiguity, spontaneity and flexibility characteristic of play' (1978: 320). However, as she states, such a distinction may be very difficult to define because play resists operationalisation and requires interpretation. Currently, therefore, play is widely held to be an attitude, disposition or stance.

Further reading: Garvey (1977), Harris (1980), Huizinga (1950), Hyland (1984; 1990), Sage (1979), Schwartzman (1978)

POLITICS

The relationship that exists between politics and sport is a difficult one to define or quantify. In many academic works that exist on the subject, such as Allison (1993), the examples that are selected to illustrate this relationship are those played out most publicly and which often focus on extreme or violent politics. As a result, there has been a wealth of work that has been produced which examines the politics of the Cold War within the Olympic setting, the **boycotts** of major sporting events caused by the apartheid controversy, or the function of sport in violent settings such as Northern Ireland or Palestine. Sport is so malleable in the cause of politics because of its high media profile and its regular setting on an international stage. Specific illustrations of the problems caused by the use of sport by political regimes and causes would include Hitler's 1936 Olympics in Berlin which were used as a propaganda exercise for his regime, the attack by Palestinian terrorists on the 1972 Olympic Games in Munich, or the British failure to officially recognise the state of North Korea during the 1966 World Cup finals. In these examples, politics has been seen as the cause of sporting conflict, and therefore worthy of investigation.

What has often been lacking in academic writing on sport, has been a thorough understanding of the workings of government within the sporting domain. Writers such as Houlihan (1991) have sought to explain the interface that exists between sport and government, and in doing so have illustrated how politics impact on sport. Through the evolution of **government policy**, the political world can transform access to sport by providing more facilities, provide better training for elite athletes, and can support bids to host major sporting events. Governments have also pursued a political agenda by mobilising sport as a method of evoking feelings of **nationalism**, in promoting sporting facilities as a way of enticing tourists to the country, and by using sport to improve the health of the nation and thereby reduce welfare and public health expenditure. These issues, which usually come under the control of a specific government ministry, are issues that are commonly viewed as mundane. However, without governments, political parties and movements recognising the huge importance of sport within society, all these things would not happen. Politics is about mobilising the population of any given country behind a system of government or a set of ideological beliefs. As sport is so popular, and such a part of so many people's lives, it has been a natural vehicle for achieving such mobilisation. Once this has been recognised and achieved, the majority of political involvement with sport is about harnessing and maintaining the relationship through the provision of facilities, the distribution of funds, and the setting up of administrative bodies such as the British Sports Council.

At the general level there is a host of other sporting issues that are political. The debate that surrounds the sponsorship of sporting events by cigarette companies has evoked a response from both national governments and the European Commission. Equally important, at the global level of politics, is the control and provision of television coverage of sport, and the rights of either sporting associations or television companies to restrict viewing on the basis of maximising their profits. Finally, sport has become politically important within the wider battles for recognition and equality that have been fought by women, ethnic minorities and disabled groups in recent decades. Issues such as equal prize money for women at major sporting events, racial abuse of black players in major team sports, and the rights of disabled athletes to compete in able-bodied sporting competitions, have become political battlegrounds.

See also: **boycotts, government policy, nationalism**

Further reading: Allison (1993), Hargreaves (1994), Houlihan (1991), Polley (1998)

POST-MODERNISM

One of the major sociological theories of the late twentieth century, post-modernism has had a profound effect on all scholarly disciplines. Post-modernism was used, from the late 1970s, as a method of describing the contemporary world. It was argued that the two concepts which underpinned modernism, truth and liberation through progress and development, had failed. Frederic Jameson argued in his *Postmodernism, or the Cultural Logic of Late Capitalism* (1984), that society had reached a stage where many aspects of development were ending, and that all remained was depthlessness. This post-modern condition, although much debated, can be seen as possessing the following features:

1 Pastiche: the development of style that no longer relies on single cultures of historical epochs.
2 Reflexivity: a belief in a self-awareness that is accompanied by a sense of irony.
3 Relativism: the absence of objective standards of truth.
4 Rejection: the dismissal of traditional forms of understanding artistic techniques, such as narrative or reality.
5 Disrespect: traditionalism is rejected in favour of radical ways of approaching artistic production.
6 Creation: a challenge to the concept of the author as the creator of text.

Modern sport, because of its connection with the media, and its reliance on spectacle and image, has been seen by many commentators, most notably the French philosopher Jean Baudrillard, as representative of post-modernism. Modern sporting events, such as the Olympics and the football World Cup finals, have been examined by post-modernists as exemplars of cultural events that have become ever more mediated, commodified and unreal. Events such as the 1996 Atlanta Olympics or the 1994 World Cup finals in the United States, have been used by academics to explore how bodies such as the IOC and FIFA, in conjunction with sponsors and television companies, manufactured an alternative sporting post-modern reality. Other areas of contemporary sporting life, such as club mascots, cheerleaders and fan behaviour, are readily used as examples of the innate post-modernity of sport.

See also: **modernisation, sociology**

Further reading: Andrews (1998, 2000), Connor (1989), Rail (1998), Redhead (1998)

PRICE

The lower the price of most goods, including those for leisure and sport, the greater will be the consumer demand. And, of course, the reverse; hence the protests about 'real fans' being excluded from Premiership football by the steep rise in the cost of season tickets. Price discrimination operates at most events, with higher prices being charged for better seats, and within sports there is a quality aspect, with higher prices for what is perceived as a better product, such as Premier League compared to non-league football, or test cricket compared to the second division of the county championship.

PRIVATE GOODS

The concept of private goods, like that of **public goods**, must not be confused with whether the source of supply is in the **private sector** or **public sector**. These are those goods and services which if consumed by one person are no longer available to another. For example, if one golfer is using a particular set of clubs then that set is not available simultaneously for another player.

See also: **public goods**

PRIVATE SECTOR

Basically the private sector of the economy is that not organised by either government or volunteers. It is commercially oriented, with profit as its motivation. For many years private sector operators have seen sport and related activities as a profitable market. However, the growth of private sector involvement in sport has, in the last two decades, been unprecedented as fitness clubs, sports stores, sport equipment manufacturers, sport sponsorship agencies, and companies promoting recreational sporting opportunities have all grown at an unparalleled rate.

See also: **public sector**

PROCESS ORIENTATION

Unlike competitive sporting scenarios, where outcomes sometimes outweigh the process through which results are achieved (goal orientation), the aims of some programmes (e.g. in **physical education**) value this process in its own right. An activity such as football might be valuable as a means of developing cooperation, self-esteem, coordination and spatial awareness, and the outcome of any game activity would be entirely incidental. Such programmes or activities would have a process orientation rather than a **goal orientation**.

See also: **goal orientation**

PRODUCT DEVELOPMENT *see* **commercialisation**

PRODUCT IMPROVEMENT *see* **commercialisation**

PROFESSIONALISM

Today the term professionalism implies the earning of money from playing sport. The modern professional sportsperson obtains monetary rewards via signing-on fees, wages, bonuses, prize-money, sponsorship and advertising. The rewards to some can be immense. Some Premiership footballers are paid over £100,000 a week but even more can be secured in individual sports such as boxing, golf and tennis.

Initially professionalism, in the sense of making money out of playing sport, was not necessarily the obverse of **amateurism**, for in the nineteenth century gentlemen were often allowed to row or race against each other for wagers. Wages, however, were another matter, for these clearly defined the recipient as being from the lower social orders. The earliest professionals were: watermen, who ferried goods and passengers between ships and the shore but occasionally participated in races for prizes; pugilists, who were supported by their patrons to participate in prize fights; jockeys, who rode as liveried servants for aristocratic and gentrified owners; and cricketers, who, if not paid directly by their employer for playing cricket, were often found employment as gardeners and the like so that they could represent the estate owner in high-stake matches.

The widespread development of professionalism in late nineteenth-century British sport led to controversy and debate in almost every sport as to whether the ruling bodies should recognise it and, if so, what safeguards should be imposed in the interests of amateur participants, the professionals themselves, and society in general. The common theme of all the major criticisms was that of class antagonism, the fear of the middle-class players and administrators that they might lose both social position and sporting supremacy. Allied to this was a belief that professionals, whose livelihoods were at stake, would commit fouls to ensure that they were not defeated, and, worse still, might be a source of corruption in what had been unsullied amateur sport. In cricket it was acknowledged that the paid players were indispensable to the game, for few amateurs could play throughout the season, and fewer still were prepared for the hard grind of county championship bowling. Nevertheless the paid player was made aware of his inferior social position both by nomenclature, in that amateurs were termed 'gentlemen' with its obvious social connotations, and by symbolic subordination in that the amateurs and professionals ate, travelled, dressed for the game, and even entered the field of play by separate entrances, as well as being distinguished on the scorecard by the initials of the amateur preceding his surname, with the reverse for the paid player.

Perhaps the greatest divide between amateur and professional lay in rowing. In 1879 the Henley authorities decided that no person should be considered an amateur who had ever competed in open competition for a stake, money or entrance fee; who had ever competed with or against a professional for any prize; who had ever taught, pursued, or assisted in the practice of athletic exercises of any kind as a means of gaining a livelihood, or who had ever been employed in or about boats for money or wages. These were perhaps reasonable conditions, but then followed a savage piece of class legislation – the so-called 'mechanic's clause' – which excluded anyone who was, or had ever been, by trade or employment for wages, a mechanic, artisan or labourer!

Rugby was late to embrace professionalism, and this occurred only after a schism which irreconcilably split the organisation of the game.

In the north of England, many talented working-class players were receiving covert broken-time payments to enable them to play by compensating them for loss of earnings. When an attempt was made to legitimise this practice, the reaction of the rugby union authorities was to declare that 'only clubs composed entirely of amateurs shall be eligible for membership', thus embedding what had been an unwritten rule into their constitution. In September 1895 it was declared that travelling expenses were the only costs that could be compensated. So strict were the new regulations that players could be deemed professionals if they did paid repair work to club premises or if they were awarded medals without the formal permission of the Rugby Football Union. Almost inevitably, this led to a breakaway by those clubs that wished to continue with working-class players, and the formation of the Northern Union (later the Rugby Football League). Equally almost inevitably, broken-time payments quickly gave way to payments for playing, though only semi-professionalism was allowed, and initially players had to demonstrate that they had been gainfully employed in the week preceding a match.

Over time the opposition to professionalism has been diluted. In the 1960s the distinction between gentlemen and players in cricket was discarded, and by the 1990s rugby union remained the last of the major sports to refuse to accept professionalism at the elite level. Finally, it too succumbed. In 1996, only days before the centenary of the breakaway of the Northern Union, a change of policy was announced which led to full-time professionalism in the leading clubs and substantial semi-professionalism elsewhere in the game.

See also: **amateurism, shamateurism**

Further reading: Smith and Porter (2000), Vamplew (2005b)

PROFIT

Any commercial organisation seeks to make profits, but there is debate about whether profit maximisation is a major aim in the sports world. Generally economists identify two ideal-type sporting organisations: the profit maximisers, who aim to make as much money as they can, and the **utility** maximisers, whose aim is to win as many matches or trophies as they can. Either raising revenue or reducing costs can increase profit, and many economists now prefer to use the term 'net revenue' rather than profit to emphasise this point.

PROGRESSIVE RESISTANCE

In developing training programmes to promote gains in both muscular strength and muscular endurance, the principle of overload is vital. Strength and endurance will only increase when a muscle performs for a given period of time against workloads greater than those normally encountered. The basis for all progressive resistance exercise is the concept of repetition maximum (RM), which is defined as the maximal load that a muscle or muscle group can lift over a given number of repetitions before fatiguing. Thus an athlete needs to assess their R1VI for any particular load and/or number of repetitions. The majority of strength training studies have found that the optimal number of repetitions is between four and eight (4–8RM) and should be practised in multiple sets (three or more). High-resistance, low-repetition exercises are used to build muscular strength; low-resistance, high-repetition exercises are used to build muscular endurance. To achieve the full benefit of such training, proper rest intervals are important both between exercises and between training sessions. Insufficient rest results in inadequate recovery and thus reduces the athlete's ability to exert force. **Drugs** such as anabolic steroids speed the recovery rate and enable athletes to train more often and thus reduce training tune to achieve specific strength and/or endurance gains.

Further reading: Fahey (1997), McArdle et al. (2000), Williams (1998)

PROTECTIVE EQUIPMENT

Concerns about the health and safety of those involved in sport and physical activity, along with growing concerns about litigation, have encouraged the increasing use of protective equipment in sports. Both the quantity and the quality of protective equipment have increased as the number, type and range of sporting activities and the numbers of those involved have increased. Thus, in cricket, no batsman wore a helmet when facing a fast bowler until the 1970s. In rugby, shoulders were not padded, nor were mouthguards *de rigueur* until the 1980s. In squash and basketball, eye protection was unseen until this period also. Protective equipment is intended to protect vulnerable parts of the body from injury. Typically this has meant the head (and particularly the temple and the eyes), the reproductive organs, the shins and the feet. However, concern over impact injuries to joints such as knees, elbows and ankles, as well as areas of soft muscle tissue such as the thigh (cricket) and forearm (lacrosse), have also led to greater use of protective equipment. For professional athletes, whose livelihood and career depends upon remaining fit and healthy, such equipment is vital. These athletes tend to set a standard that recreational and weekend athletes follow.

Further reading: Grayson (1999a), Harries (1996)

PSYCHOLOGY

Sport psychology is the study of human behaviour such as achievement or competition and the thoughts and feelings associated with this behaviour such as anxiety, self-esteem and motivation. Since its development as an academic discipline in the 1970s it has been viewed in two ways: as an applied psychology, in which the principles of psychology are applied to sport and physical activity; and as a subdiscipline of sport (and **exercise**) science requiring knowledge of the other sub-disciplines of **sport science**, such as exercise physiology, **biomechanics**, etc., and their theories, constructs and measures. Those adopting the former view have tended to focus on studying sport and physical activity as a setting in which to understand psychological theory and apply psychological principles. Those adopting the latter have tended to focus on observing, explaining and predicting behaviour in sporting contexts.

As the study of human behaviour applied to the context of sport and physical activity, sport psychology is one of the younger sub-disciplines within the field of psychology, just as it is one of the younger sub-disciplines within the field of physical education and sport studies. Medical and psychological concerns relating to health and fitness have increasingly been supplemented by interest in performance. And in pursuit of optimal or 'peak' performance, athletes, trainers and coaches have come to realise the importance of the psychological in sport performance. This interest in the relationship between the athlete and athletic performance has led to two related but distinct areas of study within the field.

The first area is concerned with understanding how psychological factors affect an individual's physical performance, and has led many coaches to search for athletes who display particular psychological traits or profiles. These coaches ask the question, 'what psychological attributes should I be looking for in a champion, to match the physiological characteristics that make a champion?' The second area has involved those coaches and educators who are less concerned about producing champions and the effects of a 'champion' on sporting performance, and are more interested in the effects of sport on psychological development and behaviour. As such they have looked at and used sport psychology very differently. They have asked, 'what are the effects of participating in sport and physical activity on the psychological development, behaviour and well-being of the participant?'

Psychologists working in the areas of sport and physical activity have adopted a wide range of theoretical and conceptual orientations for their field, often matching those in the parent discipline. However, as the field has developed, four major areas of research and three major orientations to the field have emerged, both in Europe and in the USA. The four areas of research are in the fields of personality motivation, interpersonal and group processes, and intervention techniques. The three major orientations to studying sport psychology are: the psycho-physiological, the social-psychological, and the cognitive-behavioural. These orientations also mirror methodological and measurement concerns within the field, and are thus important indicators of the types of debate taking place in the field of sport, psychology of sport, and physical activity over what constitutes legitimate and useable knowledge.

The psycho-physiological approach emphasises the use of physiological measures such as heart rate, brain wave activity, palmar sweating and muscle action potential to study behaviour (sport performances), assuming that these are good measures of psychological processes. Those adopting a social-psychological orientation assume that behaviour (sport performance) is determined as a result of complex interactions of the individuals and their psychological make-up (traits/predispositions) with the social environment in which they are performing. Those adopting a cognitive-behavioural stance focus on the cognitions or thoughts and behaviour of the performer. They focus on what an athlete is thinking about, how confident they are feeling, how relaxed/stressed they are feeling, and how this impacts performance. Such approaches lead to emphasising different psychological elements and different approaches to each of the four areas of research. Thus, with regard to intervention techniques, approaches ranging from training the mind using biofeedback for the psycho-physiologist, to social-facilitation and social reinforcement studies by social-psychological researchers, to approaches looking at causal attributions and self-efficacy by cognitive behavioural researchers, are likely to be used.

Many sport psychology researchers believe that progress in the field has been slow because new conceptual frameworks or models developed within the context of sport and exercise have not been offered. They believe that too great a reliance has been placed on the parent discipline of psychology. However, it appears that the field is moving towards a more integrated and inter-disciplinary approach to examining sport-specific questions and, while not abandoning 'grand theory', is building its own models through which to test such theory. Just as importantly, however, sport and exercise psychology is looking to larger epistemological concerns about what it means to know, and what knowledge is of most worth to the field. Use of a variety of data gathering methods, and interpretive strategies that offer different ways of knowing, is being increasingly encouraged.

The field of psychology of sport and physical activity has been dominated by research conducted in North America. And despite the similarities that exist between sporting cultures in different geographical regions, it is important that research findings from one culture or geographic location are not used to explain sporting behaviours in all other locations. Human behaviour is influenced by the society and culture in which it is located. Therefore, as Biddle has noted, the field needs to take account of the diversity and richness of sporting cultures, and not assume that globalisation will subsume cultural differences.

Further reading: Biddle (1995), Biddle and Mutrie (2006), Cox (1994), Horn (1992), Murphy (1995), Nesti (2006), Vealey (1996), Wann (1997), Weinberg and Gould (1999)

PUBLIC GOODS

Essentially, public goods are those whose benefits can be enjoyed by many people without detriment to each other's enjoyment. In contrast to **private goods**, one person's consumption of a public good does not exclude someone else from also consuming that good or service. An example of such a public good is the 'feelgood' factor engendered by the success of a national sports team. Public goods must not be confused with the idea of the **public sector**.

See also: **private goods**

PUBLIC SCHOOLS

The English public schools were central in the development of modern sport. Many such schools, including Winchester (1382), Eton (1440) and Westminster (1560), have origins that predate the key period of sporting development in the nineteenth century. The public schools, although having always experienced forms of physical recreation such as early cricket and football, were moved to embrace sport in the nineteenth century as a result of a rapid rise in the number of pupils boarding, and the increasing problems of disorder that accompanied the concentration of large numbers of young men in one institution.

The initial origins of sport in these schools lies with the boys rather than the teachers. Eton, Westminster, Winchester and Harrow all began inter-school cricket competitions in the late eighteenth century, and the Eton versus Harrow cricket fixture is the oldest continuous match on the sporting calendar. In the nineteenth century such sporting fixtures rapidly came under the control of the heads and teachers at the schools. Cricket, as a game that was already codified, was central to the growth of sport in the public schools. In the mid-nineteenth century, as increasing numbers of boys were sent to the schools, the expectation of the paying parents was that schools would produce educated gentleman. A central demand was that schools should produce boys of gentlemanly character with strong moral principles. For Thomas Arnold at Rugby School, sport was a way of achieving this goal. He oversaw the organisation of inter-house and inter-school tournaments, all of which were promoted with one eye firmly focused on the ideological message of **athleticism**. The number of sports played by the schools grew, to include football, rugby, rowing, cross-country running and rackets. By the late nineteenth century sport was dominant in many public schools, and was seen as central to the promotion of manliness, morality, health and nationalism. The popularity of sport spread beyond the elite schools, and through the work of old boys and masters, was eventually to be diffused to the universities, the workplace and across the empire.

See also: **athleticism, diffusion, muscular Christianity**

Further reading: Chandler (1996), Honey (1977), Mangan (1981), Money (1997)

PUBLIC SECTOR

The term 'public sector' generally infers the supply of goods and services by local government, central government, or a quasi-governmental agency. The role of the public sector organisations has changed over the last two decades. The initial involvement of the public sector in sport was a product of the post-war creation of a welfare state. There was an assumption that the government had a responsibility to improve the lives of individuals, including the provision of sport facilities and the facilitation of participation opportunities. In the late 1980s the public sector was transformed into a more differentiated network of independent or quasi-autonomous internal units operating with devolved control. The 'new public management', as the operational mode of these organisations became known, involved the introduction of 'market mechanisms', that is private sector operating principles, to the public sector. The principle changes involved an increase in user charges for involvement in sport, the opening up of local authority sport provision and related services to competitive tendering, the creation of internal markets in local authorities, and the devolution of control in which the providers of sport services operate as independent units and compete with each other.

See also: **private sector**

RACISM

Racism has always been a feature of sport. The origins of modern sport, and the initial control of most sporting organisations, lay with white men. The world of the nineteenth century was one where such men believed they were superior, and arenas such as the sporting club or event were their sole preserve. They could not imagine playing sport with women or people from different races. Such separatism was a feature of **imperialism**, and a product of the **public schools** ethic, which instilled a belief in superiority into the sons of empire. It was widely held that black-skinned peoples were inferior, morally corrupt and savage. It was seen as a function of imperialism to civilise the non-white populations of the empire. As well as religion, which was one of the main tools of the 'civilising' process in the empire, sport became increasingly important. Considering how strongly attached the British were to the positive values that were part of the sporting ethos, it is perhaps unsurprising that they should use the same device in the empire. Games such as cricket, most notably in India and the West Indies, were used to bridge the native and imperial populations. Not only did such sporting contact improve relations, it also allowed for the diffusion of British ideals to the native population through sport. Despite such positive goals, however, racism was still rife. When the West Indies began playing test cricket, they were forbidden, until the 1950s, to have a black captain.

Many early sporting clubs or associations explicitly excluded Jews or non-whites from membership, and backed up such bans with scientific argument. In the first half of the twentieth century the racism that existed in sport, as elsewhere in society, was underpinned by the arguments of scientists and geneticists who argued that some races were naturally superior. Such theories were central to the ideological beliefs of the Nazi movement in Germany, yet were also commonly held by many others in Britain, France and America. The 1936 **Olympics** were a showcase for the Aryan ideology of the Nazis, and were supposed to prove the supremacy of the 'Aryan' over other racial types. Such thinking was implicitly racist, and was overturned by the success of the black American Jesse Owens in the sprints.

Racism in sport found its most virulent home in South Africa. During the apartheid years, the whole of South African society was divided along racial lines. As a result, all non-whites were excluded from whites-only sports clubs, and the national representative teams were restricted to selecting their players from the white population. The racist sporting policies of South Africa, and the general abhorrence that was felt towards apartheid, led to a sporting **boycott** of games against South African teams. Beyond the concrete case of racism as part of the apartheid system, many sports analysts have argued that the positions that non-white athletes take in team games are racist. The racial stacking of players into certain positions has led to an overrepresentation of black players as running backs in American football, or as wingers in football. Such positioning was based on the simple assumption, which was reinforced by opportunities afforded by training, that black players were, because of natural ability, quicker than white players. Similarly, the over-concentration of black players in athletic sprints has led to charges that black athletes possess natural attributes that make them faster, whereas white athletes are stronger, therefore more suited to strength events. Racism has existed in other areas of sport, most notably amongst spectators. In the 1970s, as Britain was coming to terms with the impact of new Commonwealth immigration, many black football players began to emerge on the professional stage. These players were often subjected to terrible racist abuse, which was made more threatening by the pervading atmosphere of **hooliganism**. There was also evidence that this ter-race-based racism was linked to the activities of far-right political movements such as the National Front.

In the last two decades 'race' has become an increasingly margin-alised term in academia, and while there is still interest in studying and understanding acts of racism, studies have preferred to focus on the broader theme of **ethnicity**.

See also: **boycotts, ethnicity, politics**

Further reading: Booth (1998), Brooks and Althouse (1993), Coakley (1998), Cronin and Mayall (1998), Hoberman (1997), Jarvie (2006), Long et al. (2005), Polley (1998), Williams (2001)

RATIONALISED

The drawing-up of rules and regulations to control sports and games is symbolic of the nineteenth-century move towards rationalised sports. Games like mob football, and other forms of non-codified sports, which had few rules, no referee or umpire, and no time constraints, are symbolic of the pre-rational period. Once sports, largely as a result of the controls that emerged from the playing fields of the **public schools**, were placed under the control of rules, played for a fixed duration and judged by a referee, they were rationalised. This process distinguishes rationalised sports from uncontrolled pop-ular pastimes. The process of rationalisation was aided by the spread of sports out from the public schools, and through the work of organisations, such as the Football Association, whose job it was to act as custodians of the sport.

Further reading: Brailsford (1992), Holt (1989), Lowerson (1993), Tranter (1998)

RATIONAL RECREATION

The movement for rational recreation developed in the mid-nine-teenth century as a reaction to the rowdy and raucous pastimes of the working classes. Some promotion of the new activities stemmed from a genuine concern for the 'lower orders'; others feared for property and selves if social stability and economic development were disturbed by a continuation of traditional sports in an urban industrial environment. However, instead of simply attempting to suppress traditional sports or curb the excesses associated with them, the new reformists also offered counter-attractions. Drinking-, violent- and animal sports were to be challenged as leisure activities by tea parties, seaside trips, bands, choirs, libraries, museums and educational societies. Health, self-discipline and self-improvement were the keystones of the activities seen as rational and respectable. Although the proponents of **rational recreation** had some success, generally roughness was not replaced by refinement as the advocated moral standards failed to permeate deep into the working class, the majority of whom remained irreligious, intemperate, improvident and unchaste.

Further reading: Vamplew (2005b)

RECREATION

In its literal sense, recreation means 're-creation', reviving the body and mind in preparation for work. The term is often used interchangeably with **leisure**, yet the term 'leisure' is derived from the Latin word meaning 'to be free', while the term recreation is derived from the Latin word meaning 'restoration' or 'recovery'. Recreation implies the restoration of a state of being which some other activity, such as work, undermines. It is often referred to as organised activity for social ends. Thus Cheek and Burch suggest that broadly conceived, recreation is rationalised leisure: it is the routinisation of enjoyment. In a more recent review of definitions of recreation, Kelly has suggested that recreation be conceived of as voluntary non-work activity that is organised for the attainment of personal and social benefits, including restoration and social cohesion.

See also: **leisure, play**

Further reading: Cheek and Burch (1976), Kelly (1996)

REFLECTION THESIS

The reflection thesis is a concept most normally associated with **sociology**, and is one of the three main theoretical approaches in sports sociology that have dominated, along with the **reproduction thesis** and **resistance thesis**, research work in recent decades. The reflection thesis is centred on the idea that sport mirrors, or acts as a microcosm of society. As a result, sport reflects all that is good and bad in human life. The reflection thesis was especially important in the early years of sports sociology, and dominated the period of the late 1960s and early 1970s. As it was based on empirical and descriptive research, the work that emerged from the reflection thesis, although invaluable, was often basic, and relied on an examination of the big themes of the economics and politics of sport.

See also: **sociology, reproduction thesis, resistance thesis**

Further reading: Coakley (1987), Kenyon and Loy (1965), Loy and Kenyon (1969), Loy et al. (1978), McPherson (1975)

REGIONALISM

Regions can be defined by geography, politics and economics. Although British sport at the elite level has focused on inter-town and inter-urban competition, regionalism has played a role via county championships in such sports as rugby union and cricket, and occasional representative fixtures between teams from the North, South, or Midlands. To some extent the North/South divide in British sport is an emotional one in which those inside their usually self-defined region oppose any outside teams.

REGULATION

The debate in Britain over sports regulation has centred on self-regulation on a voluntary basis by the sports authorities versus legally enforceable legislation. Most clubs and associations do not give a voice to the fan, consumer, or even the player, and this may stimulate intervention by the government.

More international an issue is that the economic analysis of team sports raises a number of public policy concerns. A key one is whether government should treat the sports industry as just another industry. In many countries open collusion between the producers in an industry is forbidden, but, in team sports, the authorities often allow anti-competitive practices; in US baseball, for example, the industry receives special exemption from the government's anti-monopoly legislation.

Across the world sporting authorities have introduced many regulations designed to maintain competitive balance. That is, the authorities have taken measures to ensure that on the field competition is not too unequal. It is believed that the greater the **uncertainty of outcome** (match or seasonal) the greater will be the spectator interest, and, hence, the greater the chance of aggregate profit maximisation within the industry. Belief in the uncertainty of outcome idea explains to a large extent why sporting authorities restrict competitive behaviour in a way that would not be possible in 'normal' industries.

To some extent the rules adopted reflect the fact that the sporting league is a **cartel**. Rules are needed in order to maintain 'good practice' and for the league to operate effectively. Thus sporting authorities have to establish playing rules and generate a fixture list. The league may also be required to rule on the selection and employment of players by clubs, and control the number of clubs in a league and their precise location. Sporting leagues also determine rules for the allocation of revenues. But certain restrictions have gone beyond the basic rules for 'good practice'. Most notably, the reserve clause in North American sports and the **retain and transfer** system in English association football, served to restrict the **mobility** of labour and keep down player salaries. Recent application of European law suggests that such special treatment will not be allowed to continue.

See also: **rules**

RELIGION

Religious philosophy and practice has had a significant influence on the character and even the existence of sports in Britain, particularly in the restrictions of the Puritan age and later in the promotion of competitive sport in reaction to the Industrial Revolution.

Religion is defined as a set of beliefs, symbols and practices, which is centred around the idea of the sacred. This serves to unite the followers of any given religion into a socio-religious community. Western society has been dominated by the ideas of Christianity as centred around the established Anglican and Catholic churches. Elsewhere in the world, a host of other religions have dominated, such as Islam. During the late nineteenth century, and into the twentieth century, there was an assumption that belief in religion would wane, and that societies would become **secular**. While this is true of many Western industrialised nations, it is not the whole story. The formal churches have seen a downturn in attendance, but other informal versions of Christianity have proved very popular. Across the world, fundamentalist forms of religions such as Islam have gained in popularity, and have become increasingly powerful politically in the nations of the Middle East and Africa.

The Puritans believed that many traditional sports and games were profane, cruel and immoral. In particular they preached about the importance of hard work and the moral corruption of idle play and violent games. Whilst **recreation** which reinvigorated mind and body was considered legitimate by the Puritans, leisure activities that were regarded as wasteful and irreverent became prime targets for their denunciation. Consequently, many traditional pastimes were either suppressed or radically adapted, whilst sports on Sundays were generally banned. The Puritan philosophy proved an enduring legacy and paved the way for the civilising and modernising process of British sport. It took another century before the struggle against cruel sports, initiated by the Puritans, was completed with the outlawing of the most notorious **animal sports** in the 1830s.

During the early period of the Industrial Revolution, church leaders actively discouraged workers from any participation in sports and games. Emphasising the Puritan work ethic, most continued to preach the importance of hard work in contrast to the corruption of sport and idleness. This attitude of disapproval towards sports participation for the masses only changed when concerns were raised about the physical health of factory workers in the middle of the nineteenth century. In contrast to their traditional condemnation of sports, clerics now became advocates of physical exercise in the interest of good health, higher productivity and subservient manners. A new religious tenet emerged. Generally known as **muscular Christianity**, it asserted the positive connotation of bodily strength and power. It maintained that a strong and healthy body had religious significance, since physical fitness was required to meet the demands of godly work and obedient behaviour. Physical weakness, according to this new doctrine, was associated with moral and spiritual deficiency. By contrast, physical activities and team sports were promoted as a means to foster moral character, good health, gentlemanly behaviour and patriotism.

Organised religion played a major role in the initial development and sustenance of football in particular. Clerics from across the religious spectrum saw football as an important source of moral, spiritual and physical education, and many early clubs were in some way connected to church or chapel. Several professional clubs, including Aston Villa, Barnsley, Bolton Wanderers, Glasgow Celtic and Wolverhampton Wanderers, owe their origins to religious organisations. Although the conflicting demands placed on players by religious obligations (such as attendance at a specific place of worship) and the search for sporting success led to many sides breaking away from the host institution, religious bodies and their offshoots remained major sponsors of the amateur game well into the twentieth century. Nevertheless, the role of religion in influencing sporting activities has declined from the late nineteenth century, when the combined impetus of the Industrial and Darwinian revolutions had produced widespread urbanisation and secularisation in Britain. A prohibition on Sunday sport remained the last bastion of the Church, but this too collapsed as generally the Church has had a lessening influence on all aspects of life in modern Britain.

The promotion of Christianity through sport was also embraced by organisations such as the Young Men's Christian Association (YMCA) and by the Catholic Church for immigrants in many inner-city areas in North America and Europe. Religious groups and organisations have been keen to link the discipline and morality of sport with a belief in, and support for, the Church. At the elite level, many athletes have viewed their religious beliefs as an integral part of their athletic lives. Organisations for Christian elite athletes were first set up in the 1950s. These included the Sports Ambassadors (1952), the Fellowship of Christian Athletes (1954) and Athletes in Action (1966). Since the mid-1970s, every NFL team in the United States has employed a chaplain to minister to the players.

Many sports people have embraced non-Christian religions. In the 1960s, Cassius Clay changed his name to Muhammad Ali when he converted to Islam, and in the 1990s Mike Tyson also converted to Islam. For many elite athletes there is a clear link between their skills in their chosen sport and their religious beliefs.

See also: **muscular Christianity, secular**

Further reading: Higgs (1995), Hoffman (1992), Levine (1992), Mangan and Walvin (1987), Peiser (2000), Prebish (1993)

REPETITION TRAINING

Repetition training is a specialised form of interval training in which the work phase of the training session is as near exhaustive as possible and the recovery phase is lengthened so as to be almost complete. Thus a 400-metre swimmer might undertake two 300-metre swims at full pace but with a full recovery between the two, as opposed to an interval session in which the time between the two would be predetermined and limited.

Further reading: Dick (2002), Pate et al. (1984)

REPRODUCTION THESIS

The reproduction thesis replaced the **reflection thesis** as the major vehicle for studies of sports **sociology**, and dominated the research agenda in the decade from the mid-1970s. The reproduction thesis argued that sport, rather than merely reflecting the dominant themes of society, actively reproduced them. Sport can therefore be understood as a location for the production and reproduction of the social formations and social inequalities that exist within society. The research methodology shifted with the changing theoretical approach, and empirical studies were replaced by analyses of labour patterns, race discrimination and resource availability. Such work demonstrated that inequities in general society, for example between black and white worker salaries, were replicated in the sporting environment.

See also: **reflection thesis**

Further reading: Gruneau (1978), Loy and Segrave (1974), Luschen (1975), Luschen (1980), Snyder and Spreitzer (1974)

RESIDUAL VOLUME

After maximal deep expiration the amount of air that remains in the lungs is labelled the residual volume. In a healthy person this is around 26 per cent of total lung capacity, independent of body position. Between the ages of 25 and 30 the proportion can increase to 30–35 per cent due to increasing thoracic rigidity and a loss of elasticity in the lung tissue.

See also: **stroke volume, tidal volume**

Further reading: Jones and Poole (2004), McMurray (1998)

RESISTANCE THESIS

The resistance thesis has came to dominate the research agenda within sports **sociology** in the period after the mid-1980s, and replaced the **reproduction thesis**. Rather than arguing that sport either mirrored or reproduced themes that were dominant within society, the resistance thesis contended that sport was a site for minority groups to challenge the social order. Research work has examined the use of sport by minority groups, such as those discriminated against on the grounds of race, sex, disability or age. It has demonstrated that these groups use sport to resist the discrimination that they suffer within wider society, and that sport offers an opportunity to excel.

See also: **reproduction thesis**

Further reading: Coakley (1987; 1998), Coakley and Dunning (2000)

RESPIRATORY SYSTEM *see* **anatomy and physiology**

RESTRAINT OF TRADE

It is a fundamental principle of common law that individuals should be allowed to pursue their trade or business without interference. Hence decisions made by governing bodies in sport which affect the livelihood of players and the income of clubs can be challenged as being in restraint of trade. The leagues of many sports, for example, have instituted various restrictions on the labour market within their sport. These have included the **maximum wage** in football until 1961, residential qualifications used in county cricket to restrict player **mobility** until very recently, and **salary caps** currently operating in several British sports. Technically, all these mechanisms are in restraint of trade in that they raise impediments to the employment of individuals that could be against their wishes. The defence in law is how reasonable is the restriction, something usually defined in terms

189

of furthering the interests of all parties and the public interest. In sport the case is argued that labour market controls assist in promoting the **equality of competition**.

A prime example of a restraint of trade process was revealed when Kerry Packer, the Australian media magnate, took the International Cricket Council and the Test Cricket Control Board to the High Court. In 1977, Packer, having failed to secure exclusive rights to televise Australian test cricket, signed thirty-five elite players to participate in a new competition that he called World Series Cricket. The reaction of the ICC and the TCCB was to ban those players from county cricket and all official international cricket. The High Court ruled that these decisions were in restraint of trade as they unreasonably prevented the players from pursuing their living as professional cricketers, particularly as the authorities had never guaranteed the players' future employment, nor stipulated in their contracts that they could not play for a private promoter such as Packer.

See also: **law**

RETAIN AND TRANSFER

The retain and transfer system was a player reservation system, motivated by a desire to ensure competitive balance by reducing the concentration of star players in a few clubs. At the end of each playing season clubs drew up a list of players that they wished to retain and those that were open to transfer. Those to be retained had no option but to stay with the club or they could be excluded from playing at all at the elite level. Those open to offers could not choose which club they wanted to go to; that was a matter of negotiation between the existing employer and any potential employer. That restrictive practice has now been abandoned. Freedom of contract (and the Bosman ruling) allows out-of-contract players to move to another club if they so desire.

RISK MANAGEMENT

Participation in sport and physical activity, at any level, involves a degree of risk, because of the possibility of accident or injury to participants, spectators and property. The application of risk management to sport involves attempts to identify, evaluate and control the risks involved in sports participation as a means to the promotion of health and safety, by the provision of information and advice to ensure that the potential dangers are avoided, or at least arise less frequently, and are of a less serious nature. Those charged with risk management are required to understand the potential dangers of, and legal liability associated with, the use of sporting equipment and facilities, just as they need to understand the law as it relates to participation in sport and physical activity, and as it relates to issues of safety and health.

Further reading: Appenzeller (1998), Goodman and McGregor (1994), Grayson (1999a), Greenfield and Osborn (2000a)

RISK SPORTS *see* adventure sports

RITUAL

Many sport psychologists consider ritual to be a form of intervention technique used by athletes as a means of enhancing exercise and sport performance. One important goal of intervention strategies is to maximise the chances of achieving an ideal performance state or peak performance. Ritual is often seen as a means of focusing attention. And because the rituals that athletes select are those that are connected in their minds with past successes, ritual, like self-talk, is engaged in as a means of intentionally thinking about positive past successes. As such, athletes who employ pre-match rituals are intentionally providing themselves with behaviours that are used to convince them that they are confident, motivated and ready to perform. Ritual becomes a means of both mental preparation and constructive intervention, signifying the beginning of the athletic contest and thus the need to focus on the contest if success is to be achieved. Rituals can range from team activities such as pre-match pep talks, prayers or warm-ups, to individual activities involving the ritual laying out of one's equipment, cleaning of equipment, or listening to specific pieces of music on a personal CD or cassette player.

See also: **superstition**

Further reading: Cashmore (1996), Murphy (1995), Wann (1997)

ROTATION

Rotation or angular motion takes place when a body moves along a circular path about some line in space so that all parts of the body travel through the same angle, in the same direction, in the same time. An example would be a gymnast performing a giant swing on a horizontal bar where the centre of the bar forms the axis around which the body moves in a circular path.

Further reading: Dyson (1986), Hay (1993)

RULES

Sport is a rule-governed practice: constitutive rules, both prescriptive and proscriptive, define required equipment and facilities as well as setting the formal rules of play; auxiliary rules specify and control eligibility both to the sport but more particularly to the event; and regulatory rules such as dress codes place restraints on behaviour independent of the sport itself. Initially, rules tended to be restricted geographically, relating to a game or sport played in a particular locality, but over time the desire for regional, national and international competition led to a codification of rules so that the sport was played everywhere under the same regulations. Rule formulation is a dynamic process and over time rule changes have been influenced by gambling, fair play ideology, economic pressures and legal intervention.

Further reading: Vamplew (2007)

SAFETY

With participation in sport and physical activity, and particularly in contact sports such as rugby and boxing, comes an increased risk of accident and injury. Accordingly, those involved in **sports medicine** have directed much time and attention to increasing efforts to promote safety in sport, not only in regard to appropriate methods of training, but also in the use of equipment, and facilities to better prepare athletes for competition. Athletes who are physically fit and well prepared are less at risk of injury and less likely to incur disability. The safety of spectators has become of major importance in most professional sports, football in particular, following tragedies at Ibrox, Hillsborough and Bradford. The owners of a sports ground have a legal duty to any spectators, whether or not they have paid to watch the game, and in the event of injury on the premises could be liable for damages. Additionally, the Football Licensing Agency – created under the Football Spectators Act of 1989 – is responsible for a certification system to ensure that safety requirements are maintained. With the Health and Safety Executive insisting that organisations offer a safe working environment and the law being willing to step in if spectators are injured, **risk** assessment has become an important part of sports management.

See also: **risk management**

Further reading: Frosdick and Whalley (1997)

SALARY CAP

In many sports, including rugby, ice hockey and basketball, the league authorities have imposed a limit to the total salary bill of individual clubs. The intention is to promote greater **equality of competition** as part of an effort to maintain the viability of the league concerned. Without such a salary cap, it is feared that the wealthier clubs could dominate a competition by attracting the best players with offers of higher wages than those available at other clubs.

See also: **maximum wage**

SCHEMA THEORY

Developed by Richard Schmidt in the mid-1970s as an alternative to Adams' **closed loop** theory and the ideas of peripheral and memory trace as the mechanisms through which we control movement, schema theory could provide an answer to the question, 'how can a person respond to and perform successfully a novel task they have never experienced before?' Schema theory is based on the premise that for any given class of movements, such as throwing, catching, jumping, etc., we develop a schema or set of rules. We abstract these rules from related experiences and construct a schema that will enable us to perform throwing, catching or jumping movements successfully.

Thus a schema is an abstract rule or generalisation used to guide behaviour.

Schmidt has posited that there are four pieces of information that are pertinent to our abstractions. These are: the initial conditions related to the response; the response specifications; the sensory consequences; and the response outcome.

According to Schmidt's conceptualisation, two schemes are critical in controlling movement: a recall schema and a recognition schema. The recall schema sets the parameters necessary in the initiation and production of a movement. The recognition schema continues and terminates a movement, and is used as a means of assessing feedback about a movement. Schmidt's theory suggests that we keep generalised knowledge of movements, such as throwing and catching, stored as schema and then construct our responses to any given movement task based on our recall of similar movements and the recognition feedback we obtain either during or after completing a movement.

Further reading: Magill (1998), Schmidt (1975), Schmidt and Lee (1999)

SECULAR

Religion played a key role in supporting the early development of modern sport. In institutions such as the English **public schools**, the religious ideology that underpinned sporting activity was very important, and crystallised in phrases such as **muscular Christianity**. Such specific developments of a religious basis for sport were underpinned by a society-wide embrace, during the Victorian era, of moralistic Christian living. As a result of this religious ideology, sports were applauded for their constructive and worthwhile values. In the twentieth century, Britain, and many other countries, underwent a process of secularisation. A secular society is one where all kinds of religion, but especially the established religion of the state – in Britain, the Church of England – have become less powerful and important. Britain is now considered a secular state: for most people, religion is not an important or central part of their lives, and the Church of England has little impact on the policies of the government. The secularisation of society can be observed in sport as the ideas of muscular Christianity and the notion that recreation should have worthwhile moral values have all but disappeared. Religion is, for most people, not a part of their sporting lives.

See also: **religion**

Further reading: Holt (1989), Holt and Mason (2000), Polley (1998)

SENIORS' SPORT *see* **ageism, veterans**

SEXISM

Sexism is the term used to denote discrimination, in any aspect of life, which is based on a person's sex. Most countries have laws that legislate against sexual discrimination with respect of employment or access to opportunity. However, sport is often seen as an arena where sexism is still a regular problem.

A common criticism of the sporting world, in terms of sexist attitudes, are the differential rewards that are available to men and women athletes. In tennis for example, the winner of the men's championship at Wimbledon received prize money of £655,000 whereas the women's champion won the lesser amount of £625,000. Such attitudes are also reflected in the media coverage of sport. Men's sports receive far greater coverage than those of women. While every game was shown live on British television during the 2006 men's football World Cup, not a single game in the women's football World Cup was shown live on terrestrial television. A lack of exposure for women's sport means that attendances and the value of sponsorship deals remain low, and there are fewer high profile women role models available for girls.

Although major international sporting bodies such as FIFA and the IOC have rules that oppose sexism, leading figures in sport have often made comments that were construed as sexist. For example, in 2005, Lennart Johansson, the President of UEFA, stated his belief that women's football could be sold to a greater audience given that 'Companies could make use of a sweaty, lovely looking girl playing on the ground, with the rainy weather.' In a similar vein, the President of FIFA, Sepp Blatter, argued in 2004 that women's football needs different sponsors from the men's game and that it needed to attract fashion and cosmetics companies. To do this, he argued that women players should be kitted out in 'more feminine uniforms ... tighter shorts, for example'.

Organisations such as the Womens Sports Foundation in Britain and the United States both work to promote the involvement of women in sport, but also to ensure that sexism is eradicated from the world of sport.

SHAMATEURISM

This term was devised in the late nineteenth century to describe those sportsmen who wished to be paid for their efforts without undergoing the stigma of being labelled as a **professional**. Historically, the home of shamateurism was English county cricket, where liberal 'expenses' and jobs as assistant secretary enabled many amateurs to take home more money than most professional players. Dr W. G. Grace, the famous cricket all-rounder who regularly captained the amateur Gentlemen against the professional Players, was an **amateur** but obtained £1,500 to tour Australia as captain of the English team in 1873/1874 and £3,000 plus expenses eighteen years later, an amount almost equal to that received by the professional members of the touring party in aggregate. Perhaps this money could be considered as reasonable compensation for the employment of a locum and loss of earnings while overseas, but the ethics of an amateur pocketing nearly £1,500 from a testimonial in 1879 and over £9,000 from another in 1895 are questionable. Shamateurism continued well into the twentieth century, but then declined as the need for subterfuge was no longer necessary after a general relaxation of amateur regulations that allowed trust funds to be established for overt earnings from participation and endorsements, from which athletes could draw to meet their expenses and receive the residual on retirement from sport. Moreover as many sports became open and welcomed professionalism, the social stigma attached to being paid to play lessened almost to vanishing point.

Further reading: Vamplew (2005b)

SKELETAL SYSTEM *see* anatomy and physiology

SKILL

The term is generally used in two ways in the sport and physical education literature: (1) as an act or task employed to achieve a specific goal and requiring 'voluntary' movement to be performed. An example might be the taking of a penalty kick in soccer. And (2) as an indicator of the quality of performance such as that of a player who rarely 'misses' a penalty kick. We credit such an effective penalty-taker with having a great deal of skill.

The significant elements of (1) are that a skill has a purpose, that it is performed voluntarily and is not just a reflex action, and that it requires part or whole body movement to be accomplished. Because it requires movement it is termed a motor skill. The significant elements of (2) are that quality of performance (skill) is usually demonstrated by productivity (how often the penalty-taker scores) and/or consistency in a variety of contexts. Thus skill is 'an ability to bring about some end result with maximum certainty and minimum amount of energy' (Guthrie 1952: 136). The term 'skill' is differentiated from the concept of ability, in that ability is a general capacity for skilful behaviour in contrast to the greater specificity of 'skill'.

There have been a number of efforts at classifying motor skills into broader, more general categories, in order to facilitate the application of principles of teaching and learning to skill development in sport and physical activity. These classification systems each employ the concept of a continuum and evaluating skills in terms of that continuum. Thus one classification system uses a gross-fine continuum, where the placement of skills along the continuum is dependent on the precision of the movement and the type of musculature involved. Thus writing would be considered a relatively 'fine' motor skill, whereas throwing the discus would be closer to the 'gross' end of the continuum, because although precision is important in both movements, it is a more important component in writing.

A second classification system uses a discrete-continuous continuum, in which the nature of the beginning and end points of the skill is the salient feature of classification. Thus throwing a ball, which as a skill has a distinct beginning and end, is a discrete skill, whereas running is a continuous task because the beginning and end is not specified by the task but rather is determined by the performer. A third classification system is the open–closed continuum, where the stability of the environment in which the skill is performed is the determining factor. If the environment in which the skill is performed is stable or predictable such as in playing darts, or in shooting basketball free throws, then the skill is considered a 'closed' skill. If the environment is changing, such as in hitting ground strokes in tennis, then the skill is considered a more 'open' skill.

See also: **skill acquisition**

Further reading: Fleishman (1975), Gentile (1972), Guthrie (1952), Magill (1998), Schmidt and Lee (1999), Singer (1980)

SKILL ACQUISITION

Acquiring the ability to perform motor skills or tasks requires practice. To acquire and perform such complex skills as running, jumping, catching and throwing requires the integration of sensory and motor information. Learning such skills appears to take place in stages, as learners move along a continuum from novice to expert. Fitts and Posner proposed a three-stage model of skill acquisition. In the first or cognitive stage, the learner must understand the goal of the motor skill, and the movements and strategies necessary to accomplish that goal. This stage is marked by a large number of errors in performance; often gross errors such as 'missing' the ball in golf or tennis. In the second or associative stage, movements become more precise, errors fewer and less gross in nature. Learners begin to identify some of their own errors, as movements become more integrated and smooth, and limited motor programmes are developed. Motor programmes may be thought of as blueprints or pre-conceived plans for a motor act. The final or autonomous stage, in which the skill has become almost automatic, requiring minimal attention, is thought to be the result of the development of enhanced and better-integrated motor programmes. It is the changes in movement efficiency between novice and expert, between the cognitive and autonomous stages, and the apparent effortlessness of the highly competent performer, that distinguishes the skilled athlete.

See also: **skill**

Further reading: Fitts and Posner (1967), Magill (1998), Schmidt and Lee (1999)

SOCIAL BEHAVIOUR

With very few exceptions, sport is a social activity; participating involves some form of social interaction. As such, many of the concerns of social psychologists regarding social behaviour are of interest to sport psychologists. Answers to such questions as 'How is our behaviour and performance influenced by those around us?', 'How do we explain success and failure to ourselves and others?' and 'What makes a good team or a good team member?' are central to our understanding of social behaviour in sport. Sport psychology research suggests a number of answers to these questions. In looking at how our behaviour is affected by those around us, researchers have argued that the presence of an audience (social facilitation) leads to **arousal** which, in turn, leads to the dominant response. Thus for skilled athletes the dominant response is likely to be success, and therefore they are likely to perform better in front of an audience than are unskilled athletes, for whom increased arousal will inhibit performance. However, audiences can be both supportive (home crowd) or disruptive (away crowd) and thus lead to different levels of arousal.

Second, in assessing their own and others' success and failure, athletes adopt a range of behaviours in their desire to present themselves to others in a positive manner. As such, athletes may carefully select the activities, the teams and the settings in which they are willing to perform, in order to ensure that their self-presentation is positive and their concerns over impression management are addressed.

Finally, several factors seem to influence team dynamics, including team size, team homogeneity, feelings of cohesiveness and degree of stability of membership. The continued interaction between social psychology and sport psychology promises further advances in our understanding of social behaviour in sport.

Further reading: Goffman (1961), Kremer and Scully (1996), Wann (1997), Zajonc and Sales (1966)

SOCIAL CAPITAL

The use of the term social capital is a way of conceptualising the intangible resources of a community or group such as its shared values, the trusted relationships within the collective, and the personal networks that are drawn upon. A major example in sport would be the club and the interaction between its members. What needs to be considered is whether in community terms the sports club acts as (exclusive) bonding capital rather than as (inclusive) bridging capital. Are the groups formed not just of people interested in a particular sport but of persons of like minds, from the same social class and neighbourhood or are others reached out to from different gender, religion and social status? Another issue to be looked at is whether the positive aspects of social capital in the form of associational engagement (mutual support, co-operation, trust and institutional effectiveness) outweigh the negative ones including sectarianism, sexism and class discrimination.

Further reading: Field (2003), Hughson et al. (2005)

SOCIOLOGY

Sociology is a discipline of the social sciences, and can be best understood as the study of society or social membership. The foundations of sociology lie with Karl Marx, Émile Durkheim and Max Weber, who all raised fundamental questions about the nature of society, questions that remain at the heart of the subject. Sociology took off as a subject for university study in the post-war years, and was transformed into a series of sub-disciplines such as the sociology of medicine, the sociology of the family, the sociology of gender, and the sociology of sport. As a result of the wide range of approaches and topics, no definition of the concept is ever satisfactory. Sociology has been an important intellectual force, and has contributed much to our understanding of society. In both its empirical and theoretical forms, the subject has raised questions about the nature of individual responsibility, has contributed to work in other related fields such as history, philosophy and economics, and has often been central in defining the nature of post-industrial society.

Sports sociology emerged as a discrete sub-discipline in the 1960s, and aimed to understand the role of sport in social and cultural life through the application of sociological methodology. It was driven by a recognition that 'sport and physical education are social practices and that they are culturally and historically relative' (Coakley and Dunning 2000: xxi). Sports sociology has been dominated, though not entirely, by studies of organised and competitive sports that are both rational and institutionalised. Sports sociology has sought to understand two main areas of activity: the historical and the contemporary. The former has focused on the sociological origins and functions of sport, while the latter has examined, amongst others, pressing topics such as power structures, subcultures, violence and race.

The academic and institutional development of sports sociology took place predominantly in the United States, but has since spread across the world. The subject now has three major journals: *International Review for the Sociology of Sport, Journal of Sport and Social Issues*, and the *Sociology of Sport Journal*. There are sports sociology societies in North America, Britain, Europe and Australia, and conferences are regularly held. The field of sports sociology has been one that has created many controversies between differing theoretical approaches. The major theoretical approaches have included **functionalism**, **conflict theory**, **critical theory**, and **figurational theory**. Each approach has its own supporters and literatures, and all have focused on a wide variety of sporting types and themes.

Further reading: Coakley (1998), Coakley and Dunning (2000), Guttmann (2004)

SPECIALISATION

Three major forms of specialisation have developed in sport. First is that of role specialisation, in which specific tasks are allocated to players so that one might be a goalkeeper, another striker, positions often determined by a player's physical attributes. In effect, **modern sport** has adopted the economic concept of the division of labour. Historically there were more all-rounders in sports – players good enough, for example, to be chosen for both their batting and bowling in cricket – and more sportsmen that excelled at the elite level in several sports. The demands of modern sport at the top level have generally forced talented players to specialise in one sport and in one aspect of that sport. Second, there has been a specialisation of events so that only standard distances and formats are universally accepted for purposes of record achievements. In 1952 the International Amateur Athletics Federation recognised 64 events; by 1991 this had been reduced to 25. The mile is now the only remaining imperial distance over which official world records are ratified; everything else is metric. Third, there has been the specialisation of land use with the dedication of facilities for specific purposes rather than multi-use. Even within a sport, segmentation has occurred, as in athletics where the use of lanes was introduced for races of over 100 metres, and field events were banished from track areas.

Contemporary sports performers are rarely all-rounders who can excel at a wide range of sports. They have usually chosen to concentrate, and often from a young age, on a particular sport. This decision is one driven by the need to choose a specialisation. By specialising in a given sport, the athlete can tailor their training, select coaches, equipment and diets, specifically to bring out the best in them. Specialisation is a product of the development of modern sport, and the accompanying demands of professionalism and intense media monitoring of performance. Specialisation is not solely about the choice of sport, but is also concerned with a particular position on the field of play, or style of play and approach in individual sports. Particular positions, it is argued, have specialised skills and responsibilities that are best suited to a specific type of player. Specialised equipment, such as gloves for a cricket wicket-keeper, or types of club for a golfer, are also products of the ever increasing level of specialisation in sport.

See also: **Corinthians, modern sport**

Further reading: Bale (1992), Coakley (1998), Guttmann (2004)

SPECIAL OLYMPICS

Founded in 1968 by Eunice Kennedy Shriver, Special Olympics is a year-round sports training and competitive athletic programme for children and adults with mental retardation. In the early 1960s, Eunice Shriver started a day camp at her home in Rockville, Maryland, for people with mental retardation, a group which at that time had the greatest set of unmet needs in the US healthcare system, and quickly discovered that these individuals were capable of participating and achieving in sports and physical activities at levels beyond those that many experts thought possible or even appropriate. Mrs Shriver helped organise the First International Special Olympics in Chicago in 1968. The Special Olympics has grown rapidly and from its beginnings in the United States, now has accredited programmes in almost 150 countries around the world.

Special Olympics UK was founded in 1978 and is one of the largest Special Olympics programmes outside the US. It is the largest volunteer programme in the UK, with over half a million people involved. It is also the UK's largest sports charity for people with learning disabilities, providing year-round sports training in 24 different Olympic-type sports ranging from alpine skiing to volleyball, for athletes of all ages and all abilities. Corporate sponsorship has facilitated the development of Special Olympics. It differs from the Paralympics in that it is authorised to use the word 'Olympics' even though, unlike the Paralympics, it is for people of all abilities and not just elite level athletes.

The Special Olympics Oath is 'Let me win. But, if I cannot win, let me be brave in the attempt.'

Further reading: Klein et al. (1993)

SPEED

Simply defined, speed is distance travelled in a specific amount of time. It is an average since it does not take account of variations of speed over the entire period, and thus is expressed as distance divided by time. For human beings an average walking speed is about three miles per hour, and an average jogging speed about six miles per hour, while high level athletes can typically sprint at about 22 miles per hour over 200 metres. While resistance training and plyometric exercises are often used, speed cannot be greatly enhanced through training but by the same token nor does it decline substantially through detraining, but rather as a product of ageing. Speed or swiftness of motion is a significant component of many sports. Arm speed is an important attribute for fast bowlers in cricket and pitchers in baseball just as leg speed is an important attribute for almost all field games since speed is so difficult to defend against. Speed plays a significant role in human culture as exemplified in the Olympic motto, 'citius, altius, fortius', (Faster, Higher, Stronger). The 100 metres is often referred to as the 'blue ribbon' event of the Olympics and touted as identifying the world's fastest human. In fact our fascination with all speed records (human, animal, and machine) is indicative of the importance of speed as a cultural phenomenon.

SPONSORSHIP

Sponsorship involves a commercial decision to provide funds in cash or kind to a sports organisation or player in return for securing publicity and product awareness. In the nineteenth century, race meetings often featured races sponsored by local innkeepers and tradesmen who stood to benefit from an influx of visitors to the area. Modern sponsorship of horse racing developed from the 1950s when Whitbread brewers, Hennessey distillers and others in the alcohol trade began to fund major races. Today, as in many sports, sponsorship is indispensable to the racing industry, with jockeys, horses, courses and races all receiving this form of financial assistance. The

Institute of Sports Sponsorship estimates the sponsorship sums involved in all British sport at the end of the twentieth century as over £300 million, a significant rise from £2.2 million in 1971. Obviously sports equipment and apparel manufacturers use sports sponsorship as a means of bringing their products to the attention of potential consumers in the sports marketplace, but many other non-sport companies also have become involved in sports sponsorship. Although examples can be found from most industries, two major business groups have participated, the financial sector and the tobacco and drinks trade. Sponsorship of a team, and particularly an event, can be beneficial when television is involved. Indeed, the acceleration of sponsorship deals paralleled the growth of commercial television and of **advertising** generally from the 1950s. In return for the money, the host sport or club will be expected to advertise the product or service of the sponsors on their kit or around the ground, perhaps utilise their name in the title of the competition, team or stadium, and players might be expected to attend corporate functions. Sponsorship, however, occurs at more than the elite level of sport, and many local teams obtain sponsorship from local shops or tradesman. Sport is the chosen vehicle for sponsorship because of the numbers of adherents it has, but also because many sports are associated with a positive, healthy image. Yet there is a suspicion that sometimes sponsorship occurs because a businessman wants to be a 'super fan'; then it becomes more an expensive executive toy than effective advertising. Sport has embraced sponsorship because it can help pay for enhanced facilities, better players and improved teams, all of which can bring success. The major criticisms of the enhanced role of sponsorship in funding British sport are that it has led to changes in rules, style of play and playing costumes at the behest of the sponsor and that, via television, it caters for an audience deemed incapable of grasping the finer points of the game. Then there is the issue of whether alcohol and tobacco companies should be involved in sport, given the health hazards of their products. At the elite level, sports sponsorship has become a sophisticated marketing exercise involving both the commercial sponsor and the television broadcaster. The sports association gains an additional source of finance, and the sponsors hope to gain a return for their spending via the exposure of their name and product through the print and electronic media.

See also: **advertising**

Further reading: Polley (1998)

SPORT

A definition of sport as a structured, goal-oriented, competitive, contest-based, ludic, physical activity embraces most activities generally recognised as sports. It is located on the continuum between play and work. Most sports are played in a limited, defined space designed specifically for that activity, and take place within a prescribed timeframe. Many of them are governed by bodies that set the **rules**, goals, and the criteria by which success and failure can be judged. Sporting competition is of three forms: 'direct', in which opponents confront each other; 'parallel', in which opponents take turns or compete in separate areas; and 'attainment', where the target is a standard which has to be achieved. Unlike in **play**, where there is little regard for victory, sport places substantial emphasis on winning. 'Contest-based' infers a demonstration of superiority via relative speed, endurance, strength, accuracy or coordination. Although the physical is an essential part of sport, strategy is also commonly involved, but in varying degrees, outcomes can be influenced by chance. Those playing sport can receive **intrinsic** and **extrinsic** rewards; the more the rewards are extrinsic, the more sport becomes work in the sense of being instrumental rather than consumption. An interesting view of sport is to regard it as about achieving certain ends often using ineffective means, for in all sports artificial difficulties are introduced to allow the participants to test their skills and abilities to overcome them. Thus football has an offside rule, without which the objective of scoring goals would be more easily attained, and golf limits the number and type of club that can be used to propel a ball that is restricted in size and composition.

SPORT EDUCATION

Teachers involved in sport education attempt to use sport positively to present children with challenging and enjoyable sporting experiences. Sometimes it is associated with games played under modified rules in which skills and ethical behaviour is encouraged ahead of competitive performance. This model of physical education design was popularised in the United States and Australia and more recently has increased in prominence in the United Kingdom. Although some physical educationalists see it as a potential threat with a concern that the competition inherent in most sport might come to dominate, proponents of sport education want to ensure that the overriding educational aim is to provide all children with the opportunity to develop skills, understanding and a sense of worth as a participant in sport. Others take this further and offer students an array of roles ensuring that they also become skilled and knowledgeable as captains, coaches, managers and even match reporters. Hopefully they will also become more educated as sports spectators and critical consumers of the sports media. Ideally, although often separate from physical education in the school curriculum, it should reinforce the educational values of that discipline.

Further reading: Penney et al. (2005), Siedentop (1994)

SPORT FOR ALL

In 1972, the **Sports Council**, Scottish Sports Council and Sports Council for Wales all launched the **Sport for All** campaign. The aim was to promote, across the United Kingdom, wider public awareness of the value of sport and physical fitness. The message of **Sport for All** was a dual one: sport as part of everyone's life, and access to sport for disadvantaged or marginalised groups such as women, the disabled or the economically deprived. In addition to increasing active participation in sport, the campaign also sought to improve facilities across the country. During the lifetime of the campaign, most city, town and county councils sought to either improve existing sports and leisure facilities or build new ones.

SPORTING ASSOCIATIONS

As many Western nations have not, until recent decades, extolled the virtues of a clearly laid out policy plan for sport in their country, there has always been a plethora of different sporting associations that have effectively functioned as pressure groups in an attempt to shape government policy. In Britain, such groups have included the National Playing Fields Association (NPFA), the Central Council for Physical Recreation (CCPR), the Youth Sport Trust and a host of others covering issues such as women in sport, access for the disabled and equality for lesbians and gays. The NPFA was founded in 1925. As a charity, its aim was to protect playing fields and other open spaces that could be used for sporting and recreational activities. In 1935, George V presented 500 fields to the nation to mark his Silver

Jubilee, all of which are still administered by the NPFA. The association is currently the largest charity involved in the promotion of recreation and the protection of playing fields in the country. It actively campaigns at both the local council and central government level, and is heavily involved with securing and protecting sports spaces within the inner cities. The CCPR was formed in 1934, and was brought together by experts in the fields of health, education and sport to promote the playing of sport as a method of securing good health. In the post-war years the CCPR established national training centres for various sports across Britain, such as Crystal Palace in 1964 and the National Sports Centre for Wales in 1972. With the founding of the Sports Council, the CCPR redefined its role, and now functions as a body which lobbies and consults national government in relation to the framing of national sporting policy.

In addition to those associations that were established specifically to lobby government and protect or promote specific concerns, sporting bodies have also long been involved with the process of government and **politics**. In addition to drawing up rules, arranging fixtures and administering their own games, sporting associations and federations have had to maintain relationships with government. Often such relationships relate to central government funding for new facilities or the advance of new talent, but on other occasions they revolve around specific political issues. The Football Association in England has been heavily involved in lobbying the government over matters relating to crowd safety and hooliganism. In the 1930s, the MCC was called to account by both the British and Australian governments in response to the arguments caused by the 'bodyline' test series. In recent years, all British sporting associations and federations have become more politically astute and organised as they have had to lobby both central government and the Charities Commission for access to money from the **National Lottery**. It is therefore important to recognise the history, and current practice of those people and organisations charged with running sport in the widest context. Their function is not solely to run sport, but also to lobby for and to protect sport.

Further reading: Allison (1993), Coghlan (1990), Evans (1974), Houlihan (1991)

SPORTING CONDUCT

Sporting conduct is becoming the more modern phrase for **fair play** but can be regarded also as the process by which fair play aims are achieved. Hence it encompasses such things as the education of coaches, officials, and administrators with respect to expected standards of conduct within a sport; codes of conduct themselves; the promotion of respect, trust and honesty; rewards for appropriate behaviour; knowledge of both the written and unwritten rules; and the use of high performance athletes as role models.

See also: **fair play, sporting deviance**

Further reading: Vamplew and Dimeo (2004)

SPORTING DEVIANCE

In many respects sporting deviance is the antithesis to **fair play** or **sporting conduct** as it encompasses such activities as abuse of opponents, officials and equipment, verbal and physical intimidation, the taking of performance-enhancing drugs, gamesmanship, racial abuse and sexual disparagement, and disregard for the ethics of a particular sport. It can also cover spectator disorder and the inappropriate coaching of children and young people, However, it can be broadened to include behaviour of sportspersons outside their sporting life such as sexual misconduct, the use of recreational drugs, and alcohol-fuelled aggression and violence.

Further reading: Blackshaw and Crabbe (2004), Vamplew and Dimeo (2004)

SPORTING HEROES

For many people one of the great attractions of sport is that it creates heroes. Skilful performances, daring shots, being the successful underdog or battling through against injury, have, amongst a range of other factors, all served to create heroes. The **media** have played an instrumental role in the creation of heroes. From the first reports of sport within the pages of newspapers, through radio and **television**, the media has been at the forefront of the creation of sporting heroes and villains. Not only did sporting heroes add an extra dimension to the report of a match or event, the focus on someone who was idolised undoubtedly added to circulation, listening or viewing figures.

The first sporting heroes emerged in eighteenth-century Britain. Men such as Sam Chifney, the jockey, or Jack Broughton, the pugilist, became widely known and idolised for their sporting exploits. In the nineteenth century, and during the slow but steady development of modern sport, the **amateur** reigned supreme as the ideal sporting hero. In the Victorian era it was not solely that some-one played skilfully or bravely enough to be considered heroic, it was the manner in which they conducted themselves and what they represented that was all-important. Amateurs who combined manly attributes with gentlemanly conduct, supreme athletes who could take defeat well, and those who played solely for the love, and good of the game, echoed attributes that were applauded across wider Victorian society.

The more sport that took place, the more opportunities there were for the creation of heroes. Some heroes were only important so long as they were still active; others entered the **collective memory** and became central to the national sporting story. All events, whether national, such as the FA Cup final or the Grand National, or global as in the case of the Olympics, presented the public and the media with new heroes. With the advent of the sporting **professional**, the nature of the hero was transformed. Increasingly the hero was evident not solely on the field of play, but on advertising billboards, in the newspaper gossip columns and on film. In Britain the first such sporting hero was Dennis Compton, whose fame was added to by his skill on both the cricket field and the football pitch. Professional sportsmen and women, especially in team sports, were often only recognised as heroes in their local area. While many followers of football might recognise Jackie Milburn as a great player, it is doubtful that he would be recognised by many as a national hero. In the northeast of England however, Milburn's status as hero is unquestioned. The fascination with 'home grown' sporting talent is interesting, as it offers a different pathway for the sporting hero. Footballer Steve Bull never played in the Premier League, was selec-ted for England on only a handful of occasions, yet in his native Wolverhampton possesses the status of a living God. Bull undoubt-edly made a good living from his professional career, but his localised heroic status demonstrates the subjective nature of the sporting hero. Muhammad Ali, Mark Spitz, Jack Nicklaus or Ayrton Senna would be considered by many as global sporting heroes; others would dis-agree with that list and suggest their own. This subjectivity and the contest between the local, national and global, make any concise definition of the sporting hero difficult.

From the 1960s, the tabloid press, assisted by television and the increased interest with the celebrity, created a whole new generation of heroes. Appearances on chat shows, in films, at fashion shoots and society parties have become the norm for many contemporary sporting heroes. The ever increasing salaries paid to top sports performers serve to blur the line between hero and celebrity. The demands of fame, and the pressures of expectation that are placed on any new or aspiring hero have produced sad tales of personal excess and outlandish behaviour. George Best, Paul Gascoigne and Eric Cantona are all examples of heroes who have, in one way or another, lashed out against the expectations put upon them to conform to the ideals of the sporting hero. Time will tell whether any of the current crop of sporting heroes, be they David Beckham or Steve Redgrave, are still referred to that way in years to come, but any such judgement will have to take into account a range of issues about their lives, beyond their athletic performance.

See also: **collective memory, media**

Further reading: Duncanson and Collies (1992), Holt et al. (1996), Huntington-Whiteley (1998)

SPORT SCIENCE

By studying responses to exercise and sport, we learn about the normal function of the tissues and organs whose very functioning allows exercise to be performed. The genetic endowment of elite athletes is a major factor in their success, and they represent one end of the continuum of human performance capability. With this population, **sport science** becomes a study in the possibilities of human performance, because nowhere else do we subject the human body to such levels of intensive exercise and training on such a regular basis. The information gleaned from such study can be used in a number of ways. We can use such information to identify potential sporting talent, as has been done in Eastern Europe, Australia and elsewhere. We can also use such information for medical purposes, since we know that lack of physical activity is a major risk factor for many of the diseases that affect people in much of the world. An understanding of the body's response to exercise is therefore vital both physiologically and psychologically.

Further reading: Elliott (1998), Rogozkin and Maughan (1996)

SPORTSMANSHIP

A player who exhibits sportsmanship epitomises the best aspects of fair play. Such players obey not only the rules of the game, but also adopt a code of playing within the unwritten ones which ordain social conduct and the **etiquette** of the game. Hence footballers would not score a goal while an opposition defender was lying injured on the ground; a batsman in cricket would walk before the umpire's decision if he knew that he had hit the ball for a catch; and a yachtsman would abandon a race to rescue an opponent who had capsized. Such behaviour is admired rather than required. These days it would be more appropriate to refer to sportspersonship.

See also: **fair play, sporting conduct**

SPORTS MEDICINE

The branch of medical care that is concerned with the effects of exercise and sport on the human, and focuses specifically on the diagnosis, treatment and prevention of illness and injury associated with participation in sport and physical activity (Strauss 1984). Founded in 1928, the International Federation of Sports Medicine was the first organisation to address the various concerns of those responsible for the well-being of athletes. The American College of Sports Medicine, founded in 1954, has since become the major force in professionalising the field of sports medicine. The aim of all those involved in sports medicine has been to help athletes optimise their performance whilst minimising danger and risk of illness or injury.

Sports medicine typically encompasses four major areas of expertise: the preparation of an athlete; prevention of injury or illness; diagnosis and treatment of injury; and rehabilitation. Preparation of an athlete involves both physical and psychological readiness. Thus both physical conditioning, designed by exercise physiologists to develop appropriate strength, flexibility, speed and endurance; and psychological conditioning, involving mental preparation such as mental imaging and stress reduction techniques developed by sport psychologists, are now widely employed in the preparation of athletes.

Prevention of injury or illness has become an increasingly significant aspect of sport, as maintaining the health and well-being of highly paid professional athletes, who represent a significant investment for professional teams, has become a high priority. Concern over injury and illness prevention has fostered developments in **protective equipment**, such as the wearing of helmets in cricket, but has also led to discussions about brain damage from heading a football, and more significantly to concern about brain damage in boxing, all of which has helped fuel the current **boxing debate**. As part of the concern for an athlete's well-being, sports nutrition has also become an important area of sports medicine: Issues of what to eat and drink, and when, in order to optimise performance and minimise risk of illness and injury, are the concern of these experts.

The diagnosis and treatment of injuries is typically conducted by teams of medical personnel including physicians, athletic trainers and sports physiotherapists. While common injuries include sprains and pulls, cuts and bruises, fractures and dislocations, it is in the areas of soft tissue injuries, and torn or pulled tendons and ligaments, particularly in the knee and shoulder, that sports medicine has made the greatest advances. The development of increasingly sophisticated technology, such as computerised tomography (CT) scans, magnetic resonance imagery (MRI) and arthroscopic surgery, has enabled physicians to diagnose and treat such injuries far more effectively than in the past. In dealing with soft tissue injuries, a variety of therapeutic modalities are now used, including heat and ice, electrical stimulation and various anti-inflammatory drugs, steroids or enzymes. The use of **drugs** has also become part of the preparation of athletes. Substances such as **anabolic steroids** and amphetamines have led to a variety of controversies about **drug testing** and drug abuse. And as athletes have sought ways of enhancing their performance, the pharmacological aspects of performance enhancement have presented increasing problems for both athletes and sports medicine experts alike.

See also: **drugs, health**

Further reading: Berryman (1995), Berryman and Park (1992), Grayson (1999b), Hackney and Wallace (1999), Harries (1996), Narvani et al. (2006), Strauss (1984), Waddington (2000)

SPREAD BETTING

A form of gambling that has caught on in the past decade, spread betting differs from conventional betting in that winnings are not calculated in fixed odds, and losses can be many times the stake placed. A spread betting firm will create an index for a sporting event, e.g. the total runs scored in a cricket match, and then forecast a range within which it expects the aggregate to fall. This is called the spread. In this example it might be between 505 and 520 runs. If punters believe that the forecast is too high they 'sell' at 505, and if too low then they 'buy' at 520. Alternative terminology is to place a 'down' or 'up' bet. Winnings or losses are then determined by how far the actuality differs from the forecast. If the total runs came to 495 then those who sold would win their stake multiplied by ten (505–495) but those who bought would lose their stake multiplied by twenty-five (520–495). If the aggregate falls within the forecast range then the bookmaker wins from both those who sold and those who bought, hence accurate forecasting is of prime importance.

See also: **gambling**

STANDARDISATION

Bale has identified four major forms of **standardisation** in modern athletics. First, he sees standardisation of distances so that, for example, the steeplechase is now always over 3,000 metres. Second is the standardisation of the size and orientation of track and field space. Third is the standardisation of criteria for victory so that stopwatch and tape measure have totally replaced style. Not until the mid-1970s did Britain abandon a style prize in its annual walking championships. Finally there has been standardisation of micro-topology in an effort to reduce variations in – and neutralise the effects of – the natural environment. In pre-modern sport, running, jumping and throwing took place on roads, commons and fields, all of which could vary between venues. Now starting blocks and synthetic surfaces offset such differences. To a degree all of these kinds of example can be found elsewhere in modern sport.

Further reading: Bale (1993a)

STATE SCHOOLS

In the context of the United Kingdom this term refers to schools funded wholly by the public exchequer. This funding is normally made available through the local education authority in which the school is situated, or in the case of grant maintained schools, directly from central government. Entry to such schools is open to all young people between the ages of five and sixteen years, although in practice this extends to students up to the age of eighteen years who wish to continue their education. State schools (first known as Board Schools until the 1902 Education Act when school boards were abolished and control was transferred to county councils) were first created as a result of the (Forster) Education Act of 1870.

Many other countries use the term 'public school' when referring to state schools and this is sometimes a source of confusion when referring to the UK, where **'public schools'** are in fact independent schools, funded by endowment and student fees. The term public schools derives from the fact that some of the older foundations such as Winchester and Eton were founded for poor scholars and in theory they are open to any boy provided he wins a scholarship to cover the cost of fees.

See also: **public schools**

STRATEGY FOR SPORT

Published in 2000, the Labour Government's 'Strategy for Sport' offered a major shake-up of school sport. It included the provision of 300 multi-purpose sports and arts facilities for primary schools at a cost of £150 million, **National Lottery** sports awards worth £50 million being earmarked for youth projects, further development of club/school links, and the employment of 600 sports coordinators to develop competitive inter-school sport. The strengthening of the links between schools, clubs and governing bodies was a central feature, though some critics feared that this would accentuate the move away from schools as being the traditional identifier and developer of young sporting talent. Other criticisms included the failure to insist on more than two hours a week being devoted to sport and physical exercise in the **National Curriculum** and a reluctance to halt the sales of school playing fields. In 2002 'Game Plan', a report from the Prime Minister's Strategy Unit, set out the necessary components for a 'strategy for delivering the Government's sport and physical activity objectives' which included recommendations on developing the United Kingdom's sport and physical activity culture; enhancing the nation's international success; improving the approach to mega events and major sporting facilities; and improving the organizational structures for delivering sport and physical activity.

See also: **government policy**

Further reading: Department of Culture, Media and Sport (2004)

STRIKES AND INDUSTRIAL DISPUTES

Players and administrators may work for the same club and wish it to be successful on the field of play. Nevertheless, not all their objectives and ambitions may coincide. The former may want to be paid their **economic rent**, whereas the administrators may pay more attention to balancing the books. Sometimes the dispute may be with the controlling association rather than with the employing club on matters that affect the labour force as a whole rather than one club or team in particular. Disputes in British sport have generally been of the flashpoint variety. Instances of jockeys refusing to ride at a particular meeting because they felt conditions were dangerous, or players not turning out because they had not been paid are more common than any premeditated national campaign by a sports union, such as the threat of the Professional Footballers' Association to hold national strikes over the **maximum wage** and the **retain and transfer** system prior to the First World War, and over the distribution of television revenues in the 1990s. In the United States whole seasons have been disrupted by industrial action.

See also: **unionism**

STROKE VOLUME

This is a measure of cardiac output, basically of the amount of blood pumped out of the heart with each beat. It is controlled by a combination of hormones, the nervous system, and the amount of blood returning to the heart. During exercise the muscle pump also helps to maintain stroke volume which can increase up to twofold. In a normal healthy heart the stroke volume is the same for both sides of the heart, about 70 ml.

See also: **residual volume, tidal volume**

Further reading: Jones and Poole (2004), McMurray (1998)

STRUCTURALISM

Experts in a variety of fields of study have taken a structuralist approach in their work, although it has most often been favoured by those working in the field of literary criticism. Structuralism has its origins in the work of Ferdinand de Saussure, and his Course in General Linguistics, first published in 1916. The essence of the theory is that all language can be understood and analysed as a structural system of relationships. In this approach, meaning emerges from the relationship of the structural system of language, not from the definitions of the words themselves. Structuralism is therefore an attempt, driven by the ideas of objective science, to place all linguistic and social relations within an objective setting. The approach has been challenged by the post-structuralists, who have argued against the strict methodological framework imposed by structuralism.

See also: **post-modernism, sociology**

Further reading: Attridge et al. (1987), Clarke (1981)

SUBSIDISATION

Most commonly, subsidisation infers grants from government or quasi-government bodies to **finance** activities that are considered to be of value to the community, but which without the subsidy either could not be afforded or would operate on a lesser scale. In the nineteenth century, rifle clubs received government funding as they were regarded as useful training institutions for national defence. Today subsidies are made for purposes of national prestige (via payments to enable elite athletes to prepare for international competitions) and social well-being (through part-funding of club premises). Nevertheless until recently both central and local government subsidisation of sport in Britain has lagged behind that of most other European countries, although, since the mid-1990s, the **National Lottery** has been used indirectly by the government as a means of subsidising sporting activities without resort to taxation.

Within clubs or associations, cross-subsidisation occurs when the profits from one activity are used to underwrite financial shortfalls elsewhere in the organisation. Many football clubs use their **merchandising** income to pay playing staff whose wages could not be afforded from gate money alone. Without the redistribution of test match and one-day international cricket revenue, most county cricket teams would be in the red.

SUPERSTITION

Although generally the most skilled or determined participant will triumph, occasionally luck can also have a role in determining the winner of a game. Indeed, getting the 'rub of the green' has entered both sporting terminology and idiomatic language. This has led some players to adopt superstitions to secure good luck or prevent bad luck affecting their performance. Some like to have their set place in the dressing room, put certain equipment or garments on first, and enter the playing area in a particular order. Others will wear charms and talismans, eat the same meal before playing, or have a certain routine that must be followed. There is no evidence that any of these super-stitions influence luck, but they may assist the athlete psychologically to be in the right frame of mind to perform.

While there is unlikely to be any physical advantage to such behaviour, sport psychologists point to the psychological effect that such behaviours can bring to an athlete. First, athletes tend to go back to behaviours which have been connected with athletic success in the past, or which they believe will prevent them from having bad luck in the future. Superstitious behaviours are a means of trying to control, or at least limit, the element of luck or chance in the out-come. In terms of attributions, superstitious athletes are trying to attribute positive outcomes that can be thought of as being the result of chance or luck to their own superstitious behaviours. As such, they are attempting to gain some control over this attribute of sporting outcome.

Second, many athletes have noted that superstitious behaviours, like individual **rituals**, are means of controlling pre-contest anxiety and giving the athlete something specific to focus on over which they have some control. In some cases, the superstition is used as a means of focusing and elevating arousal, while in others it is viewed as a means of dissipating anxiety and helping to relax the athlete. As such, superstitions and rituals are individual-specific, but may also show similarities among athletes in specific sports. Thus, while for a particular cricketer having to 'pat the crease' five times before look-ing up to face the bowler may be an individual superstition, it is a widely held superstition amongst many cricketers that the score 111

217

(the 'Nelson') is unlucky, and members of the batting side in the dressing room lift their feet off the ground to counteract the negative influence.

See also: **psychology, rituals**

Further reading: Neil (1982), Wann (1997)

SUPPLY

Sport in Britain is supplied by the **public sector**, the voluntary sector and the commercial sector. Government encourages sport to improve the nation's health via mass participation, but also for a 'feelgood' factor from success at the elite level. That said, it obtains more money from taxation on sporting activities and facilities than it gives in subsidies to sport. The commercial sector operating under **capitalism** is there to make profits by meeting consumer demand, a demand, of course, that can be influenced by **advertising**. The voluntary sector relies on the efforts of unpaid labour. On the supply side, attention should be paid to the relative role of the various **factors of production** that are combined to create the sports event.

See also: **demand, subsidisation**

Further reading: Gratton (1998)

SWEDISH GYMNASTICS

Swedish gymnastics were founded by Pehr Henrik Ling, who established the Royal Gymnastic Central Institute in 1813. The basis of Swedish gymnastics was to improve health through movement. Ling's work was recognised for its health giving qualities when he was elected a member of the Swedish General Medical Association in 1831. Ling's system was based around the idea of light gymnastics and did not use apparatus. Instead it favoured callisthenics and exercises and was a system for building up the body's strength and suppleness. Swedish gymnastics proved especially popular in women's training colleges, and by the early twentieth century was the recommended form of gymnastics to be used in physical education colleges in Britain. Similarly, the Swedish system was made popular in

America from the 1880s under the guidance of Hartvig Nissen and Nils Posse.

Further reading: Trangbaek (2000)

SYLLABUSES OF PHYSICAL TRAINING

These defined the exercises and procedures demanded of **state schools** by the Board of Education. Following the review of the **model course of 1902**, a revised syllabus, written largely by Colonel G. M. Fox, who had been seconded from the War Office for the task, was issued in 1904. This embraced the **Ling** system of Swedish **gymnastics**. Although the 1909 syllabus still had the tradition of drill, it did introduce dance and games such as leap-frog, which can be regarded as a further move away from **militarism**. This syllabus also approved of the appointment of advisors for **physical education** and encouraged the provision of training for teachers to deliver the syllabus. The syllabus of 1919 was called one of **physical training**, not merely one of physical exercises. It developed aspects of physical education not included in the syllabus of the previous decade. Individual interpretation and decision-making in movements were encouraged, as was the use of music and games. The 1933 syllabus gave games a more prominent role, and emphasised outdoor education, attaining good posture, and the place of rhythm and movement. Most significantly, it stated that physical education was an integral part of overall education. Daily physical education was called for, suitable clothing was discussed, and there was a postponement of certain exercises until children's physiques were more developed.

See also: **gymnastics, physical education**

Further reading: Bailey and Vamplew (1999)

SYMBOLIC INTERACTIONISM

The roots of symbolic interactionism lie with the studies of self pioneered by George H. Mead. Mead argued that all individuals in society will imagine themselves in the roles of those with whom they interact. Symbolic interactionism can therefore be understood as the study of the relationship between self and society as a process of the symbolic communications between social actors. Social interactionism has been highly useful in analysing patterns of socialisation, deviancy, stereotypes and stigma. Symbolic interactionism has been the most prominent form of interpretive sociology in the **sociology** of sport, and absolutely vital in the investigation of sporting subcultures. Although popular in the 1970s, and ever present, this particular strand of sociological investigation has been reinvigorated by the work of the French thinker Pierre Bourdieu. The best examples of published work which adopt a social interactionist approach would include Scott's 1968 work on horse racing, and Polsky's 1969 investigation of pool hustling.

See also: **sociology**

Further reading: Donnelly (2000), Ingham and Loy (1993), Polsky (1969), Scott (1968)

TASTE

Taste is the aspect of demand most susceptible to influence by sports promoters and advertisers. This can be done via **product development** and **product improvement**, both of which offer something novel to the sports consumer, or by attaching characteristics to a sport that change its public persona. Certainly, both darts and snooker gained large television audiences when they threw off their pub and club image. Sport, like many other consumer goods, is also susceptible to fads, where taste is manipulated to render some activities more fashionable than others.

TEACHING FOR UNDERSTANDING

The philosophy of teaching for understanding is founded on the principle that the process of learning is equally as important as any intended outcome or **outcomes**. The aim is for students to understand what they learn rather than simply perform tasks, and for skills to be transferable to a range of situations and environments. The development of problem-solving and self-discovery in physical education is designed to increase student participation and interaction, both with other students and with the teacher.

Further reading: Bunker and Thorpe (1982), Mosston and Ashworth (1994), Werner et al. (1996)

TEACHING STYLES

Teaching styles vary from those that are totally teacher-directed, through those that encourage cooperation between teachers and students, to those that allow almost complete student autonomy. This continuum is probably best exemplified by the 'Spectrum of teaching styles' developed by Muska Mosston and Sara Ashworth, which illustrates the shift from absolute control by the teacher (command style) to a situation where students work independently of the teacher (self-teaching style). The 'Spectrum' embraces eleven styles as below:

- command style
- practice style
- reciprocal style
- self-check style
- inclusion style
- guided discovery style
- convergent discovery style
- divergent production style
- learner-designed individual programme style
- learner-initiated style
- self-teaching style.

Some of the above styles apply particularly to physical education scenarios. A teacher may employ the 'command style' with very large groups or beginners, even though this may be dispensed with after an initial period. 'Practice' and 'guided discovery' styles are often appropriate in the teaching of gymnastic- or games skills, and 'self-check' learner-focused styles may be utilised in today's national curriculum, where self-assessment and problem-solving can enhance the students' perception of their own involvement in the physical education process.

See also: **coaching, syllabuses of physical training**

Further reading: Mosston and Ashworth (1994)

TECHNOLOGY

Advances in technology have changed some sports and created others. Although the basic format of modern cricket would be recognisable to the players of Hambledon in the eighteenth century, much has changed because of the application of technology. The nineteenth century brought the lawnmower, heavy roller, and drainage devices to keep the pitch in good playing order. This has been followed by batting helmets as protective equipment, hollow-backed bats to provide more powerful striking of the ball, and third umpires using video replays to assist their judgement. Similarly, boxing under lights with gloves, and night race meetings on all-weather tracks, have both benefited from technology whilst maintaining their essential features. Nevertheless, new sports have emerged as a result of technological development; one of the more recent has been windsurfing, now an Olympic event. Other sports have emerged through technological development outside the sporting arena. Perhaps the most important historically has been the variety of motor sports initially sparked off by the invention of the internal combustion engine.

Technological developments in sport can be classified as having assisted participants, spectators and officials. Players have improved their performances by using better equipment, such as the disk wheel in cycling, fibre carbon in darts and vaulting poles, and streamlined running gear and swimming costumes. Such technological breakthroughs are not confined to the turn of the millennium. In golf the replacement of the feather ball by the gutta-percha in the mid-nineteenth century, and it in turn by the rubber-cored ball in the early twentieth century, revolutionised the game. Sportspersons can now test their fitness and skill levels under laboratory conditions with specially designed equipment. Safety, too, has improved: Formula One drivers and pit crews now have fire-resistant suits, and hard hats have saved the lives of jockeys and cricketers.

Spectators attending the game have gained from improved stadium architecture with better roofing to combat the worst of the weather, the use of lights to enable night-time sport to be watched, and better design to allow unobstructed viewing. Those at home have benefited from developments in newspaper, radio and television technology. Clearly, in many instances, thanks to miniature cameras, split screens and instant slow-motion replays, they now have better than the best seats in the house.

Sports officials have found their tasks eased by the coming of the photo-finish camera, electronic measuring devices, and pharmaceutical advances in drug testing. This latter point serves to emphasise that not all technological developments can be viewed positively. Drugs, blood doping, and potentially gene modification, are also technological advances.

See also: **engineering**

Further reading: Anderson (2000b), Dyreson (1996)

TELEVISION

Without television, it is doubtful that sport would have the global importance that it does. It is also unlikely that sport, especially key television games such as American football, football, tennis or golf, would be as awash with money. Sport, with its skill, movement, drama and tension is the perfect partner for television. Coverage of sporting events is, by comparison with costume drama or documentary, relatively cheap, and possesses a ready-made audience of fans and enthusiasts. In the contemporary world, the relationship between sport and television appears to be vital to the future health of both.

The British Broadcasting Corporation (BBC) launched the first public broadcast television service in 1936. In the years before the Second World War the BBC offered its limited number of viewers coverage of Wimbledon, the Derby and the FA Cup final. In 1948 the London Olympics became the first ever games to be televised. Until the opening of the Independent Television Association's ITV network in 1955, the BBC refused to pay any sporting club or organisation money for the rights to screen events, and only paid for any facilities that they used within a sporting venue. The arrival of ITV meant that the BBC, like all television companies in the future, would have to pay for the right to cover sporting events. Such competition, especially heated in the United States, would bring a huge amount of money into sport.

The attractiveness of sport for television companies, and its popularity amongst the viewing public, brought about dedicated sports programmes. In Britain the BBC began broadcasting 'Grandstand' in 1958 and 'Match of the Day' in 1964. ITV countered with 'World of Sport' from 1964 and 'The Big Match' in 1968. In the United States the 1960s witnessed the launch of the ABC's 'Wide World of Sport' and 'Monday Night Football'. In an attempt to wrest control of American football coverage from ABC, NBC and CBS entered bidding wars that saw the costs of television rights rise dramatically. In Britain, the creation of **listed events** was an attempt to avoid expensive struggles over the right to broadcast major events.

A key impetus for the growth of televised sport and its importance within the schedules has been technology. Not only has the actual coverage improved with the advent of video editing from the 1960s, colour television from 1968 and digital technology from the 1990s, but the improvements in satellite and transmitting technology have allowed for globalised live coverage and ever wider receivership. Between 1950 and 1960, television ownership in Britain increased from 2 to 82 per cent. In the US the growth was from 10 per cent in 1950 to 96 per cent by 1963.

As most television companies in the world rely heavily on advertising for income, it was inevitable that sports events would attract the attention of advertisers. In 1947, Ford and Gillette paid $65,000 to sponsor the baseball World Series, and the cost of such exclusive sponsorship has been spiralling ever since.

Two major issues have come to dominate the television/sport relationship in the past two decades. First is the issue of exclusive rights. Television companies can boost viewing figures and advertising revenue by being the sole provider of coverage of any given sports event. To win such exclusive rights costs a huge amount of money. In 1998, the US rights to the coverage of NFL football were worth $2.2 billion, while the global rights for Olympic and football World Cup finals have both exceeded $10 billion. To retain sports coverage, broadcasters have had to dedicate ever-greater proportions of their revenue to buying sport. The second major contemporary issue, that of cable, digital and satellite television coverage of sport on dedicated channels, has had an impact on the price of sporting rights. In Britain, and elsewhere across the globe, the television empires of men such as Rupert Murdoch, Kerry Packer, Silvio Berlusconi and Ted Turner have released large funds solely to secure the rights to sporting events as a way of ensuring the success of their non-terrestrial television ventures. By preserving coverage for those who have subscribed to their channels or paid specifically to watch a one-off event, the non-terrestrial providers are limiting access to sport.

The future of sport on television offers many unanswered questions. Sporting clubs and associations need the money paid to them for exclusive rights, so that they can pay wages and develop new talent. The television companies subsequently pass on to viewers and sponsors the costs of buying the rights. The global television market for sport appears to have no bounds. However, there are serious issues to be addressed about free access to television coverage of major events, and the impact that the power of television will have on minority sports such as rugby league, women's golf or Australian rules football.

See also: **listed events, media**

Further reading: Chandler (1988), Rowe (2000), Whannel (1992)

TIDAL VOLUME

Tidal volume is the amount of air moved in and out of the lungs during a normal resting respiratory cycle.

See also: **residual volume, stroke volume**

Further reading: Jones and Poole (2004)

TIME

Although most benefit obtained from sport is the pleasure from the immediate consumption of the sports product, either as spectator or participant, some benefits, particularly that of health, are more long-term in nature and can be enjoyed well after the activity itself. In the short term the time at which sporting activities are scheduled can affect participation and spectator levels. The emergence of Saturday afternoons free from work for most people in the late nineteenth century paved the way for the emergence of commercialised sport by providing it with a regular time slot, though it should be noted that Sheffield Wednesday gained its name from that being the half-day on which many businesses closed in the nineteenth century. However, the traditional Saturday afternoon football fixture has now been altered at the elite level to suit television.

TOBACCO

The evidence is overwhelming that both tobacco and **alcohol** are injurious to health, yet both have sought to link themselves with sport, usually considered to be health promoting. Unlike alcohol, tobacco has never been promoted as a benefit to sports-persons, though the tobacco trade, like the alcohol industry, has been heavily involved in sports sponsorship, for example Benson and Hedges in cricket and Marlboro in motor sport. Indeed, tobacco companies were the largest sponsors of sport in Britain until 1997 when government legislation banned tobacco **advertising** at sports events.

TOPOPHILIA

Many followers of sport are as enthusiastic about the stadium that their team plays in as they are about the sport which they have chosen to watch. This enthusiasm, romantic attachment to, or love of, a sporting venue can be understood by the term 'topophilia', which is, as Bale has defined it, literally 'a love of place' (Bale 1992: 120). The concept was developed by Tuan, who argued that topophilia applied to any intense feeling of sense of place which engendered a love and affection between people and a place or setting. It seems clear that home grounds for football supporters engender such strong feelings, but so it would seem do other sporting venues. The Grand National is inseparable from a love of Aintree, the All England Tennis Championships from feelings for Wimbledon, or the All Ireland hurling and football finals from sentimental views of Croke Park.

Further reading: Bale (1992), Tuan (1974)

TRADITIONAL SPORTS

Sports and games that are classified as 'folk' or 'traditional', are those which have a long-standing history, and are most usually associated with a period of popular recreation that preceded the birth of modern organised sport. Historians have shown that a wide range of different physical activities existed across Europe in the medieval and early modern period, and such activities were also a common feature of life on the other continents. Many of these games and recreations came under attack during the eighteenth and nineteenth centuries, as they were seen as a threat to public order. Too often traditional games were violent, and served as conduits for gambling and other illegal practices. In particular it was the folk ball games that disappeared in the years of codification and during the advent of modern sport. The organised games of football, rugby and other regional varieties such as American or Gaelic football, were too powerful and popular for the folk games to resist.

Despite the advent of modern sport, many folk games and pastimes still exist. The continued practice of folk games in certain regions can be understood as a resistance to the overpowering nature of modern sport, and a promotion of regional and national identity. Today many folk games are actively encouraged as a means of promoting a locality within the tourist market. Examples of this process would include the palio, an annual horse race in Siena, the ball game of calcio fiorentino in Florence, and the dragon boat races in Hong Kong. Many supporters of controversial blood sports, such as fox hunting and bullfighting, argue that these should be preserved and supported as folk events that celebrate traditional life.

In Britain, the most important folk events are the annual Shrove Tuesday folk football game in Ashbourne, Derbyshire, and the summer programme of highland games across Scotland. Both these events celebrate a traditional form of sporting practice, which is reputed to be little changed from that practised by the locality's forefathers, while also stressing a powerful regional, and in the case of highland games, nationalist identity. Additionally there are the Cotswold Games, first organised in 1611 by Robert Dover, and the Much Wenlock Games begun by Dr William Penny Brookes in 1850. These continuing festivals embraced contemporary sporting forms, and both sought to promote the sport for participants and spectators.

In Sweden, the throwing game, varpa, continues to be well supported in specific geographical pockets, while in Iceland, the Canary Islands, Scotland, Brittany and Cornwall, traditional forms of wrestling remain popular. In the Americas, Africa, Asia and Australasia, various folk forms of sport are celebrated, promoted and in many cases protected, as part of the traditions of indigenous culture. Such games include toli, a stick game played by North American Indian groups, the intertribal tournaments, or pruns, which take place between different Aboriginal groups in Australia, and gambling sports such as cockfighting that continue to be popular in South East Asia.

For many observers and participants, the traditions of folk sports have to be preserved. In an age of increased globalisation folk sports both represent the heritage of a particular group or region and also offer an important form of resistance to the powerful forces of sporting homogenisation.

Further reading: Collins et al. (2005)

TRAINING PRINCIPLES

Research on training has helped scientists to determine a number of important principles that need to be applied in the development of any successful training regime, if physiological changes (training effects) are to be observed. The first of these principles is the principle of specificity. Training, like fitness, is specific, and therefore if an athlete desires to increase strength, specific strength-training exercises need to be employed. And while cross-training has its own benefits, it cannot replace the effects that a specific training activity has on a specified performance gain. The second principle is the principle of progressive overload, which implies that to improve any aspect of physical fitness an individual must continually increase the level of demand placed on the appropriate body system or systems being targeted. Thus, in training to increase muscular strength, athletes must increase the weight or the resistance they are using. In training to increase endurance, runners must overload the cardio-respiratory system by running further or faster or both. It is important to remember that the overload should be progressive to avoid both injury and the retrogressive effects of **over-training**. The third principle is the principle of individual differences. Researchers have established that individuals differ in both the rate and magnitude of the adaptations that they make to training, in the same way that they enjoy or can tolerate different types of training.

Further reading: Brooks et al. (1996), Fox et al. (1987), Howley and Franks (1997)

TRANSFERS

In most occupations there is a right to give notice and then take another job, even if it is with a firm competing in the same sector of the economy. In several British professional team sports, however, the idea of restricting the free movement of players developed in the late nineteenth century. It was epitomised in the **transfer** system operated by the Football League. No footballer was allowed to play league football unless he was registered with the league, but that registration was not held by the player but by the club for which he had signed. Once a player had signed for a club it had absolute discretion over his registration, and could refuse to release him to play for another club unless a transfer fee was paid to them for his services. Alternatively, if the club did not wish to retain him as a player he could be placed on the transfer list and be open to offers. Any player who did not wish to be transferred had two options, either to give up the game or play it at the less-remunerative non-league level. Although the more oppressive aspects of the system – such as the annual **retain and transfer** list – have been modified, the transfer system itself currently remains inviolate for contracted players. European law, however, may have the last say, as it views the current transfer system as an illegal impediment to the free movement of labour within the European Union. It is likely that a system involving payment to a club for the costs of training and developing a player, or the buy-out of the unused years of a contract, will emerge.

See also: **free agents, mobility, retain and transfer**

TYPES OF PRACTICE

Research into the learning, retention and performance of motor skills has shown consistently that a variety of practice experiences is essential for learning both **open-loop** and **closed-loop** motor skills. Since both the amount of practice and the spacing of practice sessions are important factors in learning motor tasks, teachers and coaches need to assess the characteristics of the skill to be learnt and the level of the learner before selecting the type of practice (massed or distributed) and the amount of contextual interference (interference that results from practising a task within the context of the practice situation) to be employed in a practice session. They will also need to assess the complexity and organisation of the skill to be learnt, to decide whether to practise the motor skill as a whole or whether to break it down into parts. While physically practising a skill under optimal learning conditions and an appropriate practice schedule is vital, mental practice can also be helpful when learning new motor skills and when preparing to perform a skill.

Further reading: Feltz and Landers (1983), Magill (1998), Schmidt and Lee (1999)

TURNEN

Turnen was a system of **gymnastics** developed in the early nineteenth century by Friedrich Ludwig **Jahn** as part of his drive for German nationalism. Although cloaked in educational rhetoric which argued that physical exercise would provide a counterbalance to the emphasis on mental activity in schools, his main idea was to enthuse fit, young men with the desire to liberate their native land and provide them with exercises suitable for paramilitary purposes. In conjunction with Swedish gymnastics and English sports, Turnen provided the basis of modern **physical culture**.

See also: **gymnastics, physical education**

Further reading: Ueberhorst (1996)

UNCERTAINTY OF OUTCOME

Sport is unlike theatre in that the action is unscripted and the conclusion unknown to both players and the audience. This uncertainty of outcome provides the drama and excitement of sport, and many economists believe that the greater the uncertainty, the larger the attendance.

See also: **economics**

Further reading: Sloane (1980), Symanski (2003)

UNIONISM

Unionism involves the bringing together of a labour force in an enterprise or industry to bargain collectively with employers over wages and working conditions. A trade union needs members with mutual interests if it is to be successful, but such mutuality is not always apparent in the competitive industry that is modern sport. This is particularly true where earnings are concerned, for even in team sports there will be some individuals who are paid substantially more than others. Hence historically it has required restrictions on earnings power – via either the imposition of a maximum wage or impediments to labour mobility – to bring the star players into the same fold as the journeyman professional.

The first permanent grouping was that of the Professional Golfers Association in 1901, whose members were concerned about attempts of their golf club employers to annex the profits from the sale of golf balls. Next came the Association Football Players Union (now the Professional Footballers Association) in 1907, mainly a result of the imposition of the maximum wage along with the **retain and transfer** system. Two other major sports were unionised in the 1960s with the Jockeys Association and the Cricketers Association. More recently has come the Professional Boxers Association in 1993 and, as the game went professional, the Rugby Union Players Association.

Generally, professional sportsmen in Britain have tried to avoid strikes and threats of industrial disputes and, to some extent, this desire not to appear to be militant and confrontational explains the choice of the titular 'association' rather than 'union'. Although earnings have been important, many associations have sought to look after health and safety issues and provide benefits to injured and unemployed members.

See also: **strikes and industrial disputes**

Further reading: Greenfield and Osborn (2000b), Vamplew (2005b)

URBANISATION

Many sporting sites and venues became urbanised and formalised as a by-product of eighteenth- and nineteenth-century industrialisation. In the rapidly developing towns and cities of the nineteenth century space was often at a premium. As such, sporting clubs and organisations had to compete for space against demands that land be used for factories or housing. As a result of urbanisation, space had to be reserved and marked specifically for sporting pursuits. As part of the middle-class and educational promotion of sport as being beneficial to mind and body, pressure was brought to bear on town and city councils to provide spaces for sporting pursuits within the urban environment. However, many of these sporting venues within urbanised areas, developing as private clubs, became distinguished as elite venues. Therefore, despite the provision of space for golf or tennis clubs within the crowded urban setting, the majority of people were excluded. The sporting stadium was a direct product of urbanisation. London's first cinder running track was built in 1837, and its racecourse and ice rink in 1870. The demands of urban dwellers for access to professional sporting fixtures within their town or city led to the installation of the first floodlights for football in 1878. Within the urban environment there has always been a tension between the provision of space for professional sporting clubs and venues, and the demands for pitches and playing fields to be used by everyone. With the demands that football stadia meet with safety regulations, many football clubs in Britain have sought to move to a new site. For many clubs however, such as Wimbledon, this has proved impossible because of the competing demands for space and planning restrictions that have been imposed on clubs to deter them from relocating in urban residential areas. Equally, the National Playing Fields Association has been fighting a long battle in trying to preserve Britain's stock of open sporting and leisure spaces from redevelopment as towns and cities continue to grow. Urbanisation has not always been successful, and many inner-city areas have fallen into disrepair and have largely been abandoned. In an attempt to breathe new life into neglected urban areas, sport has been used as a vehicle for regeneration. This is true of the Stade de France in the St Denis area of Paris, the Homebush Olympic site in Sydney and the Commonwealth games venue in Manchester. It has been argued that the battle for sporting space within urban areas led, in part, to the popularity of running and jogging, i.e. sports that did not need specific venues and thus could adapt to an urban landscape dominated by cars and buildings.

Further reading: Bale (1989, 1992), Winters (1980)

UTILITY MAXIMISATION

Utility maximisation refers to the motivation of those club proprietors who seek to win cups and championships rather than attempt to maximise profits as a conventional business enterprise is assumed to do.

See also: **economics**

VALUES

In viewing the worth, desirability and utility of sport and physical activity, and the qualities on which they depend to create value for participants and spectators, philosophers of sport and physical activity have generally addressed two questions. The first concerns the values that sport and physical activity reflect in any particular culture. They ask: 'What can we learn about the values which are prized in a particular nation or culture by studying both the types of sport and physical activity which are practised and performed and the manner and style in which they are practised and performed?' Thus, in a society in which Sunday observance was practised, a comparison of religious values and sporting values can be assessed. In general, it is recognised that the values present in sport and physical activity are a reflection of broader social values. However, the simple 'mirror' phenomenon is too simplistic, since it is also apparent that sport and physical activity can impact on social and cultural values. As an example, the growth of athletic footwear and apparel as part of the clothing and fashion industries is indicative of the interactive nature of the relationship between sport and society, and the transfer of values from sport to the broader society.

The second question which emerges from this interactive relationship is 'If sport teaches values, can it be used as a means of instilling in participants those values on which a culture is built?' The answer to this question is generally yes. However, which values are learnt is widely contested. For those who see sport and physical activity in a positive light and stress its ability to teach positive values, sport has been used among other things as a means of building character, promoting the spirit of **fair play**, promoting identity and even nation building. Persons keen to promote the playing of sport often attribute moral values to sport that encompass such things as fair play and sportspersonship. Other aspects often admired include the self-discipline, dedication and commitment regarded as necessary to success, but it should be stressed that these are functional rather than moral values. A dedicated athlete need not be a fair-minded one. This is picked up by those who highlight negative values. For them sport promotes unhealthy competition, a disregard for the health and well-being of oneself and others, and ultimately alienation. In both positive and negative cases, the values of sport and physical activity are generally held to be both reflective of, and adding to, the values of the broader society. As such, to change the values inherent in society, it is necessary and helpful to change the values inherent in sport and physical activity.

By contrast, those who adopt the theoretical position that sport and physical activity are forms of **play** and are thus activities that are quite consciously outside 'ordinary' life since they have their own rules, see sport and physical activity as distinctive social and cultural practices, with their own distinctive internal goods and values. These internal goods or values might include the exercise of skills, the use of tactics and strategies, testing one's abilities, and the sheer joy of performing at one's peak. Some values in sport are thus **intrinsic** in that the skills that are required to participate in a sporting activity are valued by the player for their own sake. This is in contrast to those **extrinsic** values in the form of status, money or kudos, which are rewards related to the playing of the sport, not of the sport itself.

There are also aesthetic values associated with sport; indeed, in sports such as diving and gymnastics it is the manner of the performance that is judged, not its effectiveness. Grace and style earn more points than simply vaulting successfully over the horse.

The distinction that needs to be drawn here is in regard to the levels of analysis employed. At the societal level, the analysis of values is of sport and physical activity as social institutions fulfilling the needs of the society and of individuals within that society. For those who see sport as play, sport is about self-realisation and personal identity, and its value is that it is a means of fulfilling the psychological needs of the individual.

Further reading: Coakley (1994), Garvey (1977), Kew (1997), Morgan (1993), Shields and Bredemeier (1995), Simon (1991)

VETERANS

Veterans are not necessarily aged. In some contexts the term merely means those who are well above the typical age for participants in a particular sport, often perhaps approaching the end of their competitive career. Hence it could be a female gymnast in her late twenties, swimmers in their thirties, a footballer in his forties, or a jockey in his sixth decade. More generally, veterans' sport refers to games and physical activities for the middle-aged or elderly, often organised under the ambiguous title of 'Masters', or the more appropriate seniors. Declining skills and loss of body powers mean that separate sports for older individuals offer fairer competitive sport. The development of such sports since the 1960s reflects the fact that people are living longer, that there is a growing emphasis on health and fitness, and that there is a greater awareness of the benefits of physical activity for older people. Those who support the concept of veterans' sport point to these psychological and health benefits, but also note simply that sport can be enjoyable at any age.

See also: **ageism, discrimination, equality**

VIOLENCE

While we tend to use the words 'violence' and **'aggression'** interchangeably, violence is generally held to be physical in nature and an extreme form of aggression. And while many social psychologists suggest that the issue of 'intent to injure' is important to our under-standing of what constitutes violence, those viewing violence from a sociological perspective, and thus focusing more on collective than individual acts of violence, tend to be less concerned about intent and more concerned with observable behaviour.

The problem of violence in sport, and questions of intent to injure, have become increasingly significant as sports violence has come to be seen as 'real' violence, and **civil law** cases have been brought to the courts where soccer and rugby players have accused their opponents of deliberately harming them and being guilty of assault. Cases of criminal violence in sports, involving players only, are few and far between although cases of 'off the pitch' and crowd violence have resulted in criminal proceedings being enacted.

Much of the research on sports violence in Britain has centred on violence in football, and specifically football **hooliganism**. The game of football has been associated with violence from the thirteenth century onwards, and medieval and folk football have long been renowned as violent activities. However, the advent of football hooli-ganism coincided with increasing **media** (and particularly **television**) coverage of the game in the 1960s. A number of explanatory models have been developed in trying to explain the emergence and growth of football hooliganism and violence since that time. The influence of factors such as **alcohol** and **racism**, and theoretical models suggesting the proletarianisation of the game of football, and other 'class-based' approaches such as the 'civilising process', have given way more recently to explanations involving **ritual** and cultural and historical forces.

As Marsh has pointed out, football violence has probably been over-researched in Britain because of its unique social and cultural significance. However, football violence in Europe has also been drawing increased attention from researchers in Italy, the Nether-lands, Denmark and Austria. Cross-national and cross-cultural studies may help determine the differing degrees of importance of individual motivations and psychological profiles, and of the broader social and cultural determinants of football hooliganism in particular and sports violence in general.

See also: **hooliganism, sociology**

Further reading: Dunning and Sheard (1979), Elias and Dunning (1986), Grayson (1999a), Giulianotti et al. (1994), Marsh (1999), Wann (1997), Young (1991)

VO$_2$MAX

A measure of aerobic fitness, cardio-respiratory fitness or endurance potential, VO$_2$Max is the amount of oxygen that can be used by the body per minute, during maximal exercise. This is an important measure of the cardio-respiratory system, and in particular the working muscles, because the greater the quantity of oxygen the body can consume, the 'fitter' one is.

Tests of VO$_2$Max are usually conducted on a stationary bicycle or a treadmill, with the intent of bringing a person to exhaustion over a 5–10 minute period by steadily increasing the exercise load. By measuring the amount of air and oxygen taken in by the lungs and the amount of oxygen and carbon dioxide exhaled, the difference represents how much oxygen was used or consumed, VO$_2$Max.

Brooks et al. note that effective measurement of VO$_2$Max must satisfy a number of important criteria that include conducting the test under experimental conditions which avoid stressful environments that expose the subject to excessive heat, humidity or altitude; and employing at least 50 per cent of total muscle mass. They also propose that among factors limiting VO$_2$Max are cardiac output, pulmonary ventilation, lung diffusion, and oxygen utilisation. Since the effects of training to improve maximal oxygen uptake are limited by these factors, sport scientists have used such measures as important predictors of athletic success in endurance events and selected athletes to train for such events on the basis of these characteristics. Many exercise physiologists believe VO$_2$Max to be the most valid measurement of cardiovascular fitness.

Further reading: Brooks et al. (1996), Fox (1998), Fox et al. (1987)

WEATHER

Sport has been influenced by the vagaries of the British climate from its origins through to the twenty-first century, when the consequences of global warming may add another dimension to the problem. There are readily identifiable short-, medium- and long-term effects of weather on sport. Golf tournaments in Britain have been interrupted by thunderstorms, rain, blizzards, high winds, and even a sandstorm, while at times severe winters have badly disrupted the sporting programme. In the medium term, rising water tables resulting from excess precipitation have caused problems for cricket and horse racing long after the downpours ceased. In the longer term, micro-climatic changes brought about by twentieth-century urbanisation have adversely affected county cricket fixtures as teams have forsaken their rural outposts for heavily built-up areas. The impact of adverse weather on participants can force a change in the skills and tactics required on the day, and, more seriously, can increase the threat of injury, career disruption and even death. The division of matches into halves offers compensation for the adverse effect of the weather but in competitions which take place over long periods of time, such as golf tournaments and cricket matches, weather conditions could result in unfair advantages. Venues can be affected by access difficulties and impaired playing surfaces. For spectators, inclement weather may result in increased risk to health, or simply non-attendance, with the consequent loss of revenue to sport. However, many are often prepared to brave the elements to watch contests made more unpredictable by the intervention of the weather.

In the short term, particularly at local, but sometimes at national level, promoters seldom seem to have had contingency plans to cope with inclement weather until the 1970s. In the longer run, responses to the weather have often depended on the nature of the sport. Those such as skiing, outdoor curling and yachting have made use of climatic conditions as the basis of their existence. Some have accepted the vagaries of the climate and adjusted to them by altering rules or employing special equipment. Another group has attempted to combat weather conditions by better stadium design, drainage improvements, and the use of all-weather surfaces. Others have circumvented the climate altogether by shifting to indoor venues both for training and playing.

Further reading: Hignell (1999), Kay and Vamplew (2006), Schmidt (2006)

WELLNESS

A general term that covers the general well-being of the individual, wellness is concerned with general lifestyle. The pursuit of wellness encompasses many different aspects of health and fitness, and includes good diet, mental and emotional health, exercise, and relaxation. It is a term that became commonly used in the 1990s, and is part of a general interest in preventive and alternative medicine. The emergence of wellness as an idea, has been accompanied by a general change in many individual lifestyles including the growth in gym membership, heightened levels of exercise, improved diet and an increase in the consumption of herbal products, vitamins and minerals. In 2000, it was estimated that Americans spent $15.7 billion on products that promoted wellness. In the Western world, where issues such as stress and obesity have become headline news, the embrace of wellness has been seen as a positive step in improving health and lifestyle. Specific advocates of wellness have included Byllye Yvonne Avery, who opened a series of Centre for Black Women's Wellness in America to promote better health amongst low income African American women, and Dr John H. Kellogg who, as well as inventing the cornflake, promoted good living, simple diet and regular exercise at his sanatorium in Battle Creek in the late nineteenth century.

WORKER SPORT

The origins of worker sport are to be found in Germany during the 1890s. The Worker Gymnastic Association was formed in opposition to the nationalistic German Gymnastics Society that was inspired by the ideas of Turnen. The idea behind worker sport was that it would give members of the working classes the opportunity to take part in sport and leisure pursuits in a healthy, largely non-competitive and capitalist-free environment. All associations supporting the ethos were open to all, irrespective of race or gender. In the years before the First World War, worker sport groups spread throughout Europe and across the sea to the United States. In 1913, the Belgian socialist Gaston Bridoux brought together the worker sports federations from five European countries to form the Socialist Physical Culture International. Worker sport was most successful during the inter-war years, and could claim over four million members world-wide during that period. In Germany the movement was most successful, with 1.2 million members by the late 1920s. The cohesion of worker sports at the international level was shattered throughout the 1920s. The group that had been brought together by Bridoux renamed itself the International Association of Sport, and was opposed by the Red Sport International, founded in Moscow in 1921. Rather than fighting the Nazi threat, the two organisations were overly concerned with fighting each other. Nevertheless, the International Association of Sport successfully organised a series of Worker Olympics from 1921 until 1937, which were popular and well attended. The Second World War had a devastating effect on worker sport, and it has been in steady decline ever since. The main contemporary stronghold of the movement is in Israel.

Further reading: Hoberman (1984), Jones (1988), Kruger and Riordan (1996), Murray (1987), Riordan (2005), Wheeler (1978)

WORLD WIDE WEB

The 1990s witnessed a rapid growth in use of the internet, and particularly the World Wide Web (usually abbreviated to WWW or just 'the Web'). Initially developed in 1990 for the communication of scientific information between European physicists, the Web was quickly adopted by people and organisations from almost every aspect of society, including sport. In simplest terms the Web allows documents called pages stored on one computer to be distributed on request and viewed on any other computer connected to the internet. Pages can contain text, multimedia elements such as graphics, photographs, sound and video, and even interactive computer programmes. Moreover, web pages can also contain links to related information on other pages. A collection of pages on a particular subject, created and maintained by the same individual or organisation, is known as a website.

There are three main categories of website devoted to sport. The first are those created by fans. These were the first to come into existence, as much of the initial growth of the Web was due to personal pages created by people with access to the internet, particularly those within academic or research institutions. Fan sites can be seen as the electronic equivalent of fanzines, allowing their creator to voice their opinion about the team, be that positive or negative. The main difference is that the website has a potential audience across the entire globe. Many fan sites also provide features such as message boards or chat rooms which allow other fans of the club from around the world to discuss the team. Second, are the official websites run by clubs, players or administrative bodies. As would be expected, these are professionally run, and provide a wider range of features than the majority of fan sites. At their most basic, team websites offer an avenue of communication to the club's supporters similar to that provided by match programmes, but with added functionality such as video highlights of match footage. They are also increasingly being used to augment the commercial activities of the club, with most now offering online sales of team merchandise. These electronic commerce facilities extend the sales of the team shop to a world-wide audience, which is a huge potential source of revenue, particularly for teams with an international fan-base.

Finally there are sites run by organisations or businesses which are not directly involved in the sport, such as the **media** sites, created either by traditional media organisations such as newspapers and television broadcasters, or by more recent online media companies. The websites run by media outlets are for the most part an extension of traditional media organisations such as newspapers, magazines, television and radio stations. Much of the information on these sites is reproduced from these sources, with thé main bonus to the user being the ability to access archived material, such as results and match reports from earlier in the season. These sites are also often used to provide interactive competitions, such as fantasy sports contests or online versions of the traditional 'spot the ball' game. As with more traditional media, these sites are largely dependent on advertising to provide their revenue, often providing links to online suppliers of sporting equipment or memorabilia.

One use of the Web that has increased very rapidly and drawn large amounts of attention over the last few years is that of online **gambling**. Many of the websites are based in countries with liberal gambling laws, and accept wagers from international customers. Whilst some sites focus on acting as online casinos, many accept bets on a wide range of sporting events.

See also: **ALT-PE**

Further reading: Davis and Duncan (2006)

Bibliography

Abrahamson, M. (1973) 'Functionalism and the Functional Theory of Stratification: An Empirical Assessment', *American Journal of Sociology* 78, S. 1236–46.

Adams, J. (1971) 'A Closed Loop Theory of Motor Learning', *Journal of Motor Behaviour* 3, 111–50.

Adrian, M. and Cooper, J. (1995) *Biomechanics of Human Movement*, Madison: Brown and Benchmark.

Allen, M. (1993) *Dangerous Sports*, New York: Chelsea House.

Allison, L. (1980) 'Batsman and Bowler: The Key Relation of Victorian England', *Journal of Sport History* 7, 5–20.

—— (1993) *The Changing Politics of Sports*, Manchester: Manchester University Press.

—— (2000) *Amateurism in Sport*, London: Cass.

American College of Sports Medicine (1998) 'Position Stand' *Medicine and Science in Sports and Exercise* 30, 6, 975–91.

Anderson, J. (2000a) 'A Games of their Own: Stoke Mandeville', Proceedings of the 19th Annual Conference of the British Society of Sports History, Liverpool.

—— (2000b) 'Technology', in Cox, R., Jarvie, G. and Vamplew, W (eds) *Encyclopedia of British Sport*, Oxford: ABC-Clio, 394–6.

Andrews, D. (1998) 'Feminising Olympic Reality: Preliminary dispatches from Baudrillard's Atlanta', *International Review for the Sociology of Sport* 33, 1, 5–18.

—— (2000) 'Posting Up: French Post-Structuralism and the Critical Analysis of Contemporary Sporting Culture', in Coakley, J. and Dunning, E. (eds) *Handbook of Sports Studies*, London: Sage, 106–38.

Andrews, D. L. and Jackson, S. J. (2004) *Sport, Culture and Advertising*, London: Routledge.

Anshel, M. (2004) *Sport Psychology: From Theory to Practice*, 4th edn, San Francisco: Benjamin Cummings.

Appenzeller, H. (1998) 'Risk Management in Sport', in Appenzeller, H. (ed.) *Managing Sports and Risk Management Strategies*, Durham, NC: Carolina Academic Press, 5–10.

Armour, K., Jones, R. and Potrac, P. (2003) *Sports Coaching Cultures*, London: Routledge.

Arnold, P (1988) *Education, Movement, and the Curriculum*, New York: Falmer Press.

Attridge, D., Bennington, G. and Young, R. (eds) (1987) *Post-Structuralism and the Question of History*, Cambridge: Cambridge University Press.

Auweele, Y., Bakker, F., Biddle, S., Durand, M. and Seiler, R. (eds) (1999) *Psychology for Physical Educators*, Champaign: Human Kinetics.

Avedon, E. and Sutton-Smith, B. (eds) (1971) *The Study of Games*, New York: John Wiley.

Bailey, S. (ed.) 2000 *Perspectives: Competition in School Sport*, Aachen: Meyer and Meyer.

Bailey, S. and Vamplew, W. (1999) *100 Years of Physical Education 1899–1999*, Reading: PEAUK.

Bairner, A. (2001) *Sport, Nationalism and Globalization*, Albany: State University of New York Press.

Baker, A. and Boyd, T. (eds) (1997) *Out of Bounds: Sports Media and the Politics of Identity*, Bloomington: Indiana University Press.

Baker, W. J. (1982) *Sports in the Western World*, Totowa: Rowman and Littlefield.

Bale, J. (1981) *Sport and Place: A Geography of Sport in England, Wales and Scotland*, London: Hurst.

—— (1989) *Sports Geography*, London: Spon.

—— (1992) *Sport, Place and the City*, London: Routledge.

—— (1993a) 'Racing towards Modernity: A One-Way Street?', *International Journal for the History of Sport* 10, 2, 215–32.

—— (1993b) *Landscapes of Modern Sport*, London: Leicester University Press.

—— (2000) 'Geography' in Cox, R., Jarvie, G. and Vamplew, W. (eds) *Encyclopedia of British Sport*, London: ABC-Clio.

Bale, J. and Cronin, M. (eds) (2002) *Sport and Postcolonialism*, Oxford: Berg.

Bandura, A. (1973) *Aggression: A Social Learning Analysis*, Englewood Cliffs: Prentice-Hall.

Bane, M. (1996) *Over the Edge*, New York: Macmillan.

Barnett, S. (1990) *Games and Sets: The Changing Face of Sport on Television*, London: British Film Institute.

Barney, R. (1996) 'Olympic Games, Modern', in Levinson, D. and Christensen, K. (eds) *The Encyclopedia of World Sport*, Oxford: ABC-Clio, 695–705.

Barney, R. K., Wenn, S. R. and Martyn, S.G. (2002) *Selling the Five Rings*, Salt Lake City: University of Utah Press.

Baron, R. and Richardson, D. (1994) *Human Aggression*, New York: Plenum.

Bartlett, R. (1999) *Sports Biomechanics: Reducing Injury and Improving Performance*, London: Spon.

Bateman, D. and Douglas, D. (1986) *Unfriendly Games: Boycotted and Broke. The Inside Story of the 1986 Commonwealth Games*, Edinburgh: Mainstream.

Beamish, R. and Ritchie, I. (2005) 'From Fixed Capacities to Performance Enhancement: The Paradigm Shift in the Science of "Training" and the Use of Performance-Enhancing Substances', *Sport in History* 25, 412–33.

Beard, A. (1998) *The Language of Sport*, London: Routledge.

Berryman, J. (1995) *Out of Many, One: The History of the American College of Sports Medicine*, Champaign: Human Kinetics.

Berryman, J. and Park, R. (eds) (1992) *Sport and Exercise Science: Essays in the History of Sports Medicine*, Urbana: University of Illinois Press.

Best, D. (1978) *Philosophy and Human Movement*, London: George Allen and Unwin.

—— (1995) 'The Aesthetic in Sport' in Morgan, W. J. R. and Meier, K. V (eds) *Philosophic Inquiry in Sport*, Champaign: Human Kinetics.

Biddle, S. (ed.) (1995) *European Perspectives on Exercise and Sport Psychology*, Champaign: Human Kinetics.

Biddle, S. J. H. and Mutrie, N. (2006) *Psychology of Physical Activity*, Abingdon: Routledge.

Billig, M. (1995) *Banal Nationalism*, London: Sage.

Birley, D. (1993) *Sport and the Making of Britain*, Manchester: Manchester University Press.

—— (1995) *Land of Sport and Glory*, Manchester: Manchester University Press.

Birrell, S. and Cole, C. (eds) (1994) *Women, Sport and Culture*, Champaign: Human Kinetics.

Blackshaw, T. and Crabbe, T. (2004) *New Perspectives on Sport and 'Deviance'*, London: Routledge.

Blanchard, K. (1981) *Mississippi Choctaws at Play: The Serious Side of Leisure*, Urbana: University of Illinois Press.

—— (1996) 'Anthropology', in Levinson, D. and Christensen, K. (eds) *Encyclopedia of World Sport*, Oxford: ABC-Clio, 37–9.

Bompa, T. (1999) *Periodization: Theory and Methodology of Training*, Champaign: Human Kinetics.

Booth, D. (1998) *The Race Game*, London: Cass.

—— (2001) *Australian Beach Cultures: A History of Sun, Sand and Surf*, London: Cass.

—— (2005) *The Field: Truth and Fiction in Sport History*, Abingdon: Routledge.

Booth, D. and Loy, J. W (2000) 'Functionalism, Sport, and Society', in Coakley, J. and Dunning, E. (eds) *Handbook of Sport and Society*, London: Sage.

Borland, J. and McDonald, R. (2003) 'Demand for Sport', *Oxford Review of Economic Policy* 19.4, 478–502.

Brackenbridge, C. H. (1997) 'Understanding Sexual Abuse in Sport', in Lidor, R. and Bar-Eli, M. (eds) *Innovations in Sports Psychology*, Netanya: Wingate Institute. nnovation

Brailsford, D. (1991) *Sport, Time and Society: The British at Play*, London: Routledge.

—— (1992) *British Sport: A Social History*, Cambridge: Lutterworth.

Brightbill, C. (1960) *The Challenge of Leisure*, Englewood Cliffs: Prentice-Hall.

Brohm, J-M. (1978) *Sport: A Prison of Measured Time*, London: Ink Links.

Brooks, D. D. and Althouse, R. C. (eds) (1993) *Racism in College Athletics: The African-American Athlete's Experience*, Morgantown: Fitness Information Technology Inc.

Brooks, G., Fahey, T and White, T (1996) *Exercise Physiology*, Mountain: Mayfield.

Brown, W (1980) 'Ethics, Drugs and Sport', *Journal of Philosophy of Sport*, 15–23.

Buckworth, J. and Dishman, R. (2002) *Exercise Psychology*, Champaign: Human Kinetics.

Bunker, D. and Thorpe, R. (1982) 'A Model for the Teaching of Games in Secondary Schools', *The Bulletin of Physical Education* 18, 1, 5–8.

Burke, M. and Roberts, T. (1997) 'Drugs in Sport: An Issue of Morality or Sentimentality?', *Journal of Philosophy of Sport* 24, 99–113.

Bussard, J-C. and Roth, E (1999) *Which Physical Education for Which School?*, Proceedings of ASEP Congress, Neuchâtel.

Butcher, R., Hong, F. and Schneider, A. (2006) *Doping in Sport*, Abingdon: Routledge.

Cahn, S. K. (1994) *Coming on Strong: Gender and Sexuality in Twentieth-Century Women's Sports*, New York: Free Press.

Caillois, R. (2001) *Man, Play and Games*, Urbana: University of Illinois Press.

Campbell, N. (1996) *Biology*, 4th edn, Menlo Park: Benjamin/Cummings.

Cambridge Econometrics (2003) *The Value of the Sports Economy in England in 2000*, Cambridge: Cambridge Econometrics.

Cannadine, D. (1988) *Class in Britain*, New Haven, CT: Yale University Press.

Cannon, W. (1939) *The Wisdom of the Body*, 2nd edn, New York: Norton.

Capel, S. and Piotrowski, S. (2000) *Issues in Physical Education*, London: Routledge Falmer.

Cashman, R. (1995) *Paradise of Sport: The Rise of Organised Sport in Australia*, Melbourne: Oxford University Press.

Cashman, R. and Hughes, A. (eds) (2000) *Staging the Olympics*, Sydney: University of New South Wales Press.

Cashmore, E. (1990) *Making Sense of Sports*, London and New York: Routledge.

—— (1996) *Making Sense of Sports*, 2nd edn, London: Routledge.

—— (2000) *Sports Culture*, London: Routledge.

Cassidy, T., Jones, R. and Potrac, P. (2004) *Understanding Sports Coaching*, London: Routledge.

Causey, A. (1989) 'On the Morality of Hunting', *Environmental Ethics* 2, 334–43.

CCPR (2002) *Everybody Wins: Sport and Social Inclusion*. London: Central Council of Physical Recreation.

Chandler, J. (1988) *Television and National Sport: The United States and Britain*, Urbana: University of Illinois Press.

Chandler, T. J. L. (1988) 'Building and Displaying Character Through Sport', in Ross, S. and Charette, L. (eds) *Persons, Minds and Bodies*, North York: University Press of Canada, 161–9.

—— (1996) 'The Structuring of Manliness', in Nauright, J. and Chandler, T. J. L. (eds) *Making Men: Rugby and Masculine Identity*, London: Cass, 13–31.

—— (1998) 'Morality, Nationalism and Health: Rugby Football's Three Faces of Manliness at Oxbridge and the Public Schools, 1830–80', in Bailey, S. and Vamplew, W. (eds) *De Montfort International Centre for Sports History and Culture*, Occasional Papers 1, Leicester: De Montfort, 32–8.

Cheek, N. and Burch, W. (1976) *The Social Organization of Leisure in Society*, New York: Harper and Row.

Chelladurai, P (1993) 'Leadership', in Singer, R., Murphey, M. and Tennant, L. (eds) *Handbook of Research on Sport Psychology*, New York: Macmillan, 647–771.

Clarke, D. and Eckert, H. (eds) (1985) *Limits of Human Performance*, Champaign: Human Kinetics.

Clarke, S. (1981) *The Foundations of Structuralism: A Critique of Lévi-Strauss and the Structuralist Movement*, Brighton: Harvester.

Coakley, J. (1987) 'Sociology of Sport in the United States', *International Review for the Sociology of Sport* 22, 63–79.

—— (1994) *Sports in Society*, St Louis: Mosby.

—— (1998) *Sport in Society: Issues and Controversies*, Boston, MA: Irwin McGraw Hill.

Coakley, J. and Dunning, E. (eds) (2000) *Handbook of Sport and Society*, London: Sage.

Coghlan, J. (1990) *Sport and British Politics since 1960*, London: Falmer Press.

Collins, T. (1998) *Rugby's Great Split: Class, Culture and the Origins of Rugby League*, London: Cass.

—— (2001) 'Codes of Football', in Cox, R., Russell, D. and Vamplew, W (eds) *Encyclopedia of British Football*, London: Cass.

—— (2005) 'Invented Traditions' in Collins, T., Martin, J. and Vamplew, W., *Encyclopedia of Traditional British Rural Sports*, Abingdon: Routledge.

Collins, T. and Vamplew, W. (2002) *Mud, Sweat and Beers: A Cultural History of Sport and Alcohol*, Oxford: Berg.

Connell, R. (1987) *Gender and Power*, Stanford: Stanford University Press.

—— (1990) 'An Iron Man: The Body and some Contradictions of Hegemonic Masculinity', in Messner, M. and Sabo, D. (eds) *Sport, Men and the Gender Order, Champaign: Human Kinetics*, 83–95.

Connor, S. (1989) *Postmodernist Culture*, Oxford: Blackwell.

Cook, T. (1908) *The Rules of Sport*, London: Archibald Constable.

Cooper, K. (1968) *Aerobics*, New York: Evans.

Corbin, C. and Lindsey, R. (1984) *The Ultimate Fitness Book*, Champaign: Human Kinetics.

—— (1997) *Concepts of Physical Fitness with Laboratories*, 9th edn, Dubuque: Brown and Benchmark.

Cox, R. H. (1994) *Sport Psychology: Concepts and Applications*, 3rd edn, Madison: Brown and Benchmark.

Cox, R. W. (1995) *History of Sport: A Guide to the Literature and Sources of Information*, London: Sports History Publishing.

—— (1996) *Index to Sporting Manuscripts in the UK*, London: Sports History Publishing.

Cox, R. W., Jarvie, G. and Vamplew, W. (2000) *Encyclopedia of British Sport*, Oxford: ABC-Clio.

Cox, R. W., Russell, D. and Vamplew, W. (2001) *Encyclopedia of British Football*, London: Cass.

Crawford, S. (1996) 'Exercise', in Levinson, D. and Christensen, K. (eds) *Encyclopedia of World Sport*, Oxford: ABC-Clio, 300–4.

Cronin, M. (1999) *Sport and Nationalism in Ireland: Gaelic Games, Soccer and Irish Identity*, Dublin: Four Courts Press.

—— (2005) 'Sam Maguire: Forgotten Hero and National Icon', *Sport in History* 25, 2, 189–205.

Cronin, M. and Holt, R. (2001) 'The Imperial Game in Crisis: English Cricket and Decolonisation', in Ward, S., *British Culture and the End of Empire*, Manchester: Manchester University Press.

Cronin, M. and Mayall, D. (1998) *Sporting Nationalisms*, London: Cass.

Crum, B. (1999) 'Changes in Modern Societies: Consequences for PE and School Sport', in Bussard, J-C. and Roth., E, *Which Physical Education for Which School?*, Proceedings of ASEP Congress, Neuchâtel.

Culin, S. (1907) *Games of the North American Indians, Twenty-fourth Annual Report of the Bureau of American Ethnology*, Washington, DC: Government Printing Office.

Curry, T. (1991) 'Fraternal Bonding in the Locker Room: A Profeminist Analysis of Talk about Competition and Women', *Sociology of Sport Journal* 8, 1991, 119–35.

Dale, J. and Weinberg, R. (1990) 'Burnout in Sport: A Review and Critique', *Journal of Applied Sport Psychology* 2, 67–83.

Davis, N. W. and Duncan, M. C. (2006) 'Sports Knowledge is Power; Reinforcing Masculine Privilege Through Fantasy Sports League Participation', *Sport and Social Issues* 30, 3, 244–64.

DCMS (2004) *Bringing Communities Together through Sport and Culture*, London: DCMS

Deci, E. (1975) *Intrinsic Motivation*, New York: Plenum.

DeGrazia, S. (1964) *Of Time, Work and Leisure*, Garden City, NJ: Doubleday.

Department for Education (2001) *Physical Education: The National Curriculum for England, jointly published by the Department for Education and Employment and the Qualifications and Curriculum Authority*. This document can be downloaded from: www.nc.uk.net.

DfEE/QCA (1999) *The National Curriculum Handbook for primary teachers in England*, London: DfEE/QCA

Department of Culture, Media and Sport (2004) *First Game Plan Delivery Report*, London: Department of Culture Media and Sport.

DePauw, K. and Gavron, S. (1995) *Disability and Sport*, Champaign: Human Kinetics.

Dheenshaw, C. (1994) *The Commonwealth Games: The First 60 Years, 1930–1990*, Victoria: Orca.

Dick, F. (2002) *Sports Training Principles*, 4th edn, London: A&C Black.

Dimeo, P. (2006) *Drugs, Alcohol and Sport*, Abingdon: Routledge

Dirix, A, Knuttgen, H. G. and Tittel, K. (1988) *The Olympic Book of Sports Medicine*, Oxford: Blackwell.

Dishman, R. (1994) *Advances in Exercise Adherence*, Champaign: Human Kinetics.

—— (2001) 'The Problem of Exercise Adherence: Fighting Sloth in Nations with Market Economies', *Quest* 53, 279–94.

Dixon, P. and Garnham, G. (2005) 'Drink and the Professional Footballer in 1890s England and Ireland', *Sport in History* 25, 375–89.

Dobson, S. (2000) 'Economics of Sport', in Cox, R., Jarvie, G. and Vamplew, W (eds) *Encyclopedia of British Sport*, Oxford: ABC-Clio, 119–21.

Doggart, H. (1999) 'The Corinthian Ideal', in Grayson, E. (ed.) *Sport and the Law*, London: Butterworth.

Donnelly, P (2000) 'Interpretive Approaches to the Sociology of Sport', in Coakley, J. and Dunning, E., *Handbook of Sports Studies*, London: Sage, 77–91.

—— (2006) 'Studying Extreme Sports: Beyond the Core Participants', *Journal of Sport and Social Issues* 30.2, 219–24.

Donohue, J. (1994) *Warrior Dreams: The Martial Arts and the American Imagination*, Westport: Bergin and Garvey.

Duda, J. (ed.) (1998) *Advances in Sport and Exercise Psychology Measurement*, Morgantown: FLT

Dumazedier, J. (1967) *Toward a Leisure Society*, New York: Free Press.

Duncanson, N. and Collies, P (1992) *Tales of Gold*, London: Queen Anne Press.

Dunning, E. (2000) *Sport Matters: Sociological Studies of Sport, Violence and Civilization*, London: Routledge.

Dunning, E., Malcom, D. and Waddington I. (2004) *Sport Histories: Figurational Studies of the Development of Modern Sports*, London: Routledge.

Dunning, E. and Sheard, K. (1979) *Barbarians, Gentlemen and Players: A Sociological Study of the Development of Rugby Football*, Oxford: Robertson.

Dyreson, M. (1996) 'Technology', in Levinson, D. and Christensen, K. (eds) *Encyclopedia of World Sport*, Oxford: ABC-Clio, 1014–17.

Dyson (1986) *Mechanics of Athletics*, 8th edn, New York: Holmes and Meier.

Eichberg, H. (1986) 'The Enclosure of the Body: On the Historical Relativity of Health, Nature and the Environment of Sport', *Journal of Contemporary History* 21, 99–121.

Eisen, G. and Wiggins, D. K. (eds) (1994) *Ethnicity and Sport in North American History and Culture*, Westport: Greenwood Press.

Eitzen, D. (1995) 'Classism in Sport: The Powerless Bear the Burden', *Journal of Sport and Social Issues* 20, 1, 95–105.

Elias, N. and Dunning, E. (1986) *The Quest for Excitement: Sport and Leisure in the Civilising Process*, Oxford: Blackwell.

Elling, A., De Knop, P. and Knoppers, A. (2003) 'Gay/Lesbian Sport Clubs and Events: Places of Homo-Social Bonding and Cultural Resistance?' *International Review for the Sociology of Sport*, 38.4, 441–56.

Elliott, B. (ed.) (1998) *Training in Sport: Applying Sport Science*, New York: Wiley.

Ellis, M. (1973) *Why People Play*, Englewood Cliffs: Prentice-Hall.

European Commission DG Education and Culture, Studies on Education and Sport (2004) Sport and Multiculturalism (Lot 3) Final Report. European Union: Brussels.

Evans, J. H. (1974) *The Story of CCPR 1935–72: Service to Sport*, London: The Sports Council.

Evans, J. and Davies, B. (1999) *Physical Education, Pedagogy and Identity*, London: Falmer Press.

Fahey, T. (1997) *Basic Weight Training for Men and Women*, Mountain View, CA: Mayfield

Feltz, D. and Landers, D. (1983) 'The Effects of Mental Practice on Motor Skill Learning and Performance: A Meta-analysis', *Journal of Sport Psychology* 5, 25–57.

Fewell, M. (ed.) (1995) *Sports Law: A Practical Guide*, North Ryde: LBC.

Field, J. (2003) *Social Capital*, London: Routledge.

Finn, M. (1988) *Martial Arts: A Complete Illustrated History*, Woodstock, New York: Overlook Press.

Fitts, P. and Posner, M. (1967) *Human Performance*, Belmont: Brooks/Cole.

Fleck, S. and Kraemer, W. (1997) *Designing Resistance Training Programs*, 2nd edn, Champaign: Human Kinetics.

Fleishman, E. (1975) 'Toward a Theory of Human Performance', *American Psychologist* 30, 1127–49.

Fletcher, S. (1984) *Women First*, London: Athlone Press.

Foss, M. (1998) *Fox's Physiological Basis for Exercise and Sport*, Boston, MA: WCB/ McGraw-Hill.

Fox, E., Kirby, T. and Fox, A. (1987) *Bases of Fitness*, New York: Macmillan.

Fox, E. and Mathews, D. (1974) *Interval Training*, Philadelphia: Sounders.

Franklin, A. (1999) *Animals and Modern Cultures. A Sociology of Human/ Animal Relations in Modernity*, London: Sage.

Franks, I. and Goodman, D. (1992) 'Motor Control, Motor Learning and Physical Activity', in Bouchard, C., McPherson, B. and Taylor, A. (eds) *Physical Activity Sciences*, Champaign: Human Kinetics, 71–80.

Frosdick, S. and Whalley, J. (1997) *Sport and Safety Management*, London: Butterworths.

Gardiner, E. (2006) *Athletic of the Ancient World*, Chicago: Ares.

Gardiner, S., Felix, A., James, M., Welch, R. and O'Leary, J. (1998) *Sports Law*, London: Cavendish.

Garvey, C. (1977) *Play: The Developing Child*, Cambridge, MA: Harvard University Press.

Gavin, J. (1992) *The Exercise Habit*, Champaign: Leisure Press.

Gearing, B. and MacNeil, P. (1999) *Seventy Years of BBC Sport*, London: André Deutsch.

Geertz, C. (1972) 'Deep Play: Notes on the Balinese Cock Fight', in Geertz, C. *The Interpretation of Cultures*, New York: Basic Books, 412–53.

Gentile, A. (1972) 'A Working Model of Skill Acquisition with Application to Teaching', *Quest* 17, 3–23.

Gibney, M. J., Vorster H. H. and Kok, F. J. (2002) *Introduction to Human Nutrition*, Oxford: Blackwell.

Gill, D. (1986) *Psychological Dimensions of Sport*, Champaign: Human Kinetics.

Gillmeister, H. (1981) 'The Origin of European Ball Games: A Re-evaluation and Linguistic Analysis', *Stadion* 7, 119–51.

Girginov, V. and Parry, J. (2004) *The Olympic Games Explained*, London: Routledge.

Giulianotti, R., (2005) 'The Sociability of Sport: Scotland Football Supporters as Interpreted through the Sociology of Georg Simmel', *International Review for the Sociology of Sport* 40, 289–306.

Giulianotti, R., Bonney, N. and Hepworth, M. (1994) *Football, Violence and Social Identity*, London: Routledge.

Goffman, E. (1961) *The Presentation of Self in Everyday Life*, New York: Archer.

Goodman, S. and McGregor, I. (1994) *Legal Liability and Risk Management*, North York, Ontario: Risk Management Associates.

Gould, D. and Damarjian, N. (1998) 'Mental Skills Training in Sport', in Elliott, B., *Training in Sport*, London: Wiley, 69–116.

Gratton, C. (1998) 'The Economic Importance of Modern Sport', *Culture, Sport, Society* 1, 1, 101–17.

Gratton, C. and Taylor, P (1985) *Sport and Recreation: An Economic Analysis*, London: Spon.

Grayson, E. (1996) *Corinthians and Cricketers: Towards a New Sporting Era*, London: Yore.

—— (1999a) *Sport and the Law*, London: Butterworth.

—— (ed.) (1999b) *Ethics, Injuries and the Law in Sports Medicine*, Oxford: Butterworth-Heinemann.

Greenfield, S. and Osborn, G. (2000a) *Law and Sport in Contemporary Society*, London: Cass.

—— (2000b) 'Unions and Strikes', in Cox, R., Jarvie, G. and Vamplew, W. (eds) *Encyclopedia of British Sport*, Oxford: ABC-Clio, 406–8.

Greenfield. S., Osborn, G. and Taylor, M. (2001) in Cox, R., Russell, D, and Vamplew, W (eds) *Encyclopedia of British Football*, London: Cass.

Grisognono, V (1991) *Children in Sport*, London: John Murray.

Groves, D. L. (1987) 'Sport and Leisure and Its Use in Television Programmes and Commercials – Model', *Psychology – A Quarterly Journal of Human Behaviour* 24, 12, 13–21.

Gruneau, R. (1978) 'Conflicting Standards and Problems of Personal Action in the Sociology of Sport', *Quest* 48, 98–120.

Gruneau, R. and Cantelon, H. (1988) 'Capitalism, Commercialism and the Olympics', in Segrave, J. and Chu, D. (eds) *The Olympics in Transition*, Champaign: Human Kinetics, 345–64.

Guthrie, E. (1952) *The Psychology of Learning*, New York: Harper and Row.

Guttmann, A. (1978) *From Ritual to Record*, New York, Columbia

—— (1992) *The Olympics: A History of the Modern Games*, Urbana: University of Illinois Press.

—— (1994) *Games and Empire*, New York: Columbia University Press.

—— (2004) *From Ritual to Record: The Nature of Modern Sports*, New York: Columbia.

Hackney, R. and Wallace, W. (eds) (1999) *Sports Medicine Handbook*, London: BMJ.

Hain, P. (1982) 'Politics of Sport and Apartheid', in Hargreaves, J. (ed.) *Sport, Culture and Ideology*, London: Routledge, 232–48.

Haldane, J. and Wright, C. (eds) (1993) *Reality, Representation and Projection*, New York: Oxford University Press.

Hall, C. M. and Page, S. (2005) *Geographical Tourism and Recreational*, Abingdon: Routledge.

Hall, D. (ed.) (1994) *Muscular Christianity: Embodying the Victorian Age*, Cambridge: Cambridge University Press.

Hall, M. A. (1987) 'Women Olympians in the Canadian Sport bureaucracy', in Slack, T. and Hinings, C. R. (eds) *The Organisation and Administration of Sport*, London ONT: Sport Dynamics, 101–26.

—— (1996) *Feminism and Sporting Bodies: Essays on Theory and Practice*, Champaign: Human Kinetics.

Hanin, Y (ed.) (2000) *Emotions in Sport*, Champaign: Human Kinetics.

Hardman, K. and Green, K. (1998) *Physical Education – A Reader*, Aachen: Meyer and Meyer.

Hardy, L. (1990) 'A Catastrophe Model of Performance in Sport', in Jones, J. and Hardy, L. (eds) *Stress and Performance in Sport*, Chichester: Wiley, 81–106.

Hargreaves, J. E. (1986) *Sport, Power and Culture*, New York: St Martin's Press.

Hargreaves, J. A.(1994) *Sporting Females: Critical Issues in the History and Sociology of Sport*, London: Routledge.

Harries, M. (ed.) (1996) *Oxford Textbook of Sports Medicine*, Oxford: Oxford University Press.

Harris, J. (1980) 'Play: A Definition', *Journal of Sport Psychology* 2, 46–61.

Harris, J.P., (2000) *Health Related Exercise in the National Curriculum – Key Stages 1–4*, Champaign: Human Kinetics.

Harris, J. and Park, R. (eds) (1983) *Play, Games and Sports in Cultural Contexts*, Champaign: Human Kinetics.

Harris, M. (1998) 'Sport in the Newspaper before 1750: Representations of Cricket, Class and Commerce in the London Press', *Media History* 4, 1, 19–27.

Harvey, A. (2005) *Football: The First Hundred Years*, Abingdon: Routledge.

Hay, J. (1993) *The Biomechanics of Sports Techniques*, 4th edn, Englewood Cliffs: Prentice-Hall.

Henderson, R. (1947) *Ball, Bat and Bishop*, New York: Rockport.

Henschen, K. (1986) 'Athletic Staleness and Burnout: Diagnosis, Prevention and Treatment', in Williams, J. (ed.) *Sport Psychology: Personal Growth to Peak Performance*, Palo Alto: Mayfield, 328–37.

Higgs, R. J. (1995) *God in the Stadium: Sport and Religion in America*, Lexington: University of Kentucky Press.

Hignell, A. (1999) 'Crowds, Clouds and the Raining Champions: A Locational View of County Cricket in England and Wales', *Culture, Sport, Society* 2, 2, 58–81.

Hillman, S. (2000) *Introduction to Athletic Training*, Champaign: Human Kinetics.

Hoberman, J. (1984) *Sport and Political Ideology*, London: Routledge.

—— (1992) *Mortal Engines: The Science of Performance and the Dehumanisation of Sport*, New York: Free Press.

—— (1997) *Darwin's Athletes: How Sport Has Damaged Black America and Preserved the Myth of Race*, Boston, MA: Houghton Mifflin.

Hoffman, S. J. (ed.) (1992) *Sport and Religion*, Champaign: Human Kinetics.

Holt, R. (1989) *Sport and the British*, London: Oxford.

Holt, R., Lanfranchi, P and Mangan, J. A. (eds) (1996) *European Heroes: Myth, Sport, Identity*, London: Cass.

Holt, R. and Mason, T. (2000) *Sport in Britain, 1945–2000*, Oxford: Blackwell.

Honey, J. (1977) *Tom Brown's Universe: The Development of the Victorian Public School*, London: Millington.

Horn, T. (ed.) (1992) *Advances in Sport Psychology*, Champaign: Human Kinetics.

Houghton, W. (1957) *The Victorian Frame of Mind*, New Haven: Yale.

Houlihan, B. (1991) *The Government and Politics of Sport*, London: Routledge.

Howe, P. D. (2004) *Sport, Professionalism and Pain*, London: Routledge.

Howley, E. and Franks, B. (1997) *Health/Fitness Instructor's Handbook*, 3rd edn, Champaign: Human Kinetics.

Hudson, D. (2000) 'Marketing', in Cox, R., Jarvie, G. and Vamplew, W. (eds) *Encyclopedia of British Sport*, Oxford: ABC-Clio, 238–40.

Huggins, M. (2000) 'Second Class Citizens? English Middle-Class Culture and Sport, 1850–1910: A Reconsideration', *International Journal of the History of Sport* 17, 1, 1–35.

Hughes, T. (1964) *Tom Brown's Schooldays*, London: Macmillan.

Hughson, J. (2001) *Sporting Tales: Ethnographic Fieldwork Experiences*, Canberra: Australian Society for Sports History.

Hughson, J., Inglis, D. and Free M. (2005) *The Uses of Sport*, London: Routledge.

Huizinga, J. (1950) *Homo Ludens*, Boston, MA: Beacon.

Huntington-Whiteley, J. (1998) T*he Book of British Sporting Heroes*, London: National Portrait Gallery.

Husman, B. and Silva, J. (1884) 'Aggression in Sport: Definitional and Theoretical Considerations', in Silva, J. and Weinberg, R. (eds) *Psychological Foundations of Sport*, Champaign: Human Kinetics, 246–60.

Hyland, D. (1984) *The Question of Play*, Lanham: University of America Press.

—— (1990) *Philosophy of Sport*, New York: Paragon.

Ingham, A. and Loy, J. (eds) (1993) *Sport in Social Development: Traditions, Transitions and Transformations*, Champaign: Human Kinetics.

James, C. (1963) *Beyond a Boundary*, New York: Pantheon.

Jarvie, G. (2006) *Sport, Culture and Society*, Abingdon: Routledge.

Jarvie, G. and Walker, G. (eds) (1994) *Scottish Sport in the Making of the Nation: Ninety Minute Patriots*, Leicester: Leicester University Press.

Johnes, M. (2000) 'Advertising', in Cox, R., Jarvie, G. and Vamplew, W (eds) *Encyclopedia of British Sport*, Oxford: ABC-Clio, 2–3.

Johnes, M. and Mason, R. (2003) 'Sport in Public History: Soccer, Public History and the National Football Museum', *Sport in History* 23.1, 115–31.

Jones, A. M. and Poole, D. C. (2004) *Oxygen Uptake Kinetics in Sport, Exercise and Medicine*, London: Routledge.

Jones, S. (1988) *Sport, Politics and the Working Class in Modern Britain*, Manchester: Manchester University Press.

Jordan, B. (ed.) (1993) *Medical Aspects of Boxing*, Boca Raton: CRC Press.

Kahneman, D. (1973) *Attention and Effort*, Englewood Cliffs: Prentice-Hall.

Kallus, K. and Kellman, M. (2000) 'Burnout in Athletes and Coaches', in Hanin, Y. (ed.) *Emotions in Sport*, Champaign: Human Kinetics, 209–30.

Karinch, M. (2000) *Lessons from the Edge*, New York: Simon and Schuster.

Karlis, G., (2003) 'Volunteerism and Multiculturalism: A Linkage for Future Olympics', *The Sport Journal* 6, 3 (www.thesportjournal.org/2003Journal/Vol6-No2/Karlis.asp)

Kay, J. and Vamplew, W. (2006) 'Under the Weather: Combating the Climate in British Sport', *Sport in Society* 9, 94–107.

Kean, H. (1998) *Animal Rights: Political and Social Change in Britain Since 1800*, London: Reaktion.

Keele, S. (1968) 'Movement Control in Skilled Motor Performance', *Psychological Bulletin* 70, 387–403.

Kelly, J. (1996) *Leisure*, 3rd edn, Boston MA: Allyn and Bacon.

Kelso, J. (1982) *Human Motor Behavior: An Introduction*, Hillsdale: Erlbaum.

Kenyon, G. S. and Loy, J. W (eds) (1965) *Sport, Culture and Society: A Reader on the Sociology of Sport*, New York: Macmillan, 36–43.

Kerr, J. (1997) *Motivation and Emotion in Sport: Reversal Theory*, Falmer: Psychology Press.

—— (2004) *Rethinking Aggression and Violence in Sport*, London: Routledge.

Kew, F. (1997) *Sport: Social Problems and Issues*, Oxford: Butterworth-Heinemann.

Kingsley, C. (1921) *Yeast*, London: Macmillan.

Kirk, D. (2006) 'The Obesity Crisis and School Physical Education' in *Sport, Education and Society* 11, 2, 121–33.

Klein, A. (1991) *Sugarball: The American Game, the Dominican Dream*, New Haven CT: Yale University Press.

Klein, T., Gilman E., and Zigler, E. (1993) 'Special Olympics: An Evaluation by Professionals and Parents', *Mental Retardation* 31.1, 15–33.

Koppett, L. (1981) *Sports Illusion, Sports Reality: A Reporter's View of Sports, Journalism and Society*, Boston, MA: Houghton Mifflin.

Kreider, R., Fry, A. and O'Toole, H. (eds) (1998) *Overtraining in Sport*, Champaign: Human Kinetics.

Kremer, J. and Scully, D. (1996) *Psychology in Sport*, London: Taylor and Francis.

Kruger, A. and Riordan, J. (eds) (1996) *The Story of Worker Sport*, Champaign: Human Kinetics.

Kuipers, H. and Keizer, H. (1988) 'Overtraining in Elite Athletics: Review and Future Directions', *Sports Medicine* (Hong-Kong) 6, 2, 79–92.

Kyle, D. (1996) 'Olympic Games, Ancient', in Levinson, D. and Christensen, K. (eds) *The Encyclopedia of World Sport*, Oxford: ABC-Clio, 689–95.

Kyle, D. G. and Storks, G. D. (eds) (1990) *Essays on Sport History and Sport Mythology*, College Station: Texas A and M Press.

Landers, D. and Boutcher, S. (1986) 'Arousal–Performance Relationships', in Williams, J. (ed.) *Applied Sport Psychology*, Palo Alto: Mayfield, 163–84.

Lanfranchi, P and Taylor, M. (2001) *Moving With the Ball: The Migration of Professional Footballers*, Oxford: Berg.

Larson, J. E and Heung-Soo, P. (1993) *Global Television and the Seoul Olympics*, Boulder: Westview Press.

Lavallee, D., Thatcher, J. and Jones, M. (eds) (2004) *Coping and Emotion in Sport*, New York: Nova.

Lavin, M. (1987) 'Sport and Drugs: Are the Current Bans Justified?', *Journal of the Philosophy of Sport* 14, 34–43.

Lehman, C. (1981) 'Can Cheaters Play the Game?', *Journal of the Philosophy of Sport* 8, 41–6.

Lepper, M. and Green, D. (1975) 'Turning Play into Work: Effects of Adult Surveillance and Extrinsic Rewards on Children's Intrinsic Motivation', *Journal of Personality and Social Psychology* 31, 479–86.

Levine, P. (1992) *Ellis Island to Ebbetts Field: Sport and the American Jewish Experience*, New York: Oxford University Press.

Levinson, D. and Christensen, K. (1996) *Encyclopedia of World Sport*, Oxford: ABC-Clio.

Lewis, A. and Taylor, J. (2003) *Sport: Law and Practice*, London: Butterworths.

Lewis, G. and Appenzeller, H. (eds) (1985) *Successful Sport Management*, Charlottesville: Michie.

Lewis, R.W. (1996) 'Football Hooliganism in England Before 1914: A Critique of the Dunning Thesis', *International Journal of the History of Sport* 13.3, 310–39.

Loland, S. (1998) 'Fair Play: Historical Anachronism or Topical Ideal?', in McNamee, M. and Parry, S. (eds) *Ethics and Sport*, London: Spon, 79–103.

—— (2005) 'The Varieties of Cheating: Comments on Ethical Analysis in Sport', *Sport in Society* 8.1, 11–26.

Long, J., Robinson, P. and Spracklen, K. (2005) 'Promoting Racial Equality Within Sports Organisations', *Sport and Social Issues*, 29.1, 41–59.

Lowerson, J. (1993) *Sport and the English Middle Classes*, Manchester: Manchester University Press.

Loy, J. W., Andrews, D. L. and Rinehart, B. (1993) 'The Body in Culture and Sport', *Sports Science Review* 2, 1, 257–84.

Loy, J. W. and Kenyon, G. S. (eds) (1969) *Sport, Culture and Society: A Reader on the Sociology of Sport*, New York: Macmillan.

Loy, J. W., McPherson, B. D. and Kenyon, G. S. (1978) *The Sociology of Sport as an Academic Speciality: An Episodic Essay on the Development and Emergence of an Hybrid Subfield in North America*, Vanier City: University of Calgary Press.

Loy, J. W and Segrave, J. O. (1974) 'Research Methodologies in the Sociology of Sport', *Exercise and Sport Sciences Reviews* 2, 289–333.

Luschen, G. (1975) 'The Development and Scope of a Sociology of Sport', *American Corrective Therapy Journal* 29, 39–43.

—— (1980) 'Sociology of Sport: Development, Present State and Prospects', in Inkeles, A., Smelser, N. J. and Turne, R. H. (eds) *Annual Review of Sociology* 6, 315–47.

Lyle, J. (2002) *Sports Coaching Concepts*, London: Routledge.

MacAloon, J. (1981) *This Great Symbol: Pierre de Coubertin and the Origin of the Modern Olympic Games*, Chicago: University of Chicago Press.

—— (2006) 'Muscular Christianity after 150 years', *International Journal of the History of Sport* 23.5, 687–700.

MacClancey, J. (1996) *Sport, Identity and Ethnicity*, Oxford: Berg.

MacKenzie, J. M. (1989) *Imperialism and Popular Culture*, Manchester: Manchester University Press.

Maehr, M. and Braskamp, L. (1986) *The Motivation Factor: A Theory of Personal Investment*, Lexington: Lexington Books.

Magill, R. (1998) *Motor Learning: Concepts and Applications*, Dubuque: Brown.

Maguire, J. (2000) *Global Games*, London: Polity.

Malcolmson, R. W (1973) *Popular Recreations in English Society, 1700–1850*, Cambridge: Cambridge University Press.

Malina, R. (1983) 'Menarche in Athletics', *Annals of Human Biology* 10, 1–24.

Malina, R. and Buschang, P (1985) 'Growth, Strength, and Motor Performance of Zapotec Children, Oaxaca, Mexico', *Human Biology* 57, 163–82.

Mangan, J. A. (1981) *Athleticism in the Victorian and Edwardian Public School*, Cambridge: Cambridge University Press.

—— (ed.) (1992) *The Cultural Bond: Sport, Empire, Society*, London: Cass.

Mangan, J. A. and Ritchie, A. (2005) *Ethnicity, Sport, Identity: Struggles for Status*, London: Routledge.

Mangan, J. A. and Walvin, J. (eds) (1987) *Manliness and Morality: Middle-Class Masculinity in Britain and America 1800–1940*, Manchester: Manchester University Press.

Marcus, B. and Forsyth, L. (2004) *Motivating People to be Physically Active*, Champaign: Human Kinetics.

Marsh, P. (1983) *Tribes*, Toronto: McGraw-Hill, Ryerson.

—— (1999) *Football Violence in Europe*, www.sirc.org.

Marsh, P. and Fox, K. (1993) *Drinking and Public Disorder*, Oxford: CSIR.

Mason, T. (1980) *Association Football and English Society, 1863–1915*, Brighton: Harvester.

—— (1986) 'Sporting News 1860–1914', in Harris, M. and Lee, A. (eds) *The Press in English Society from the Seventeenth to Nineteenth Centuries*, London: Associated University Press.

—— (1989) (ed.) *Sport in Britain: A Social History*, Cambridge: Cambridge University Press.

McArdle, D. (1999) 'Can Legislation Stop Me From Playing? The Distinction Between Sport Competitors and Sport Workers under the United Kingdom's Sex Discrimination Laws', *Culture, Sport, Society* 2, 2, 44–57.

—— (2000) *From Boot Money to Bosman: Football, Society and the Law*, London: Cavendish.

McArdle, W., Katch, E. and Katch, V. (2000) *Essentials of Exercise Physiology*, Philadelphia: Lippincott, Williams and Williams.

McConnell, R. and McConnell, C. (1996) 'Leadership', in Levinson, D. and Christensen, K. (eds) *Encyclopedia of World Sport*, Oxford: ABC-Clio, 573–6.

McIntosh, P. (1979) *Fair Play: Ethics in Sport and Education*, London: Heinemann.

McLatchie, G. (2000) *ABC of Sports Medicine*, London: BMJ.

McMillen, R. (1998) *Xtreme Sports*, Houston: Gulf.

McMurray, R. G. (1998), *Concepts in Fitness Programming*, Boca Raton: CRC Press.

McNamee, M. and Parry, S. (eds) (1998) *Ethics and Sport*, London: Spon.

McPherson, B. D. (1975) 'Past, Present and Future Perspectives for Research in Sport Sociology', *International Review of Sport Sociology* 10, 55–72.

Mellor, G. (2001) 'Football and the Community', in Cox, R., Russell, D. and Vamplew, W. (eds) *Encyclopedia of British Football*, London: Cass.

Messner, M. A. (1992) *Power at Play*, Boston, MA: Beacon Press.

Messner, M. A. and Sabo, D. (eds) (1992) *Sport, Men and the Gender Order*, Champaign: Human Kinetics.

Middleton, L. (1999). *Disabled Children: Challenging Social Exclusion*, Oxford: Blackwell Science Ltd.

Miller, D. (2003) *Athens to Athens*, Edinburgh: Mainstream.

Miller, D. and Allen, T. (1995) *Fitness: A Lifetime Commitment*, Boston, MA: Allen and Bacon.

Money, A. (1997) *Manly and Muscular Diversions: Public Schools and the Nineteenth-Century Sporting Revival*, London: Duckworth.

Moore, K. (1988) 'The Pan-Britannic Festival: A Tangible but Forlorn Expression of Imperial Unity', in Mangan, J. A. (ed.) *Pleasure, Profit, Proselytism: British Culture and Sport at Home and Abroad, 1700–1914*, London: Cass.

Morgan, W. (1985) 'Selected Psychological Factors Limiting Performance: A Mental Health Model', in Clarke, D. and Eckert, H. (eds) *Limits of Human Performance*, Champaign: Human Kinetics, 70–80.

Morgan, W. P (1993) *Leftist Theories of Sport*, Chicago: University of Illinois Press.

—— (1996) 'Philosophy', in Levinson, D. and Christensen, K. (eds) *The Encyclopedia of World Sport*, Oxford: ABC-Clio, 740–2.

Mosston, M. and Ashworth, S. (1994) *Teaching Physical Education*, New York: Macmillan USA.

Mottola, M. (1992) 'Anatomy and Physical Activity', in Bouchard, C., McPherson, B. and Taylor, A. (eds) *Physical Activity Sciences*, Champaign: Human Kinetics, 33–42.

Mullin, B. J., Hardy, S. and Sutton, W. A. (1993) *Sport Marketing*, Champaign: Human Kinetics.

Munting, R. (1996) *An Economic and Social History of Gambling in Britain and the USA*, Manchester: Manchester University Press.

Murphey, M. and Tennant, L. (eds) (1993) *Handbook of Research on Sport Psychology*, New York: Macmillan.

Murphy, S. (ed.) (1995) *Sport Psychology Interventions*, Champaign: Human Kinetics.

Murray, W. (1987) 'The French Workers' Sport Movement', *International Journal of the History of Sport* 4.

Narvani, A .A., Thomas, P. and Lynn, B. (2006) *Key Topics in Sports Medicine*, Abingdon: Routledge.

Neil, G. (1982) 'Demystifying Sport Superstition', *International Review of Sport Sociology* 17, 99–124.

Nesti, M. (2006) *Existential Psychology and Sport*, Abingdon: Routledge.

Newsome, D. (1961) *Godliness and Good Learning*, London: John Murray.

Oriard, M. (1993) *Reading Football: How the Popular Press Created an American Spectacle*, Chapel Hill: University of North Carolina Press.

Pate, R. (1983) 'A New Definition of Youth Fitness', *Physician and Sports Medicine* 11, 4, 77–83.

Pate, R. and Hohn, R. (1994) *Health and Fitness through Physical Education*, Champaign: Human Kinetics.

Pate, R., McClenaghan, B. and Rotella, R. (1984) *Scientific Foundations of Coaching*, Philadelphia: Saunders.

Patmore, A. (1983) *Recreation and Resources: Leisure Patterns and Leisure Places*, Oxford: Blackwell.

Pearson, K. (1990) 'Methods of Philosophic Inquiry in Physical Education', in Thomas, J. and Nelson, J., *Research Methods in Physical Activity*, 2nd edn, Champaign: Human Kinetics, 229–46.

Peiser, B. (2000) 'Religion', in Cox, R., Jarvie, G. and Vamplew, W (eds) *Encyclopedia of British Sport*, Oxford: ABC-Clio, 321–3.

Penney, D., Clarke, G., Quill, M. and Kitchen, G. (2005) *Sport Education in Physical Education*, Abingdon: Routledge.

Peronnet, F. and Gardiner, P. (1992) 'Physiology and Physical Activity', in Bouchard, C., McPherson, D. and Taylor, A. (eds) *Physical Activity Sciences*, Champaign: Human Kinetics, 43–50.

Peterson, L. and Renstrom, P. (2001) *Sports Injuries*, London: Routledge.

Phares, E. (1991) *Introduction to Personality*, New York: Harper Collins.

Plummer, D. (2006) 'Sportophobia: Why Do Some Men Avoid Sport?', *Journal of Sport and Social Issues* 30.2, 122–37.

Polley, M. (1998) *Moving the Goalposts: A History of Sport and Society since 1945*, London: Routledge.

Polsky, N. (1969) *Hustlers, Beats and Others*, New York: Anchor.

Pope, S. W (1997) *Patriotic Games: Sporting Traditions in the American Imagination, 1876–1926*, New York: Oxford University Press.

Pope, S. W and Rinehart, R. (eds) (2001) *Encyclopedia of Extreme Sports*, Oxford: ABC-Clio.

Powers, S. and Howley, E. (2004) *Exercise Physiology: Theory and Application to Fitness and Performance*, Boston: McGraw Hill.

Prebish, C. S. (1993) *Religion and Sport: The Meeting of Sacred and Profane*, Westport: Greenwood.

Rader, B. (1984) *In Its Own Image: How Television Has Transformed Sports*, New York: Free Press.

Raglin, J. and Wilson, S. (2000) 'Overtraining in Athletes', in Hanin, Y. (ed.) *Emotions in Sport*, Champaign: Human Kinetics, 191–208.

Rail, G. (ed.) (1998) *Sport and Postmodern Times*, New York: State University of New York.

Ramsamy, S. (1984) 'Apartheid, Boycotts and the Games', in Tomlinson, A. and Whannel, G. (eds) *Five Ring Circus: Money, Power and Politics at the Olympic Games*, London: Pluto, 44–52.

Redhead, S. (1998) 'Baudrillard, Amerique and the Hyperreal World Cup', in Rail, G. (ed.) *Sport and Postmodern Times*, New York: State University of New York, 221–38.

Renson, R., De Noyer, P. P. and Ostyn, M. (eds) (1976) *The History, the Evolution and Diffusion of Sports and Games in Different Cultures*, Brussels: BLOSO.

Rink, J. (2002) *Teaching Physical Education for Learning*, St Louis: Mosby.

Riordan, J. (2005) 'Worker Sport' in Levinson, D. and Christensen, K. Berkshire *Encyclopedia of World Sport*, Great Barrington: Berkshire.

Roberts, J. and Sutton-Smith, B. (1962) 'Child Training and Game Involvement', *Ethnology* I, 2, 166–85.

Rogozkin, V. and Maughan, R. (1996) *Current Research in Sport Sciences*, New York: Plenum.

Rose, W. (1988) *The Combat Sport: Boxing Yesterday and Today*, Community Film Group: Videocraft.

Rowe, D. (2000) *Sport, Culture and the Media*, Buckingham: Open University Press.

Rowland, T. (1996) *Developmental Exercise Physiology*, Champaign: Human Kinetics.

Roy, B. (1992) 'Biomechanics and Physical Activity', in Bouchard, C., McPherson, B. and Taylor, A. (eds) *Physical Activity Sciences*, Champaign: Human Kinetics, 65–70.

Sage, G. (1979) 'Sport and the Social Sciences', *The Annals of the American Academy of Political and Social Science* 455, 1–14.

Sansone, D. (1988) *Greek Athletics and the Genesis of Sport*, Berkeley: University of California Press.

Scheerder, J., Vanreusel, B., and Taks. M. (2005) 'Stratification Patterns of Active Sport Involvement Among Adults: Social Change and Persistence', *International Review for the Sociology of Sport* 40, 139–62.

Scherer, D. (1995) 'Existence, Breeding and Rights: The Use of Animals in Sports', in Morgan, W. J. and Meier, K. V. (eds) *Philosophic Inquiry in Sports*, Champaign: Human Kinetics.

Schmidt, C. W. (2006) 'Putting the Earth in Play: Environmental Awareness and Sports', *Environmental Health Perspectives* 114, 286–95.

Schmidt, R. (1975) 'A Schema Theory of Discrete Motor Skills Learning', *Psychological Review* 82, 225–60.

Schmidt, R. and Lee, T (1999) *Motor Control and Learning: A Behavioral Emphasis*, Champaign: Human Kinetics.

Schneider, A. and Butcher, R. (1993–94) 'Why Olympic Athletes Should Avoid the Use and Seek the Elimination of Performance-Enhancing Substances and Practices from the Olympic Games', *Journal of the Philosophy of Sport* 20–21, 64–81.

Schwartzman, H. (1978) *Transformations: The Anthropology of Children's Play*, New York: Plenum.

Scott, M. (1968) *The Racing Game*, Chicago: Aldine.

Segrave, J. (1988) 'Toward a Definition of Olympism', in Segrave, J. and Chu, D. (eds) *The Olympic Games in Transition*, Champaign: Human Kinetics, 149–61.

—— (ed.) (1996) 'Perspectives on the Modern Olympics', *Quest* 48, 1–101.

——Segrave, J. and Chu, D. (eds) (1988) *The Olympic Games in Transition*, Champaign: Human Kinetics.

Senn, A. (1999) *Power, Politics and the Olympic Games*, Champaign: Human Kinetics.

Shank, M. (1999) *Sports Marketing; A Strategic Perspective*, Englewood Cliffs: Prentice-Hall.

Sherry, E. and Wilson, S. F (1998) *The Oxford Handbook of Sports Medicine*, Oxford: Oxford University Press.

Shields, D. and Bredemeier, B. J. (1995) *Character Development and Physical Activity*, Champaign: Human Kinetics.

Shilling, C. (1994) *The Body and Social Theory*, Thousand Oaks, CA: Sage.

Siedentop, D. (1994) *Sport Education*, Champaign: Human Kinetics.

Simon, R. (1991) *Fair Play: Sports, Values and Society*, Oxford: Westview Press.

Simon, V and Jennings, A. (1992) *The Lords of the Rings: Power, Money and Drugs in the Modern Olympics*, Toronto: Stoddart.

Singer, P. (1975), *Animal Liberation*, New York: Avon Books.

Singer, R. (1980) *Motor Learning and Human Performance*, New York: Macmillan.

Slack, T. (1996) *Understanding Sports Organizations*, Champaign: Human Kinetics.

—— (2000) 'Management', in Cox, R., Jarvie, G. and Vamplew, W. (eds) *Encyclopedia of British Sport*, Oxford: ABC-Clio, 235–7.

Sloane, P. (1980) *Sport in the Market*, London: Institute of Economic Affairs.

Smith, M. (1983) *Violence in Sport*, Toronto: Butterworth.

Smith, A. and Porter, D. (2000) *Amateurs and Professionals in Post-War British Sport*, London: Cass.

Snyder, E. E. and Spreitzer, E. (1974) 'Sport Sociology and the Discipline of Sociology: Present Status and Speculations about the Future', *Review of Sport and Leisure* 4, 467–87.

Stainback, J. (1998) *Alcohol and Sport*, Champaign: Human Kinetics.

Steenberger, J. and Tamboer, J. (1998) 'Ethics and the Double Character of Sport', in McNamee, M. and Parry, S. (eds) *Ethics and Sport*, London: Spon, 35–53.

Steinberg, L. (1991) 'The Role of Sports Agents', in Standohar, D. D. and Mangan, J. A. (eds) *The Business of Professional Sports*, Urbana: University of Illinois Press, 247–63.

Stogdill, R. (1974) *The Handbook of Leadership*, New York: Free Press.

Stoll, S. K. (1996) 'Ethics', in Levinson, D. and Christensen, K. (eds) *Encyclopedia of World Sport*, Oxford: ABC-Clio, 285–92.

Strauss, R. (1984) *Sports Medicine*, Philadelphia: Saunders.

Struna, N. L. (1996) 'Leisure', in Levinson, D. and Christensen, K. (eds) *Encyclopedia of World Sport*, Oxford: ABC-Clio, 576–80.

Sugden, J. (1996) *Boxing and Society: An International Analysis*, Manchester: Manchester University Press.

Sugden, J. and Tomlinson, A. (2000) 'Theorising Sport, Social Class and Status', in Coakley, J. and Dunning, E. (eds) *Handbook of Sport and Society*, London: Sage.

Symanski, S. (2003) 'The Economic Design of Sporting Contests', *Journal of Economic Literature* 41, 1137–87.

Taylor, D. J. (2006) *On the Corinthian Spirit*, London: Yellow Jersey.

Taylor, P. and Gratton, C. (2000) *The Economics of Sport and Recreation*, London: Routledge.

Thomas, K. (1983) *Man and the Natural World: Changing Attitudes in England, 1500–1800*, London: Allen Lane.

Tindall, B. (1975) 'Ethnography and the Hidden Curriculum in Sport', *Behavioral and Social Science Teacher* 2, 2, 5–28.

Tomlinson, A. and Sugden, J. (1998) *FIFA and the Contest for World Football*, London: Polity.

Townes, J. (1996) 'Gay Games', in Levinson, D. and Christensen, K. (eds) *Encyclopedia of World Sport: From Ancient Times to the Present*, Santa Barbara: ABC-Clio.

Trangbaek, E. (2000) 'One system, several cultures: a comparative study of Swedish gymnastics for women', *International Sports Studies* 2, 42–56.

Tranter, N. (1998) *Sport, Economy and Society in Britain, 1750–1914*, Cambridge: Cambridge University Press.

Tuan, Y-F. (1974) *Topophilia*, Englewood Cliffs: Prentice-Hall.

Tylor, E. (1879) 'The History of Games', *Fortnightly Review* (London) 25, 735–47.

Ueberhorst, H. (1996) 'Turnen', in Levinson, D. and Christensen, K. (eds) *Encyclopedia of World Sport*, Oxford: ABC-Clio, 1110–14.

Vamplew, W. (1998) 'Facts and Artefacts: Sports Historians and Sports Museums', *Journal of Sports History* 24, 2, 268–82.

—— (2004) 'Taking a Gamble or a Racing Certainty: Sports Museums and Public Sports History', *Journal of Sport History* 177–91.

—— (2005a) 'Alcohol and the Sportsperson: An Anomalous Alliance', *Sport in History* 25, 390–411.

—— (2005b) *Pay Up and Play the Game*, Cambridge, Cambridge University Press.

—— (2007) 'Playing with the Rules: Influences on the Development of Regulation in Sport', *International Journal of the History of Sport* 24

Vamplew, W. and Dimeo, P. (2004) *Sporting Conduct Initiative: An International Perspective*, London, UKSport.

Vamplew, W. and Sandiford, K. (1999) 'County Cricketers' Benefits and Testimonials 1945–85', *International Journal for the History of Sport* 6, 1, 87–116.

Vamplew, W. and Stoddart, B. (eds) (1994) *Sport in Australia: A Social History*, Cambridge: Cambridge University Press.

Vance, N. (1985) *The Sinews of the Spirit: The Ideal of Christian Manliness*, Cambridge: Cambridge University Press.

Vealey, R. (1996) 'Psychology', in Levinson, D. and Christensen, K. *Encyclopedia of World Sport*, Oxford: ABC-Clio, 774–81.

Vertinsky, P. and Bale, J. (2004) *Sites of Sport: Sport, Space and Experience*, London: Cass

Waddington, I. (2000) *Sport, Health and Drugs: A Critical Sociological Perspective*, London: Spon.

—— (2005) 'Changing Patterns of Drug Use in British Sport from the 1960s', *Sport in History* 25, 472–96.

Wade, M. (1996) 'Sports and Speciesism', *Journal of the Philosophy of Sport* 23, 10–29.

Wagner, Eric (1989) *Sport in Asia and Africa*, New York: Greenwood Press.

Wann, D. (1997) *Sport Psychology*, Upper Saddle River: Prentice-Hall.

Wearing, B. (1995) 'Leisure and Resistance in an Ageing Society', *Leisure Studies* 14, 4, 263–79.

Weinberg, R. and Gould, D. (1999) *Foundations of Sport and Exercise Psychology*, 2nd edn, Champaign: Human Kinetics.

Weiss, P. (1969) *Sport: A Philosophic Inquiry*, Carbondale: Southern Illinois University Press.

Wells, K. and Luttgens, K. (1976) *Kinesiology: Scientific Basis of Human Motion*, London: Sounders.

Werner, P., Bunker, D. and Thorpe, R. (1996) 'Teaching Games for Understanding: The Evolution of a Model'. *Journal of Physical Education, Recreation and Dance* 67 (1), 28–33.

Whannel, G. (1992) *Fields in Vision: Television, Sport and Cultural Transformation*, London: Routledge.

Wheaton, B. (2004) *Understanding Lifestyle Sport*, London: Routledge.

Wheeler, K. and Nauright, J. (2006) 'A Global Perspective on the Environmental Impact of Golf', *Sport and Society* 9, 427–43.

Wheeler, R. (1978) 'Organised Sport and Organised Labour: The Worker Sports Movement', *Journal of Contemporary History* 13.

White, A. (2001), 'Brighton Declaration' in Christensen, K., Guttmann, A. and Pfister, G., *International Encyclopedia of Women and Sports*, New York: Macmillan.

Whitehead, M. (2001) 'The Concept of Physical Literacy', *The British Journal of Teaching Physical Education* 32, 1.

Whiting, H. (ed.) (1975) *Readings in Human Performance*, London: Lepus.

Wigglesworth, N. (1992) *A Social History of English Rowing*, London: Cass.

—— (1996) *The Evolution of English Sport*, London: Cass.

Wiley, M. (1996) 'Martial Arts, Philippines', in Levinson, D. and Christensen, K. (eds) *Encyclopedia of World Sport*, Oxford: ABC-Clio, 610–13.

Williams, A. and Hodges, N. (eds) (2004) *Skill Acquisition in Sport*, London: Routledge.

Williams, J. (2001) *Cricket and Race*, Oxford: Berg.

Williams, J., Dunning, E. and Murphy, P (1984) *Hooligans Abroad*, London: Routledge.

Williams, M. H. (1996) *Lifetime Fitness and Wellness*, Dubuque: Brown.

—— (ed.) (1998) *Ergogenic Aids in Sport*, Champaign: Human Kinetics.

—— (ed.) (2005) *Nutrition for Health, Fitness and Sport*, New York: McGraw Hill.

Wilmore, J. (1982) *Training for Sport and Physical Activity*, Boston, MA: Allyn and Bacon.

Wilmore, J. and Costill, D. (2004) *Physiology of Sport and Exercise*, 4th edn, Champaign: Human Kinetics.

Wilson, J. (1994) *Playing by the Rules: Sport, Society and the State*, Detroit: Wayne State University Press.

Winters, C. (1980) 'Running', *Landscapes* 24, 19–22.

Yerkes, R. and Dodson, J. (1908) 'The Relation of Strength of Stimulus to Rapidity of Habit Formation', *Journal of Comparative and Neurological Psychology* 18, 459–82.

Yesalis, C. (ed.) (2000) *Anabolic Steroids in Sport and Exercise*, Champaign: Human Kinetics.

Young, D. (1984) *The Olympic Myth of Greek Amateur Athletics*, Chicago: Ares.

—— (1996) *The Modern Olympics*, Baltimore: Johns Hopkins University Press.

Young, K. (1991) 'Sport and Collective Violence', *Exercise and Sport Science Reviews* 19, 539–86.

Zajonc, R. B. and Sales, S. M. (1966) 'Social Facilitation of Dominant and Subordinate Responses', *Journal of Experimental Social Psychology* 2, 160–8.

Zarrilli, P (1996) 'Martial Arts, South Asia', in Levinson, D. and Christensen, K. (eds) *Encyclopedia of World Sport*, Oxford: ABC-Clio, 613–16.

Index

intervention processes 112–13
intrinsic motives 50, 75, 113, 124,
    143, 167, 205, 233
invented tradition 104, 113–14
inverted U theory 21
investment 51, 64, 92, 109, 114, 116,
    151

Jahn 33, 114–15, 127, 229
Johnson, B. 14, 62, 72
Jordan, M. 98
journalism 115–16

key stages 116–17, 149, 164
Kick it campaign 117
Krebs cycle 65, 68, 117–18

lactate threshold 118
landscape 5, 69, 95–96, 118–19, 232
language 120–21, 132, 164, 216–17
law 3, 7, 18, 38, 42, 50, 91, 92,
    121–22, 145, 185, 189, 191, 193
leadership 23, 123, 166
leisure 18, 38, 56, 64, 73, 105, 108,
    123–24, 129, 171, 183, 186, 206,
    232, 238
L'Equipe 116
levers 26, 124–25
limited channel capacity 125
Ling 126–27, 218–19
listed events 126–27, 223–24

Maclaren 127
management 8, 110, 127–28, 148,
    166, 193
manliness 23, 36, 94, 128, 147, 179
marketing 3, 31, 58, 98, 128–29,
    136, 204
MCC 3, 43, 94, 97, 207
martial arts 85, 130–32
masculinity 53, 79, 94–95, 132–33
mass culture 53, 133
material culture 133–34
maximum wage 34, 64, 134, 189,
    193, 215, 230
media 3, 5, 10, 30, 34, 39, 41–42,
    44, 53–54, 59, 72, 80, 82, 86,
    97–98, 106, 132, 134–36, 156,
    168, 170, 195, 202, 204, 206, 208,
    235, 240
merchandising 31, 44, 82, 129, 136, 216
metabolism 15, 67–68, 117, 137, 152

militarism 48, 137, 219
mobility 34, 137–38, 185, 189, 230
model course of 1902, 219, 137–38,
    219
modernisation 25, 138–39
modern sport 25, 31, 38, 41, 46, 50,
    58, 76, 80, 85, 94, 105, 119, 134,
    139, 156, 159, 170, 179–80, 194,
    201–2, 209, 213, 226, 230
moments 139–40
momentum 140
monopoly 34, 126, 140–41, 185
motion 27, 90, 141, 192
motivation 4, 25, 35, 65, 75, 101,
    112, 142–44, 171, 177, 232, 235
motor control 16, 109
motor skill 16, 36, 109, 125, 144,
    197–98, 229
motor units 144–45
multicultural 145–46
muscular Christianity 22, 42, 76, 80,
    94, 128, 146–47, 166, 186, 194
muscular system 16
museums 21, 104, 106, 147–48, 183

National Coaching Foundation 40,
    148, 164
National Curriculum 22, 55, 84,
    102, 116–17, 149, 221
National Lottery 92, 100, 151, 207,
    214, 216
nationalism 45, 48, 114, 146, 149–
    51, 155, 157, 161, 169, 179, 229
nervous system 26, 103
North American Society for Sport
    History 106
nutrition 28–29, 87, 151–52, 160, 212

obesity 102, 152–53, 238
Olympics (ancient) 153–55, 158
Olympics (modern) 8, 14, 18, 30, 42,
    45–46, 59, 62, 69, 80, 94–95,
    98–100, 114, 119, 126–27, 131,
    135, 149–50, 155–56, 168, 170,
    181, 209, 223
Olympism 153, 155–58
open loop 39, 78, 158, 229
origins of sport 80, 96, 158–59, 179
outcomes 12, 21, 54, 102, 143, 160,
    172, 205, 217, 220
over-training 47, 77, 160–61, 228

Related titles from Routledge

Secondary Education: the Key Concepts
Jerry Wellington

A comprehensive critical survey of the controversies, theories and practices central to secondary education today, this book provides teachers, researchers, parents and policy-makers alike with a vital new reference resource.

Secondary Education: The Key Concepts covers important topics, including:

- Assessment
- Citizenship
- Curriculum
- E-Learning
- Exclusion
- Theories of learning
- Work experience.

Fully cross-referenced, with extensive suggestions on further reading and on-line resources, *Secondary Education: The Key Concepts* is the essential guide to theory and practice in the twenty-first-century classroom.

ISBN 10: 0-415-34404-2
ISBN 13: 978-0-415-34404-3